AF292029

Amphibious Warfare Post WWII

A Royal Marine's Anthology

Military histories and biographies

Falkland Islands Shores
Reasons in Writing: A Commando's View of the Falklands War
Amphibious Assault Falklands: The Battle for San Carlos
Blondie: A Life of Lieutenant Colonel HG Hasler, DSO, OBE
The Next Moon. A Special Operations Executive Agent in France
HMS Fearless: The Mighty Lion
3 Commando Brigade, Helmand
Commando Assault, Helmand
Nothing Impossible. A Portrait of The Royal Marines 1664 – 2010 (Editor)
Exocet Falklands
Paid to Predict. Duplicity and Deceit Among 'Allies'
A Life in Letters
A Life Under Sail

Fiction

Skeletons for Sadness. A Story of Espionage, Love and War in the Falklands
Death's Sting. Duplicity and Deceit in the Balkans

Reference

Jane's Amphibious Warfare Capabilities (Editor)
Jane's Special Forces Equipment Recognition Guide (Editor)
Jane's Amphibious and Special Forces (Editor, bi-annual)

Amphibious Warfare Post WWII

A Royal Marine's Anthology

Ewen Southby-Tailyour

Pen & Sword

MILITARY

AN IMPRINT OF PEN & SWORD BOOKS LTD.
YORKSHIRE – PHILADELPHIA

First published in Great Britain in 2026 by
Pen & Sword Military
An imprint of
Pen & Sword Books Ltd
Yorkshire - Philadelphia

Copyright © Ewen Southby-Tailyour, 2026

ISBN 978 1 03614 544 6

Typeset in INDIA by IMPEC eSolutions
Printed and bound in England by CPI Group (UK) Ltd, Croydon, CRO 4YY

The Publisher's authorised representative in the EU for product safety is Authorised Rep Compliance Ltd., Ground Floor, 71 Lower Baggot Street, Dublin D02 P593, Ireland. www.arccompliance.com

For a complete list of Pen & Sword titles please contact:

PEN & SWORD BOOKS LIMITED
George House, Units 12 & 13, Beevor Street,
Off Pontefract Road, Barnsley, S71 1HN, UK
E-mail: enquiries@pen-and-sword.co.uk
Website: www.pen-and-sword.co.uk

or

PEN AND SWORD BOOKS
1950 Lawrence Road, Havertown, PA 19083, USA
E-mail: uspen-and-sword@casematepublishers.com
Website: www.penandswordbooks.com

Contents

Introduction

From 1960 to 1992 I served in the Royal Marines and specialised as a landing craft officer closely involved with amphibious warfare. I was also privileged to have been attached to the French Navy's *Commandos Marine*, the Sultan of Muscat's Armed Forces' Northern Frontier and Desert Regiments and the United States Marine Corps' 4th Marine Amphibious Brigade. My career included working in or with British, Dutch, French, Norwegian, German and United States amphibious ships. On retirement, I was employed by the UK Government's Foreign and Commonwealth Office as a monitor with the European Community Monitoring Mission (ECMM). Unofficially, and certainly unpaid, I was tasked by the Secret Intelligence Service (MI6) to 'keep an eye' on one or two named individuals. Chapter 1 of this book, originally written in 1961, includes language relating to race which may be considered offensive. Although this language is unacceptable, we have opted to leave this in the book for the purpose of historical accuracy.

The following essays have been written over the last years for various publications including *Jane's Amphibious and Special Forces* and a number of nautical and military magazines.

Chapter 1

Excerpts from a Second Lieutenant's Journal, HMS Wizard, 1961

All Royal Navy and Royal Marines' Young Officers under training were required to keep a journal which was inspected weekly by the training officer who would scribble derogatory or (less often) encouraging comments in the margins. The following two excerpts are from my journal, as written and unchanged apart from some tidying up.

At 0945 on the morning of 22 January 1961, thirty-one Young Officers under training embarked in HMS *Wizard* lying off Britannia Royal Naval College, Dartmouth.

Wizard was one of three ships that made up the Dartmouth Training Squadron (DTS) in that era. She had begun her life in 1944 as a W-class destroyer. In April that year she joined the 3rd Destroyer Flotilla and two months later she gained an unenviable reputation when she blew off her stern with her own depth charges. Following repairs, in April 1945 she joined the 27th Destroyer Flotilla for service with the United States Navy in the Far East. In February 1946 she was with the local flotilla at Plymouth until selected for conversion to a Type 15 anti-submarine frigate in 1951. Recommissioned in 1954, she served in the Mediterranean with the 5th Frigate Squadron and took part in the Suez operations in November 1956. On return to the UK in May 1957, she refitted at Chatham before joining the DTS.

22 January

Twenty-seven midshipmen and four Royal Marine second lieutenants joined the ship at 0915 and began stowing their kit. The ship's total complement, including those of us under training, was about 230 with fourteen officers. After lunch we were briefed by the training officer followed by a lecture from the navigating officer. The accommodation would appear to be very good for a frigate and the food extremely good especially considering the difficulties the cooks have to put up with in such a tiny galley. The gunroom is towards the stern and stretches from the port side to the starboard side with bunks/sofas and tables around the edges, otherwise it is hammocks for the rest of us, which I prefer.

23 January

The ship slipped her moorings on the River Dart and proceeded to sea in company with HMS *Roebuck* and HMS *Venus*. We, the Royal Marines Young Officers, were not on deck as we were still having difficulty finding stowage space for our issued large, tin trunks, eventually finding room in the Bofors magazine.

Throughout our first night at sea we were station keeping in a V formation towards the Bay of Biscay, which was very much as expected with a fairly heavy sea running in from the west. Happily I have never been seasick but quite a few were not so lucky. We have been warned of a Force 8 gale but it passed quickly with not much increase in the sea state.

25 January

The first time, I was conning the ship under the most careful eye of the Officer of the Watch (OOW) which I found instructive and enjoyable. Far better than the previous night when I had stood for four hours in the lower enclosed bridge, doing nothing! The second night, after a four-hour watch, was also the first night that I have slept soundly, as over the previous nights I had fallen out of my hammock a total of eleven times, due I hope, to my lack of *savoir-faire*. However I am now organised in this respect and able to sleep well. *Wizard* put into Lisbon to land a very sick midshipman.

27 January

This evening the four of us Young Officers went on a run ashore in Gibraltar to window shop as we had no money, until Gieves, the ubiquitous British naval outfitters and tailors, very kindly cashed our cheques. At 2030 a party of about twenty-five midshipmen and we four second lieutenants were invited to a dance by Admiral A.F. Powlett, the Flag Officer. It was tremendous fun and we returned on board exhausted at 0045.

29 January

Rear Admiral and Mrs Powlett invited myself and three midshipmen to a picnic 15 miles into Spain at a place called the Devil's Eye. This is a fascinating example of weathering where a huge hole has been worn through the soft interior of a tall hard-rocked pinnacle. We returned on board at 2000 as the ship is under sailing orders.

31 January

The smaller islands of the Canaries were visible this morning, rising majestically out of the Atlantic, form part of a volcanic ridge which once started in the Atlas Mountains. They are rather barren and extremely rocky. We passed close to Gran Canaria, leaving it to starboard with Tenerife rising to 12,000 feet beyond.

2 February

We are due into Mindelo on St Vincent Island in the Cape Verde Islands at 1700 tonight. The order for entering the anchorage is *Roebuck*, *Wizard* and *Venus*. I am amazed to find so many warships anchored in what I always thought was an out-of-the-way place. Apart from our three ships of the DTS there are also HMS *Scorpion*: two Portuguese frigates; one Italian built (to a NATO design) frigate plus a second built in 1952; a Portuguese destroyer built in 1928 and a Spanish-built cruiser *Canarias* (based on the British County-class) whose sister ship was sunk in the Spanish Civil War in 1936. At 1830 *Wizard* hosted a cocktail party on the quarterdeck.

6 January

Nine years ago today, King George VI died in his sleep. So to commemorate the accession of Queen Elizabeth II, a 21-gun salute was fired by each of the three DTS frigates at 1200. There were 'evolutions' this afternoon – tasks set to test our ingenuity and initiative, one of which included the captain being pulled across to HMS *Roebuck* in the sea-boat. Not an easy task for there was quite a chop running in mid-Atlantic.

10 February

Anchored off Port of Spain, Trinidad, at 0900. About fifty midshipmen and all eight Royal Marines Young Officers from across the squadron, dressed in our best tropical uniforms, were taken to the American base at Chaguaramas to witness the handing over of the base to Trinidad and Tobago.

11 February

We sailed last night at 1800, and following OOW manoeuvres, arrived at Bridgetown Barbados this morning and in time for a dance at the Royal Barbados Yacht Club.

21 February

Managed to find time to sort out the final preparations for our landing after lunch. The first lieutenant did not know what to do with us four Royal Marines while the ship went to sea for four days of OOW manoeuvres, so has decided to send us ashore to survey Friendship Bay in Bequia. He also sent some sailors with us for a spot of leave. After a hurried lunch, we carried our stores up to the boat deck to load them into the 3-in-1 whaler, [an open sea boat that can be sailed, motored or rowed.] There are sixteen of us in the party with twelve petty officers and ratings. At last zero hour came when we were put ashore at Paget Farm through slight surf. Almost immediately we were surrounded by hundreds of shouting, laughing, native children, as we formed a human chain to carry our stores through the surf to above the high-water mark.

At this point it began to rain with typical, tropical ferocity, so, having covered our stores with two tarpaulins supplied by the locals, we took shelter in the Gospel Hall. It was here that we were introduced to the people who would influence us most during our stay. One was an albino negro who was every inch a negro, but completely white. [This text was written in 1961 and reflects its time of writing. The word 'negro' refers historically to people of Black African heritage, and while it was once considered a proper English-language term it is now outdated and inappropriate.] The second was a small, youngish man who claimed to have done everything from whaling to deer stalking, although he admitted that no whale had been caught for some years and we were not sure where he stalked deer. He turned out to be incredibly useful and, unasked, would help produce several hot meals during the middle of these tropical rainstorms.

While two of us enquired at the Gospel Hall where we could obtain permission to camp temporarily for the night, the two other Royal Marines carried out a reconnaissance of the route to Friendship Bay and where to hire a jeep. Having camped for the night in the village schoolroom – above the bar – we were now in a fit state to set off for Friendship Bay, one-and-a-half miles east, along the coast road. We were keen to get there soon as it has the reputation for being the most beautiful beach throughout the Grenadines.

At 0800 the advance party of six sailors and three Royal Marines set off on foot to prepare the camp while the remainder loaded the jeep and bought vegetables and fruit to see us through the next few days.

On arrival at Friendship Bay, one Royal Marine in the advance party had called on the most respectable house in the area to enquire about a camping area and from whom permission should be obtained. He was rather surprised to find that he had called on Sir Anthony and Lady Eden, [Sir Anthony Eden. British Conservative Prime Minister between 1955 and 1957] who could not have been kinder and advised on every conceivable subject.

Eventually the jeep appeared and we set up camp at the eastern end of the palm grove running along the edge of the bay. With the help of local boys we constructed palm roofs to keep the worst of the rain off us and our stores. Then followed a rudimentary beach survey of the bay's underwater gradients and, in land, escape routes for a supposed amphibious landing but, as I discovered to my painful cost, the undergrowth was nigh impenetrable in every direction.

22 February

The highlight of today was the visit of Sir Anthony to our camp, dressed only in swimming trunks (displaying multiple abdominal scars). This was followed by an invitation for six of us to join him and Lady Eden for drinks in the evening. We were thankful to find him and his wife in most excellent health. On our return, after two fascinating hours we joined the beach celebration of our last night ashore.

24 February

Up early to break camp and remove all traces of us having been there. The jeep was due back at 0730 but by 0800 there was no sign. The problem was, we soon discovered, that a whale cow and calf had been caught and so all transport on the island – a total of five cars, three jeeps and a motor cycle – were required to collect and distribute the whale meat. We had a problem but one that was solved by an American who owned one of the three jeeps on the island. We hired his for three dollars, so we would not be late for the ship.

Through good fortune, by the time we arrived at the landing beach, HMS *Wizard* was not in sight so we spent a most interesting time observing island life after a whale is caught.

Thereafter the training cruise followed the normal pattern of gunnery practice, depth charge dropping, coastal navigation, OOW duties, engine room watches, communications practice along with visits to the United States Navy at San Juan (including an evening in the Black Angus night club) plus many social visits to, among others, Bermuda – including a day of demolition training with the Royal Bermuda Regiment. Finally, after a rough Atlantic crossing we berthed in Campbeltown in the snow prior to our arrival at Devonport at the end of March. All in all a great introduction to life at sea in the Royal Navy – as it then was.

Chapter 2

Excerpts from a Second Lieutenant's Journal, 45 Commando, Aden, 1961-1962

16 November

After many false starts I was at last on my way to join Zulu Troop as one of two troop officers stationed at Dhala, approximately 70 miles north of Little Aden. The plane left RAF Khormaksar at 0930 and landed at the Dhala strip at 1000. The 20-minute ride in a 3-tonner gave me the first opportunity to see the type of country that Z Troop patrolled over.

The first thing to be noticed is the amount of green trees and shrubs. Although the ground is dry and dusty, during the summer season it rains heavily allowing the vegetation to store up water for the rest of the year. It is a rugged mountainous country surrounding small valleys which, themselves, are dotted with small, rocky hills. Dhala itself is a medium-sized village at just over 5,000 feet above sea level, sitting on the side of a north-facing hill looking towards the Yemen.

There are two military camps, the one to the east occupied by the 4th Battalion Aden Protectorate Levies (APL). [By the end of November they had reformed as the Federal Regular Army (FRA)] while in the western camp there are Alpha and Zulu Troops of 45 Commando. Both tented camps are overshadowed by the Jebel Jihaf which towers over the valley from a height of 8,000 feet. Our camp is about 200 yards long and 50-60 yards wide, straddling a small ridge with downward slopes all round.

On arrival I was taken to the west end of the camp where the officers' mess tent and accommodation were and introduced to my own tent which, surrounded by sandbags, housed a camp bed, canvas chair, folding desk, wardrobe and a storage box. The sandy floor was part covered by a brightly coloured, goat's hair 'camel rug'. Outside stood a metal bowl perched on a wooden frame. The marines live two or three to a tent, all of which have been dug down to a depth of about three feet. As it happens today, Thursday, is a stand-down following yesterday's administration inspection.

Security in the camp is extremely strict. There are three sangers which are permanently manned by three men each during night and day with light machine guns (LMG) and the standard issue 7.62 Self-Loading Rifle (SLR). Their arcs of fire cover the immediate area around the camp and give supporting fire along two sides of the neighbouring APL camp, about 200 yards away. Leave is restricted to Dhala village only and expires at 1700. Parties must be at least four strong and always in uniform.

The generators for electricity are turned on at 1730 and off at 2230, after which we use Tilley lamps. Hot water for washing and shaving is brought to the officers' tents by the MOAs. (marine officers attendants, or 'batmen' in army speak) at 0700 and 1730.

Operationally, for patrolling, we are under command of Lieutenant Colonel W. Thomas, DSO MC, the CO of the APL battalion in the neighbouring camp. All patrols must be over twenty men including at least one officer and, usually, a Royal Artillery Forward Observation Party to control the 24-pounders based in the APL camp. Simple training patrols over the Jebel Jihaf, known as 'the milk run', must abide by these regulations as well. However, the more usual patrols are to the APL forts at Karna, As Saria, Haib and Shima to the north-east, and occasionally to others in the west and south.

Haib was one of the longer patrols and usually the main objective. My first patrol, in command (in effect the SNCOs are in command as us second lieutenants are under training) was to this fort. At 0600 on Thursday 21 December we set off in vehicles to the start of what was called, for reasons I never knew, as the 'Turkish road', which was impassable to vehicles. All I carried were two water bottles, an SLR, spare ammunition and a pair of mini binoculars.

From here we set off on foot in a tactical formation for Haib, about 5 miles to the north-east via the fort at Karna. The rough, winding track led up the side of the jebel (the Arabic word for mountain) to the fort. The usual procedure at the forts is for the officers and SNCOs to have tea with the Arab officer in charge and then after twenty minutes or set off again having reassured him that we were here for his security in return for his intelligence update.

However, most of our patrols are to ensure law and order between the tribes who are continually fighting each other while refusing to pay taxes. Our presence is supposed to maintain that law and order, and while this may be the case when we are actually in an area, as soon as we have left 'normality' returns!

We bypassed As Saria on this outward leg and set off straight for Haib set on the edge of an escarpment overlooking a great plain, with the Yemen border marked by a river that runs down the middle. I was told that this view from Haib looking straight across the valley to the Yemen and the hills beyond is claimed to be the most beautiful and impressive in the whole of the Aden Protectorate. Not difficult to see why.

After a stop of one hour we moved off to As Saria, almost always in single file, due to the terrain, where the fort was once the palace of a dissident Emir who is now in the Yemen. In some rooms there are still beautiful carvings of local scenes and faded paintings. The fort stands guard over a wide valley and many neighbouring farms. The country here, behind the jebel, is, for the most part, good arable ground producing, apart from wheat and qat, a large variety of fruits. Qat (or khat) is a thick, juicy leaf which is chewed slowly in the side of the mouth with, I was told, the same effect as alcohol, which is of course, forbidden by Muslims. I tried some but was unimpressed and have decided to stick to beer or gin! Dhala and the surrounding countryside is one of the largest qat producing areas across the Protectorate.

Leaving As Saria, and more strong black tea, we moved off towards Shima, a small fort perched on the eastern edge of the jebel with commanding views over the north of the Dhala valley, our camp and the airstrip.

From Shima we dropped down (almost literally) towards the valley floor via a very steep, winding rocky path known as 'the donkey trail'. The fast descent was an exhilarating mix of scree-riding and abseiling without ropes until we reached the airstrip, having walked about 15 miles over rough, stony ground.

In addition to these continuous foot patrols, one of Zulu Troop's other duties is to picket the notorious Kariba Pass, where the road to Aden drops 1,000 feet over about half a mile of twisting graded track, cut into the hill side. The numerous hairpin bends make it ideal ambush country. Whenever a convoy is due, either to the coast or from it, our job is to drive the length of the pass to make sure it is clear of mines, obstacles or stranded civilian trucks that might be blocking the way. We also post three armed lookouts covering the whole pass then block each end to ensure a one-way system is in place.

The pickets must be in position at least half an hour before the convoy is due, having laid out on the ground a large, bright red 'air panel' of light cotton as confirmation for the distant convoy commander that all is in place. Every troop-carrying vehicle must disembark its passengers, who have to walk up or down an adjacent foot path for the road is narrow and fatal accidents are not unknown.

28 November

There are still one or two areas which are regarded as hostile and among these, the *Asanti* tribal territory is one of the most well-known. Four years ago a patrol by the Cameron Highlanders was ambushed while returning from Wa'lan (about 5 miles to the south of Dhala), which is regarded as the capital of the area. The regiment suffered two dead and a number of wounded.

This morning at 0600 Zulu Troop set off for Wa'lan with one section of the APL (now known as the FRA) as point section, and one section from Alpha Troop covering our rear. We debussed a mile or so south of Dhala and set off as planned, with the Federal National Guard (FNG) a tactical bound ahead of our HQ, which not only included the Political Resident but also the FOO party and one rifle section with an LMG. Another tactical bound behind this group came two sections, before Alpha's troop commanded by Second Lieutenant Anthony Langdon. The empty vehicles now following some distance behind

After about twenty minutes we dropped down a steep and most impressive gorge that quite suddenly opened out onto a vast, flat country with just one wadi running down the middle. The troop had been briefed about thus Asanti region so, because of the likelihood of an ambush, morale in Zulu Troop was at its peak and all movement and field craft carried exactly as trained at the Infantry Training Centre, Lympstone. [Later Commando Training Centre.]

Suddenly, probably not by coincidence, just where the Cameron Highlanders had been ambushed, there was a loud crack which sounded close enough – the whole troop was given the order to take cover and it was marvellous to see the speed and thoroughness that each marine put into the drill and fieldcraft that they had so often practiced.

However no shots followed and the patrol set off again, a bit disappointed that that was that!

On arrival at Wa'lan we were met by the local FNG captain who explained that the shot was fired by an Arab chasing baboons! We all, including the Arab officer, laughed.

One of the reasons for our patrol to Wa'lan was to ensure that the village was paying its taxes, which perhaps understandably for a self-sufficient, almost feudal, fiefdom, were not considered obligatory. As it turned out all was well, although the villagers did not appear friendly. None of them came forward to great us except for the Imam who looked untrustworthy anyway.

During most of December, Sergeant R.V. Shellard, Zulu Troop's Assault Engineer, was 'building' a road down the eastern side of Asanti country, then through Zaned and on to the west of Wa'lan. Godfrey Meynall, the resident Political Officer, had decided to open up Asanti country by road so that civilian vehicles could export Wa'lan's goods. Godfrey had been a National Service Royal

Marine, whose father, also Godfrey, had won a VC and an MC. To build the road mostly entailed blowing up obstacles such as the larger boulders and smoothing, by hand, the result. It is considered good training for us Young Officers to take part and watch the usefulness of plastic explosive.

By today, Tuesday 12 December, the road is ready to accept the first vehicles. However, our setting off to open the road was delayed until after lunch, as all our officers were invited to a *fuddle* by the Emir of Dhala in his palace. *Fuddles* are ceremonial Arab feasts where the food is eaten sitting cross-legged on the floor around huge dishes of rice, goat and sweetmeats.

We met the Emir outside his palace and after we had all been introduced were ushered upstairs to the first floor where we removed our shoes. We sat for about half an hour in what could be described as his drawing room or *majlis* which is furnished with modern G-Plan furniture. The Emir does not speak English and so all conversation took place through an interpreter. When the meal was ready we moved into the dining room which is about forty feet long. There was no furniture in the room except cushions propped along the walls. Running down the centre were long, brightly coloured, goat-hair blankets covered with the most incredible array of food.

The main dish was a number of whole goats that had been roasted over spits and was extremely delicious. With the goats was rice and millet over which was poured a form of curry sauce. The whole meal must be eaten with the right hand which is difficult, especially the rice. It is advisable to wear old clothes! We had to sit cross-legged without the soles of our feet facing anyone. There is only one way to do this and that is to buy a 'Behan chair' – a long loop of coloured woven goat hair about four inches wide, which goes round your back and knees and is most comfortable. I will buy my own. [I did and still use it – as a sling.]

After the fuddle, which ended with thick, black, bitter coffee served out of the Arabian, long curved-spouted coffee jugs, we dashed back to the camp and immediately embussed for our patrol. We left the camp at 1530 in one 1-tonner, two quarter-tonners (one of them being the Royal Artillery's Forward Observation Officer's party – the 24-pounders remaining on call in the FRA camp) and two 3-tonners. I was in the leading vehicle, the 1-tonner, with a section of FRA troops. I was told to lead as I had driven or walked down most of the road during construction.

Progress was extremely slow, little more than walking pace, if that, for the whole way as there was in practice, no track at all. All Sergeant Shellard had done was to blow a path clear of the larger boulders and rocky outcrops. As we were the first vehicles to enter this part of the world and the area being hostile, every precaution was taken. We were not sure how the locals would react to a military vehicle patrol, as they had been told that the road was specifically for civilian use. Many of the locals suspect that this is only an excuse to build the road to a part of the country that is hostile in order to move troops swiftly.

There was only one place where we had to debus the troops. At one point the road suddenly drops 300 feet to a wadi bed and, in part, a 1:2 gradient (so we were told) which required all the vehicles to be emptied, apart from the drivers. Once in the wadi the going was easier on soft shingle. It was just beginning to get dark when we arrived at Wa'lan before driving a further 200 yards to the FNG 'fort' – a camp consisting merely of five tents commanded by a captain.

The vehicles were laagered in a square on the ground next to the fort while the officers were kindly given a tent, which we preferred not to take up as our men were sleeping in the open. After compo supper we went to visit the Emir's representative in the village. Unfortunately we choose a bad time to call as he was in the middle of a qat-chewing session. 0600 the next morning. An early start. The return journey as far as Zamad was uneventful apart from having to walk up the wadi side while the vehicles struggled with such a steep gradient.

We reached Zamad at about 0800. Then, because of the very real danger of ambushes, we set off for Ad Dubiyet on foot in tactical bounds and leaving two sections to guard the vehicles. This segment of the patrol had been kept secret from the men for reasons not divulged to us subalterns. Ad Dubiyet is a little village of great religious significance for, the locals believe, Job is buried here and so is usually considered to be the religious capital of the whole Dhala region. The Tomb of Job is also said to be situated in Jebal Qarah outside the city of Salalah in southern Oman. The village is situated on the edge of a most impressive escarpment on one of the higher plateaux in the area.

The footpath from Zamad south to Ad Dubiyat is rough and barely recognisable as such so at the cost of a few cigarettes and tins of compo we hired a local guide. The path turned out, in many places, to be very beautiful as it passes by clear mountain streams and through small, fertile re-entrants. On our arrival Captain Ted Carroll – Zulu Troop commander – was met by the deputy head of the village and was escorted into the main public building. In the meantime the men played with the numerous children that appeared as soon as their suspicions were overcome about seeing their first white men. Captain Carroll was told that we were among the first white men to be seen, the last being a number of years ago and so, of course, before the children had been born.

Once again the return journey was uneventful, except for visiting Job's grave which is an impressive square of stone about six feet high, twelve feet long and four feet wide. Back at Zamad we prepared and ate lunch before setting off at 1430 for Dhala. On the way we were faced by a number of boulders that had been rolled across the track but luckily nothing too big for a few marines to heave out of the way.

Christmas Day 1961

Luckily there are no photographs of Christmas Day at Dhala, probably due to the photographer's inability to even recognise a camera let alone knowing which button to press. Yesterday, Christmas Eve, we were warned to prepare to move to Little Aden in preparation for a unit move to an undisclosed location. To execute the move a certain code word would be signalled from Commando HQ. However, today saw the usual run of entertainment. The main one being the SNCO's party in their mess at midday. In a way this was unfortunate for it meant that we ate a cold Christmas lunch in our own mess tent at 1600. It did mean though that we all turned in at 1800 and stayed there until breakfast on Boxing Day.

On Boxing Day there began the first of five days of bad weather. Aircraft were cancelled and the top of the Jebel Jihaf was not seen until Zulu Troop returned 24 days later. The code word came the following day, 27 December, so all this afternoon we have spent packing up all troop and personal stores. An empty RASC convoy arrived well after dark so much of the night we were all busy loading up the 3-tonners ready for a 0600 start in the morning.

We all have the greatest admiration for the RASC drivers who were under a great deal of strain (and tiredness) and yet never once complained.

At 0605 the convoy set out from Dhala camp bound for Little Aden, leaving behind Second Lieutenant Arthur Williams and twelve marines as camp guards and rear-party. I was in the second quarter-tonner with Captain Ted Carroll and as we passed the entrance to the FRA camp, a guard of honour of Arab soldiers with their rifles at the 'present' stood alongside the saluting British officers. An extremely nice gesture indeed. The convoy was one of the fastest yet to Little Aden (about five-and-a-half hours) and no breakdowns.

On our arrival at 45 Commando's camp in Little Aden we learned that we were at six hours notice to move to Kuwait – all non-local leave has been cancelled. The marines are permitted to take leave in Little Aden, providing they clear it with their Troop Sergeants.

Little Aden is 25 miles from Aden itself by road, and consists basically of the BP oil refinery, its offices and accommodation plus a small hospital and the nurses quarters. There are two military camps in what were the refinery workers quarters. These camps straddle the road with their guard rooms on opposite sides. Our neighbours are the Queen's Royal Irish Hussars.

12 January
45 Commando has relaxed to 12 hours' notice to move, leave returned to normal and the general atmosphere has become less expectant.

On Sunday, for the first time, I managed to get out of the camp when Lieutenant Gerard Gandy asked me if I would like to drive with him up to the FRA fort at Tor al Bahr on the Yemen border west of Dhala. Naturally I agreed immediately so this morning after a very early breakfast we set off in his privately owned, diesel Land Rover.

Gerard is preparing to drive home to the UK via the Sahara and so he needs to test his machine and long-distance driving skills on a trial run off the road and across the Aden desert. Tor al Bahr is also an area never visited by foreigners which appeals to me.

Having turned right off the coast road we entered the proper sand desert and soon lost all sight of 'land' – just mile upon mile of sand with the Land Rover (and Gerard) coping superbly. I felt almost at home as we steered, as best we could, towards the north. Eventually land was sighted roughly where we wanted it to be, and so as planned, we entered the Wadi Amriga. This is a wide, flat-bottomed wadi with steep sides fifteen to twenty feet high. About 100 yards across in places, there are numerous outcrops of thick acacia bushes and small trees. Soon Amriga village was passed on the port side then, following some hastily scribbled instructions on the back of an officers' mess wine chit, and after half a mile from the village we climbed to the left out of the wadi and onto flat ground. Wadi M'Adin was easy to identify as it is most fertile with a wonderful, cooling stream running down its centre and was our final turning point for the border.

The FRA border fort is very prominent. The locals appeared friendly although a little shy at first – or perhaps nervous at seeing their first white men. By now we had used far more diesel than Gerard had anticipated and as there was no diesel available (nor had we expected any), we took a risk of running out of fuel halfway across the desert but managed to reach Little Aden, despite the fuel gauge being firmly on empty. A good lesson for Gerard before his drive back to the UK.

18 January

My birthday and to celebrate, Zulu Troop returned to Dhala by convoy. My 3-tonner, at the rear, broke down no less than four times with radiator and ignition problems so we left it at Fort Thumier (the halfway halt). Captain Edwards, the Troop Commander, was flying to Dhala in a helicopter. As he passed overhead he tried to lower some champagne on the end of a long piece of string but the pilot did not think it such a good idea, which was unusual for a Fleet Air Arm pilot as they will always attempt anything! And so we prepared to settle back into the pleasant Dhala routine.

At 0845 the next day the duty signaller dashed into Zulu Troop's office tent to inform us that 100 men were on the airstrip firing rifles. At the time our troop commander was having breakfast with 45 Commando's CO who had spent the night with us. When the troop commander arrived, the troop was already fallen in and fully armed. The next signal we received said that there were now three wounded. Just before two sections were despatched the final signal came through: 'The Arabs are singing and dancing on the airfield!' It was a wedding party that had got out of hand, but it proved just how quickly the troop could react in an emergency – especially as we thought it was only a hoax arranged by the CO to test our reactions.

29 January

The first shots for some time were fired at the camp this evening and were returned with three bursts of machine-gun fire.

2 February

I was due to fly to Little Aden today to see my parents who were passing through on their way back to the UK from Singapore, at the end of father's time as Commander 3 Commando Brigade. One of the engines of the RAF's Twin Pioneer would not start, so eventually after half an hour, the passengers were turned out and made to turn the propeller ourselves – by hand! It started second time.

4 February

Drove into Aden in the morning to wait for the arrival of the troopship SS *Nevasa*. Then in HMS *Sheba*'s captain's barge to Little Aden so that my father could say farewell to 45 Commando. I made a serious mistake as I insisted that an army brigadier got into the launch first, whereas the most senior officer gets in last and is first off. I should have remembered this from Dartmouth. Lesson relearnt!

There followed routine patrols at Dhala both by foot and by vehicle – also by helicopters from 845 Naval Air Squadron until 16 February. The helicopters left this morning after the pilots had drunk the officers' mess completely out of wine and gin.

19 February

The Bishop of Maidstone flew in and gave a very good talk to the Troop for half an hour in the afternoon. To begin with this was not welcome as we are working 'tropical routine' which means an early start at 0600 until 1300 then lunch and stand down. Nevertheless the talk was extremely good and well received by the marines.

1 March

At 1450 this afternoon the office tent caught fire and was totally destroyed in three minutes. I was ordered to hold a preliminary Board of Inquiry with six marines as witnesses. Suspicion is that it was arson by someone who wanted his poor service records to be eliminated.

6 March

Today was the last day of Ramadan. We were warned that at dusk there would be much firing with the odd stray round into the camp. The first bonfire was lit in Dhala village at last light and soon the whole place was alight from every rooftop. Then began the rockets, powerful bangers and fireworks. The whole officers' mess stood and watched oblivious to the odd stray round over the tent, fascinated that an Arab village could produce anything so beautiful and orchestrated.

7 March

A very great many shots have been fired at the camp during today, all in celebration of Ramadan although a noticeable number certainly appeared malicious.

8 March

This was the day of our second Ad Dubiyet patrol and deserves a special mention. We have been to Ad Dubiyet before but never by the route taken today. The walk in was normal and without interest, except that we were encased in fog which made following the track difficult, as it is not really a track, and even in full sun is difficult to follow. Having reached the village and checked that all was well, the plan was to march due east to find a mountain pass, which we had been told about by the FRA guides, that led down through the hills, with me leading the way with guides immediately behind.

All went well to begin with and then we found ourselves scrambling along a knife-sharp ridge with the ground dropping away each side for thousands of feet into the valley. Slowly and delicately, as the surface was loose shale, we manoeuvred past this obstacle until we had a sheer drop on just one side. By now the FRA guides had given up hope, leaving us entirely to our own intuition as to which was the best route to take – not that there was much choice! After a short discussion we decided to retrace our steps but just then the mist lifted allowing us to see a better way down the precipitous slope. I am certain the guides had never been here before.

15 March

Zulu Troop has now left Dhala after 15 months, and so today in Little Aden I have been appointed sports officer as well as fire and hygiene officer. It is unfortunate that life in here is certainly not exciting and very little is worthy of a place in a journal. Nevertheless, apart from my duties of sports, fire and hygiene I am now also the assistant adjutant.

27 May

Yesterday Major Wharfe (the Commando's operations officer) had asked me – I presume in my capacity as sports officer – if I would like to climb the Jebel Shamsan, the highest peak in Aden that forms the western edge of the Aden crater. I agreed to do so and we met a retired Royal Marines major, Jeff Douglas, who lives on Flint Island in Aden harbour. There were two aims to this climb: the first is that any European who reaches the summit will never again be posted to Aden. [This did not work for me as I was to be posted to Aden twice more in my career. During an Arabic language course in 1966, I held the local record for the base to summit to base.] The second and more laudable aim, is to teach Arab instructors how to run an endurance course and rock scramble. The instructors then pass on this knowledge and experience to Arab boys taking part in the Duke of Edinburgh's Award Scheme.

25 June

Flying Officer Martin Webb, one of the few Hawker Hunter pilots that I knew, was killed this morning when his aircraft failed to pull out of a dive. There followed many Land Rover expeditions into the interior when we always tried to find somewhere that, to our knowledge, had never been visited before by Europeans – at least not within living memory. As sports officer and with the help of my PTI (physical training instructor) – a Judo black belt – we put on three wrestling evenings. So popular did this quickly become that the final one was in the colony's sport stadium which attracted an audience of nearly 2,000. I also introduced gliding to the marines at the RAF's gliding club, with a number going solo. And so ended my first commission. I hope the others are as pleasant and interesting. [They were!]

Chapter 3

Les Commandos Marine, 1963

In the early 1960s, having seen action from Dien Bien Phu to Algeria, the French Navy's Commandos Marine were, in numerous respects, the envy of many fighting men anxiously retained at home. France had converted FS *Arromanches*, the ex-British aircraft carrier previously HMS *Colossus*, into what we called a Landing Platform Helicopter (LPH) while, their helicopter cruiser *Jeanne d'Arc*, was being built and trials completed on the 1 July 1963. [Our HMS *Bulwark* had been commissioned as an LPH (or, originally a Commando Carrier) in 1960.] Five, company-sized *Commandos Marine* were already well-versed in the intricacies of amphibious operations as we then knew them.

Two of their Commandos, *Commando Hubert* and *Commando Clemenceau*, were stationed at Toulon in the south of France, while the remaining three were at their more permanent base in the north.

The *Commandos Marine* were then an unknown quantity to us in England as there was little or no liaison at working level. Our first assault ships (later designated Landing Platform Dock or LPD), HMS *Fearless* and HMS *Intrepid*, were still under construction. *Fearless* was completed on 25 November 1965 and *Intrepid* on 11 March 1967, and yet we regarded ourselves as the acknowledged experts in this style of warfare. Suez was under our belt, and despite what else may be said about that affair, the helicopter-borne landings by 45 Commando (the first opposed helicopter landing in history and commanded by my father) and the seaborne landings of 40, 41 and 42 Commando were a success. My father had been Commanding Officer of 45 Commando and so I am biased – along with every other Royal Marine!

In 1963, I had been commissioned just three years in the Royal Marines after attending a three month, intensive French language course at Grenoble University in the foothills of the French Alps. I can't pretend that I learnt much French formally, but as the only Englishman living in a pension and spending all my time skiing in places that were shortly to become fashionable, famous and expensive, I had managed to practice what I had learnt as a child cruising on yachts between Cherbourg and the Spanish border.

Even so, it came as a surprise when my adjutant at the Joint Services Amphibious Warfare Centre at Poole (on the south coast of England) told me I was to be the accompanying officer for two *Commandos Marine* officers who were to arrive shortly for a fortnight's tour of our training establishments, commandos and amphibious fleet. I thought that I was rather young and too junior for this privilege but kept my mouth shut. It was an unexpected assignment, for although I was the seamanship training officer of the landing craft branch, I had yet to command a detachment at sea in an assault ship. My only commando experience at that stage had been on the Yemen border with 45 Commando, which was as far removed from helicopters and amphibious assault craft as was possible. However, like so much appointing, I was selected for my availability rather than my suitability.

I was very keen to be involved. The spin-off from the non-stop work involved as a liaison officer was the chance to see and hear things out of the normal ken of an acting lieutenant. I would be able to listen to senior officers (of whom I had only heard) explaining their experiences and theories, and I would visit establishments and ships to witness demonstrations of a higher classification than dreamt of at that stage of a career.

University and ski-slope French does not prepare an officer for in-depth discussions of amphibious tactics and equipment capabilities, but I needn't have worried. The visiting officers spoke perfect English and were supreme professionals who had already studied the British way of doing things. One, Bruno de la Maisoneuve, had been awarded the Croix de Guerre five times, three from Dien Bien Phu and two from Algeria. His companion, who was only ever known to me by his nickname of 'Pollop', was the French free-fall champion in an age when the sport was still in its infancy. Pollop was violently antide Gaulle, which made his Algerian service in support of the General's policies a source of amusement to his fellows. Being a professional soldier, he carried out his duties impeccably – so he told me – although I was surprised to discover later, that as a protest, he had removed with a metal file the Cross of Lorraine from the top left corner of his cap badge. He was not the only French commando to have done so.

The officers arrived early one October day in 1963. For the next months my feet hardly touched English or French soil, and although there was no action, some of the experiences required as much adrenaline.

After a fascinating fortnight touring Royal Marines and Royal Naval establishments and ships, the two French officers flew back to Toulon. In return, the Royal Marines had asked that I should visit the *Commandos Marine* stationed there, to see if there was anything at my level with which we could help – or learn. It was also an opportunity (and a much more likely event, considering the French experience and state of their art) for me to see if there was any firsthand knowledge I could bring back. Probably to make sure I behaved myself, I was accompanied by a Royal Marine captain who sadly, as he didn't speak French and did not seem to enjoy himself, left after ten days.

A car met us at Toulon station, and although it was November, the warmth after Poole Harbour was stifling. When I saw my quarters I was not too sure that this was a good thing, for the French ship *Les Deux Mondes* was a wooden-decked aircraft carrier converted during the war from, I think, an ex-US merchant ship. She was a reasonably permanent fixture on the western shore of Toulon harbour, joined to the mainland by a floating 'walk-ashore'. The plumbing was 'continental' and there was no air conditioning. Even at the onset of winter the air below was warm, fetid and very French!

We had arrived on a Friday with the naval base almost closed. However our conscript driver and his gallant little *deux chevaux* (2CV) motor car were at our disposal until Monday morning. We were warned not to be late, as work would start in earnest. We weren't and it did.

The main autumn exercise testing the embryo French amphibious forces was to take place that year in Corsica, using Toulon as the mounting base. The overall plan was to launch a helicopter assault onto high ground to the south of the Golfe de Sagone, on the west coast of the island, with a view to leapfrogging inland against guerrillas hiding in the valleys.

Covert parties were to land in advance, block the approaches to the helicopter landing zone, then establish ambush positions as a forward protective perimeter. A submarine was allocated to *Commando Hubert* for this task, and I was asked to sail in her while the Royal Marines' captain remained with the main assault group on board FS *Arromanches*. We were to launch from the submarine four hours before dawn by Zodiac rubber assault craft, paddle ashore by H-2, and make an RV with friendly 'agents' supplied by the resident Foreign Legion battalion. These agents would guide us to selected bridges that were to be blown before taking us to prepared ambush positions covering tracks and ravine crossings. After H-Hour, I was to join the main assault group on the mountain top and follow the counter-insurgency operations with the CO.

Once the briefings were over I was kitted out for four days in the field. The French ration pack was the first surprise. It was designed to be eaten cold, there was no issued heating equipment, the individual supplying his own. The bulk of the 24-hour pack consisted of tins of corned beef and anchovies, together with numerous packets of lemonade powder, milk and coffee powder (but, of course, no heating) and a small bottle of cognac. Each man was also issued a yard of French bread, which was either broken into smaller pieces for the inside of our large packs or more usually, lashed to the top of the pack so that it stuck out each side. A handful of small, boiled sweets were thrust into pockets along with a further handful of sugar lumps. The daily menu was completed by a packet of Gauloise cigarettes, a Camembert cheese and an orange. The chance to fill up one of the two, issued water bottles with white wine was taken by every marine.

I joined the submarine FS *Astrée* alongside in Toulon harbour with 20 of the commandos plus their three Zodiac inflatable rubber craft. *Astrée* had had an interesting career for she had been laid down by the French in 1938 before being captured, unfinished, by the Germans in 1940, and renamed *U-F3*. At the war's end she rejoined the French navy. At 900 tons she was not a large submarine with a top submerged speed of 9 knots. Her captain was deeply proud of her and took delight in pointing out all the dials written in German – and how a few did not work. His depth sounder certainly did not operate accurately which was to cause some concern later. Immediately forward of the conning tower, outside (but joined to the pressure hull within the casing) was the submarine's escape compartment, allocated to me for the voyage. There was just room to fit a camp bed, which by the standards of the day was a luxury. Apart from the captain, I was the only member with his own private space, for which I was grateful; it allowed me room to lay out my sketch books and write up my notes. The marines were spread about the boat in any cranny they could find. We sailed that night and dived almost immediately.

Everyone smoked whether dived or not. Luckily in those days I smoked Gauloise, a legacy from my university days at Grenoble, and so could hold my own at that. The off-duty naval officers played French card games almost incessantly in the wardroom.

There was time to fill, for these were before the days of rehearsals and demonstration or turn-away landings. We surfaced and dived, carrying out naval evolutions, including a communications exercise with the Corsair aircraft which were to support the operation. During the first afternoon at sea the captain took us on the surface, close to a well-known nudist beach (rare in those days even for the south of France). The crew were allowed on the casing with binoculars, while others took it in turn to stare through the periscopes from below. That night we made contact again with a Corsair for a final communications check before diving for the approaches to Corsica.

Five hours before dawn the marines were woken. The boat went to surface stations as we prepared for our long, dark paddle. As the depth sounder was faulty, the captain ran in slowly towards the distant beach at periscope depth until we slid gently onto the sandy bottom. He would then bring the submarine up slightly and move forward until we touched again a little further inshore. This process was repeated many times until the casing was a few inches above sea level with the submarine sitting firmly on the sand. The order was given for the forward hatch to be opened, and we struggled into the cool, damp, sticky air with our folded and deflated craft and our awkward, bulky, large packs. Each dinghy was quickly inflated and launched. We embarked and pushed off into the darkness after receiving a final course check from the navigating officer. As we paddled away, the submarine slowly and silently moved astern, submerging with the Gulf's deepening bottom contours as she did so – a diminishing, but still malevolent, black slash against the blacker night. We started our two–hour paddle towards the southeast corner of the bay.

I remember little of that paddle, similar to so many before and a few since, except for one phenomenon which kept me amused. As the spray, rhythmically flung back from our paddles, soaked into the long loaves of French bread, the crusts softened and the ends drooped slowly until each pack was neatly embraced in soggy dough. It was a rather bizarre and unexpected sight in the dim starlight.

The beach was approached with caution for fear that our guides had been captured or were simply not there. All was well however, as a single red light flashed the agreed code and we slid noiselessly onto the sand. As soon as the Zodiacs had been hidden in the shrub at the back of the beach there was instant relaxation. Longed-for Gauloise were lit; there was laughing and joking between old friends, and the non-water, water bottles, were passed a number of times. It struck me, as it certainly struck my companions, that two hours of hard paddling was a long time for a Frenchman, even a commando, to be without his national sustenance.

This interlude over, we split into previously arranged groups and set off silently towards our various objectives. My party was to blow up an important road bridge leading to the hill that was to be the objective of the dawn helicopter assault. The bridge was a likely route for an enemy who might want to move quickly in counterattack, and yet its loss would not be felt by the commandos whose further objectives lay in the opposite direction. Our orders were to destroy the bridge with plastic explosives – and destroy it we did. I learnt then that realism played a great part in these training exercises, even if I had already been surprised by some of the non-tactical aspects. The real loss of the bridge also produced excellent training for the Legion or Commando engineers, who would be required to rebuild it in time for the civilian, dawn traffic. Everyone benefited.

The different groups, having completed their tasks, lay up in prearranged ambush positions to thwart any further enemy ambitions. They too would re-join their fellows at dawn. When the helicopter assault came it was on time and impressively fast and efficient, from a darkened and apparently empty western horizon. The main hilltops were quickly seized, patrols were dispatched to keep any enemy at arm's length while the build-up of stores and command facilities continued. Enemy opposition was light, as the main concentration was expected to be in the mountains of inner Corsica, against which we were to operate using the Mont Sebastiano area as a support base. When this position had been consolidated, I moved tactically, to join the force commander in his hilltop command post.

There was a brief lull in the exercise, that to a British Royal Marine, was unusual but was of good value. The exercise was halted at various stages so that lessons learnt thus far could be evaluated and re-emphasised if necessary This was useful, for each evaluated event was fresh in the participant's mind. An added benefit, which was so often missing in our own exercises, was the junior commanders' ability to see, immediately, how their small sub-units were affecting the larger picture.

The battle plan was explained to me as were the future intentions of the force emphasised by much Gallic waving of arms towards the distant, steep-sided and thickly vegetated mountains.

The commandos were to leapfrog forwards in helicopters, while the dominating heights were picketed by men controlling their own dedicated, fixed-wing aircraft. Beneath the heights the advance would be in an 'advance to contact' formation, as far as the rugged ground allowed, using a combination of helicopters over the sheer ravines and fast foot patrols where tactically prudent.

I suggested that I might follow the progress of the advance on foot so that I would not take up valuable helicopter space. This would keep me out of the way and yet allow me to observe closely the tactics and drills. The CO agreed, and after much consulting of maps, I set off with full pack and a replenished non-water, water bottle.

Immediately the going was terrible. Defiles thickly covered with undergrowth well above head height made navigation difficult and the going very slow. After about an hour it was obvious that I would not make the RV with the final lift-off by helicopter, which was scheduled for a few hours before dusk (assuming that the enemy had been soundly beaten by then). However I could not return to the headquarters, for they and the small supply base had already moved to avoid enemy observation. I had to push on and hope that the going would ease.

There was to be no such luck that day. It was hot (it was November). It was very tiring (I was as fit as I had ever been). It was difficult to navigate (I was an experienced navigator, albeit a nautical one) and it was extremely rough under foot (I was commando trained!).

I arrived at the foot of the final objective at about 1600 that day, just in time to watch an impressive display of close air support – very close air support – by the piston-engined Corsair aircraft. It was a perfect example of why, against criticism, the *Commandos Marine* insisted on keeping the Corsairs. No jet could have carried out the sorties in such narrow valleys, where success lay in the tightness of the turns between mountain peaks. In the narrow valleys of Corsica the piston aircraft were supreme.

The Corsairs carried out strafing runs against the enemy, preventing them from mounting counterattacks. Unable to break for cover, the 'terrorists' were surrounded by hastily deployed troops while others simultaneously began the lift off from the peaks back to a rear concentration area. It was glorious watching the differing activities dovetail into each other, emphasising vital lessons in command and control that I was never to forget.

As the last helicopters began the withdrawal, I was still 2,000 feet away in an adjacent valley bottom. I waved, I tried to light a fire, I even shouted, but as I was to learn later on in my career, there is nothing one can do to attract the attention of a busy, friendly aircraft 600 yards away. Paradoxically, I was also to learn that despite lying in the bottom of a camouflaged slit trench two miles away, the brain will insist that one is always highly visible to enemy aircraft. Such is the psychology of the imagination under combat conditions.

Immediate action was needed. By chance there was a village straddling the track that ran down the side of my valley. Ducks, goats and forlorn-looking cattle wandered the paths and scrub. I weaved my way through these onlookers as unprovokingly as I could.

The next few hours are best left unrecorded for they were not very military and involved the help of a Corsican mountain family (eventually the whole village); the contents of my whisky flask and non-water, water bottle; a mad drive in a police car through the mountain passes; Ajaccio's chief gendarme; a night club;

another wild dash with yet more police cars, and a last moment rendezvous with the Commando's CO on a mountain plateau two hours before dawn. I had arrived just in time to join the tactical withdrawal to the beach area and the helicopter LZ.

Our withdrawal was as well conducted as the landings. The last helicopter stick arrived on *Arromanches'* dew-glistening flight deck as she was already hull down on the western horizon, steaming at 20 knots with the mountains already barely visible. Another display of fine timing and close coordination.

The exercise wash-up was difficult to follow as it was conducted in colloquial military French. I was, naturally, at the back of the crowded briefing room and hardly within earshot of the participants. However I was able to gather that the general opinion was that the exercise had been a success, which was hardly a surprise. Despite some practices which to my fresh-from-training mind were unusual if not down-right risky, it had been efficiently conducted from beginning to end. Of course, I was to discover soon enough that safe training standards are necessary, but in the field, risks, daring action, improvisation, initiative, practical common sense and real adrenaline are the prime movers.

We arrived back in Toulon in time for the weekend. This was fine for most of my French brother officers as they either lived ashore with their families or in well-appointed quarters, but for me there was a new complication. During our brief absence from Toulon the venerable *Deux Mondes* had been towed across the harbour to a floating dry-dock close to the town. The French sanitation, ventilation and cooking facilities were suddenly even more French (if that was possible) and I felt that my decision to live ashore in the officers' club was a justified expense to the British Crown. In fact I was to be seldom there, for another intensive period of training began that Monday.

In those days, all *Commandos Marine* were parachute-qualified, with much of their training taking place at a naval air station close to Saint Tropez. It seemed an opportunity not to miss, not that my French hosts were going to let me. I stayed in the naval air station wardroom, the weather was glorious and the Riviera beckoned although, in practice, we did not get ashore as the officers' mess was very lively.

All commandos had to complete ten jumps before being allowed to free-fall, and although this was not a required military skill, most did qualify. That Monday, we mustered at the airfield, were issued with parachutes and our equipment checked. It was then that I had to admit that I was not para-trained. The French had assumed that, like themselves, all British commandos had attended a basic parachute school. I was keen to jump, indeed I was on line for a course in England, but at that precise moment I had not attended one. There was much discussion.

I appealed to their apparently relaxed interpretation of regulations, but there was to be no bending of this particular rule and on this matter they were determined. However, I was allowed to watch the training from the aircraft and was instructed (with a wink) to remain fully kitted with my parachute, 'in case you fall out!'.

The Nord Noratlas 17 transport aircraft circled the field as I watched the novices jump – all faultlessly – before we climbed to a better altitude for the freefallers. As soon as the aircraft was empty we landed, and those who had jumped packed their own 'chutes before climbing back in again. Everyone completed three jumps. There was on that day no tactical setting but just straight-forward parachute training. That night was different, with a jump into a DZ deep in the Alpes Maritimes. My abiding memory was the low-level flight between the mountain peaks guided only by the faint light from the moon's first quarter. It was an impressive if hair-raising performance for this untutored passenger in the rear of the aircraft.

We returned to Toulon for the final two phases of my brief but crowded look at the *Commandos Marine* and where I immediately accepted an invitation to attend a *combatant nageur* [combat swimmer] course, for here was a skill in which I was already reasonably proficient and I was certain that my participation this time, would not cause embarrassment.

Their divers, unlike our Special Boat Squadron who used closed-circuit oxygen sets, were using new equipment named the DC55. It operated on compressed air, but to prevent telltale bubbles breaking the surface the exhaled air was forced through thousands of tiny holes in an outer glass fibre casing. One of the main advantages was the greater operating depth, thirty-three feet being the limit for oxygen.

This course was immense fun, the water beautifully clear and not cold. The French were masters at eating 'on the march', as it were, and would often peel off from a line of swimmers to grab a tasty Mediterranean crustacean and then swim back in line, munching behind their mouthpieces.

We carried out beach surveys, ship attacks across Toulon harbour, and bottom searches. Days of swimming in Toulon and the surrounding waters spoilt me for any further military swimming. The muddy, slimy waters of Devonport Dockyard did not quite match those of the Riviera.

My final attachment of the tour was to a commando group in an anti-guerrilla patrolling exercise across the Alpes Maritimes. For this four-day yomp I was attached as a supernumerary officer to one of *Commando Hubert*'s platoons and it was here that I was to meet my first and only disappointment of the sojourn.

Before that I was now asked to wear their distinctive cap badge, and as they wore the same green beret as ours (also pulled down to the right, unlike other French military units, as a nod to their connections with the British commando forces in the Second World War) it was just a question of changing the badges.

All the movement was on foot, unsupported by logistic back-up, and designed to practice the confrontation of rural terrorists on their own terms and using their own tactics. But there were many occasions when we had to go non-tactical to sort out minor and low-level problems that should not really have occurred.

I never quite got used to the lighting of fires at night, especially when in open country and in likely contact with the enemy. Much movement was along the hillsides or even on the crests and yet we did not use scouts ahead or to the sides, nor did we picket the heights when moving through the valleys. And I certainly never understood the necessity of urinating on the camp fires to douse them before we moved on. The steam and stench would have attracted any worthwhile enemy from miles around.

Nevertheless, it was an instructive period enlivened by the French military humour, the ration packs to which I had quickly adapted, and the sudden snow storms without adequate equipment. However this was a good test of personal endurance for each man.

On return to base at Toulon I was bold enough to mention my surprise at the sudden difference in standards from the previous week. The explanation was Gallic: They had recently returned from arduous active service in Algeria, were at home for a rest, and the turnaround of conscripts was due. The exercise was really a method of filling in time and was not to be taken too seriously, after all, it was explained: 'It is November!'.

With sadness I returned my stores (except the beret badge I had been proud to wear) and began my farewells before catching *Le Train Bleu* for Paris. But I had yet to learn the most important lesson of my visit. On returning to Toulon and while preparing to take my leave of the CO, I was asked if I would like to accompany the *Commandos Marine* on its next tour in Algeria. Of course I would! For appearances' sake I was already used to wearing the cap badge and uniform of the *Commandos Marine*, I spoke enough French, had begun to know the men and their officers, and I understood their modus operandi. I would not have had any official or executive function, yet I would be passed off as a French officer. In an internal security situation such as Algeria, it is rare indeed for any country to accept foreigners, but I enjoyed their company and they were keen for me to see themselves on active service.

It was then that I made one of the more naive decisions of my life. Algeria was very much a French problem (although it had been granted independence in July 1962). It was clear it would not have been diplomatically excusable for an Englishman to serve there, so I felt that a telegram to my adjutant in England would appear audacious if not impudent. I declined the CO's offer without even checking, in a guarded manner, with friends at Poole.

Back with the Royal Marines, I waited a few days before choosing a suitable moment in the officers' mess to broach the subject of Algeria. Instead of receiving thanks from the adjutant for not putting him in an embarrassing position, I was rounded on for not taking an opportunity that many officers would have given an arm for. Sometimes it is difficult not to lose. I resolved there and then, that in the future I would always (when prudent) act first on the premise that it is less painful, and takes less time, to receive retribution after an action, than it is to obtain permission in the first place!

Chapter 4

The Oman: Memories of Service with the Sultan's Armed Forces, Northern Frontier and Desert Regiments, 1966-1968

Written in 1992

The name Oman conjures up a romantic image that few other countries can match. In legend, the Queen of Sheba negotiated with King Solomon over the purchase of frankincense from the south coast; the Biblical Ophir and Sephar are generally accepted as being Oman while, some say, it is the home of the unicorn. It remains the most mysterious and unknown corner of that land the Romans named Arabia Felix.

The country only entered the twentieth century in 1970, when it jumped two thousand years of development. It is still a country of tribesmen. Over 250 separate tribes with a significant number of them nomadic Bedouin (or Bedu as they refer to themselves), who roam the edges of the Empty Quarter or Rubha al Khali; known by the Bedu as simply, the Sands. This desert is the desert of imagination and fable – a million square miles of sand, gravel and scrub. It is a sea of majestic dunes, marching from the fertile Jebel Akhdar, or Green Mountain of the east coast, to the dry and barren hills of the Yemen in the south and west. The Oman is the crescent-shaped littoral mass that divides this vastness from the Indian Ocean. Since biblical times it has remained a comparatively small and simple country acting as a vital trading route between the orient and the west. More recently its geographical, political and strategic position has given it further prominence.

No man can live among the nomadic tribes of the Oman and come away unmoved. No man can lead these fierce and independent men in a battle for their freedom, and remain unconvinced of their cause, and no man can endure this unforgiving and harsh land without falling under its spell. The need to return is compelling, for the call of the desert is as powerful as the call of the sea – and just as romantic.

Lawrence of Arabia (T.E. Lawrence) wrote in *Seven Pillars of Wisdom* 'Bedouin ways were hard, even for those brought up in them and for strangers terrible: a death in life'. Fifty years later, a younger generation of Britons were to discover that nothing had changed since Lawrence mobilised General Allenby's desert flank during the approach to Damascus. This next generation were fighting the Dhofar War over the moon country of southern Oman in a bitterly contested campaign of tribesman versus tribesman. The enemy, or Adoo, eventually backed by Chinese communists, matched the drama of the climate with its own equally cavalier treatment of opponents. The Oman government forces were led and supported by British, Baluchi, Iranian and Jordanian officers and men with this mix of mercenary and regular troops fighting, at the beginning, with little more than their ingenuity and professionalism. Before the present ruler, Sultan Qaboos, came to power in 1970 there was little money to spend on essentials for the community, let alone the armed forces and it was also suggested by some that the previous Sultan, Said bin Taimur, had been keen to keep the war in progress for strange reasons of status. Certainly the oil revenues which became available in 1967 were not initially used for either the military or the civil sectors, until the nearly bloodless coup changed the face of the country forever. The second half of the war from 1970 onwards was most certainly difficult, and costly in casualties, but it was a more formal affair, with the military commander able to call on many outside agencies for help as the seriousness of the situation became clearer to the western nations.

However, for all the old Sultan's faults, his small and backward country held sway in a political theatre renowned for turmoil. For ten years, his insular realm stood against sophisticated infiltration from a revolutionary movement backed by a vast arsenal.

The turning point came on 23 July 1970 with the arrival of a man prepared to lead his country forward. It is still a remarkable achievement that for the five years before this event, the Sultan's Armed Forces kept an increasing threat at bay with precious little equipment – which was vastly outdated by most weapons used by the Adoo. Those British officers who served after the coup often regard the earlier part of the war, in effect pre-Qaboos, as a minor affair, but to those of us who had the privilege to serve under Sultan Said bin Taimur, it was no ersatz campaign. We fought against the odds of poor arms, no medical support, no replaced uniforms or shoes, and rudimentary intelligence, as well as an astute Adoo whose territory it was. For instance, although in the future, I was to buy a number of my company combat trousers out of my own pocket, and had them flown out for my soldiers, it was also quite usual for my men to patrol without boots or shoes. Many British officers bought their own rifles or as I did, their own pistols. We were often outgunned by small arms and mortars, and yet the morale of our men never wavered.

We must make no mistake, if the Oman had lost her (initially) lone struggle against communism, the entrance to the Gulf would have become dominated by those who do not hold the interests of the western world closest to their hearts. If that had been the case, oil would not have flowed to where we would have preferred it to flow, and a confrontation would have taken place dwarfing the present internecine feuding between Iraq and the rest. It is as simple as that. Yet few know of the war that, with hindsight, was crucial to the West. It may take some more years yet for us to appreciate this.

To understand the 1965-1975 Dhofar War it is useful to appreciate the political and social background of the country as a whole. British political relations with the Oman date back to 1798, when Britain was at war with France which was expected to seize Muscat, the capital, in order to attack British and Indian shipping. It was even suggested at the time that France might have invaded India from this safe haven. A treaty of friendship was therefore concluded between the Oman and Britain that has existed ever since. This friendship manifested itself a number of times over the years with practical and political support. There was the Buraimi Oasis crisis, involving Saudi Arabia between 1952 and 1955, and a revolt led by the religious ruler of the interior in 1957. In this later incident, Saudi Arabia and Egypt lent arms while offering refuge and training facilities in their own countries. The aim was to re-establish an Imamate (religious ruler) of Oman, which in fact would have been a Saudi puppet government. It was a long and rough struggle for the Sultan's Armed Forces (SAF) against well-motivated and trained fanatics which ended in the Jebel War across the Jebel Akhdar (the Green Mountain) high above the capital of Muscat.

When the Omani forces, helped by the British, finally routed the Imam's supporters, a delicate peace reigned, broken by spasmodic mining and sniping. Rebels continued to be recruited and trained abroad, although their training camps had moved from Saudi Arabia to Iraq. Apart from the long-standing treaty of friendship there were underlying reasons why Britain was so keen to oppose the Saudi occupation of Buraimi and the Oman's interior. An American company held the oil concessions in Saudi and believed that if the Oman could be deemed Saudi territory – through the Imam's presence and the claim to ownership of Buraimi by Saudi – it would ensure further riches. For the British and the Sultan of Oman, it was vital to prove, that despite the Treaty of Sib signed in 1913, the Sultan was seen to rule the interior, de facto as well as de jure, and not the Imam. Through this treaty the Sultan agreed not to interfere with the internal affairs of the Oman. Some argued that this meant, in practice, the establishment of two states, with the Sultan only having jurisdiction over the coastal region. At that time the British agreed with the Imam in this respect and had it not been for oil, forty years on, this lack of concern by the British would probably have remained.

The Sultan granted oil rights to a British company and both the British and Omani governments determined that these should be exploited to their mutual benefit. The potential oil reserves were particularly exciting to the British as it had become well established that the Gulf oil fields were a mainstay of Britain's post-war economy. The added attraction of the Omani oil was that it could be piped direct to an oil terminal on the Indian Ocean coast, by-passing the strategic problems associated with a nearly landlocked gulf.

However it is in the hitherto peaceful south, that trouble with the possibility of international consequences, actually began in 1964. For ease of description, the Dhofar region of the Oman can be split into three geographical and tribal regions: the coastal plains and foothills inhabited in the main by the Kathir tribe; the Qara mountains to the north, inhabited by the Qara tribe; and the great gravel plains running north to the Empty Quarter, inhabited by the Rashid. There are numerous other tribes but it is these that were at the centre of the troubles.

The Kathir tribe had for centuries assumed control over the whole of Dhofar until relations with the Qara reached difficult proportions in the nineteenth century. Help from the Sultan in the north was sought and was given in the form of a *Wali* or local governor. This *Wali* arrived in 1880 as the Sultan's representative, with orders to maintain peace throughout the area but this control from the distant capital was only a partial success. Sultan Said bin Taimur had succeeded his father in 1932, married a Dhofari woman in 1939 and sired a son, Qaboos in 1941. Sultan Said was an articulate, educated man who viewed with distaste the effects of oil money on his neighbouring states.

Sultan Said believed that doctors, teachers and scientists were all subversive and should have no place among the traditions of his country. Even Qaboos, on return from a conventional upper-class schooling and short period in the British army, was banished to the hills of Dhofar, presumably to prevent him from exercising western influence. Whilst it was possible for those aspiring to higher education abroad to leave the Oman they could not obtain permits for return. Inevitably some did return, bringing with them glimpses of the outside world.

Thus, especially in Dhofar where another vast oilfield to match that in the north of the country was expected to be discovered, were the seeds for discontent sown.

Before the oil flowed to the newly built oil port outside Muscat in late 1967, the plea of poverty for the lack of government enterprise was almost understandable. Sultan Said wanted change, but he wanted it to be natural and unhurried. There were many aspects of life under Said bin Taimur that were admirable that must be seen in the context of an old and proud country and not judged against western standards. There was no crime of any significant nature and there was a real fear that the rural way of life, once gone, would never be replaced. The adherence to religion was absolute. For these aspects alone one must respect the old Sultan's stance.

The Dhofar Liberation Front (DLF) was formed on 9 June 1965. Its aims were no to begin with, the destruction of the Omani government, but in very simple terms, the achievement of some autonomy, with recognition of Dhofar as a viable province. Of course a slice of any oil revenue and the right to determine their own affairs formed a large part of these demands. The DLF had its first headquarters across the border from Salalah astride an important trade route at Hauf. Britain was due to leave Aden in November 1967, thus allowing the People's Democratic Republic of South Yemen (PDRSY) to become established. But the birth of the new country was not a happy one, with Britain being blamed for what was an inevitable disaster. As a diversion, the PDRSY were therefore only too happy to give succour to the emerging 'liberation' movement beyond its eastern border. Here was ideal breeding ground for communism, with PDRSY strategists quick to realise that although the domination of the Oman with its oil revenues, would be a difficult task, a third party involvement would make the whole project most attractive and possible.

Allowing Eastern Bloc countries an entrée was also expected to produce a further spin-off in technical and military aid, in recognition of the part played in helping to secure communist control over the entrance to the Persian Gulf. Russia and China had long realised this. Opportunities were suddenly available for young Dhofaris to be taken away for training and indoctrination. With Britain leaving Aden, the way was paved for this closer attention and practical influence.

The revolution, for that is what it fast became, had all the hallmarks of the perfect communist-backed insurrection. A textbook example indeed, except perhaps, for one vital aspect that the communists overlooked. The Omani is a deeply religious person and the replacing of his Islamic faith by a communist doctrine was doomed to failure. In the end, this religious aspect, coupled with careful manipulation of captured or surrendered Adoo by the British and Omani forces, brought about the end of the war in Oman's favour. It was a classic example of the successful hearts-and-minds campaigns of Malaya and Borneo. This was helped by the new sultan insisting on a pragmatic approach to modernisation and the sensible use of oil revenues for the benefit of all.

My part in all this was less-than minimal but to me, fascinating. In 1966, the Royal Marines were asked for the first time by the British Army to help supply volunteer officers for secondment on loan service with the SAF. By coincidence at that time, I was a lieutenant serving as a troop commander with 43 Commando, Royal Marines, in Plymouth, while my father was the Commandant General (then a four-star appointment) in London. This loan service tour presented me, if selected, with an ideal opportunity to leave the corps for a short period in order to avoid embarrassment on either side of the family, while at the same time experiencing some real soldiering. I had served twice before in the Middle East and had a rudimentary knowledge of the Arabic language. With my commanding officer's ready agreement I applied to the military secretary to be considered as a volunteer for eighteen months loan service with the SAF and was accepted with almost suspicious alacrity. Two courses were deemed necessary, and after three months at the Royal Naval College, Greenwich, and a further three at the Command Arabic Language School in Aden, I joined the Northern Frontier Regiment (NFR) stationed at Nizwa, the old capital of the interior.

Aden was its well-remembered hot and smelly self. The British were leaving and the final troubles had started some time before, in an attempt to force forward their departure.

For those of us attending the Command Arabic Language School, life was fun. Not for us the daily toil of guard and picket duties nor, in illegal practice, the restrictions of curfews. Instead we lived in comparatively palatial quarters in the Federal Regular Army's barracks at Seedaseer Lines. The mornings were spent in formal lessons, while the afternoons were filled with homework, which we learnt before testing each other while lying on the beach. We were fortunate, for ours was the last course to be taught using Arabic script. Subsequent courses would be confined to transliteration and shortly moved to England.

I even managed an operational weekend in the Radfan, flying in the left-hand seat of a Fleet Air Arm Wessex helicopter piloted by my father's former ADC from Plymouth days and my future best man, Johnny Ackroyd-Hunt.

So much fun was it all that I ended up being interviewed by a pompous RAF provost martial squadron leader, who took a grave and probably jealous dislike to my erratic driving within the confines of the naval base in a car I shared with a fellow Royal Marine, James Devereaux, bound for the Gulf. We had just passed our colloquial Arabic exams (in my case, rather surprisingly) and were between celebrations, driving in bathing trunks from the officers' Tarshin Club up the hill to the Royal Navy's chief of staff's house for a very late lunch. The car also contained the cream of the garrison's beauties: the daughters of the admiral, his chief of staff, the army chief of staff and two army lieutenant colonels. As it was a diminutive Fiat 500, it was top heavy with everyone standing out of the rolled-back sunroof.

Regrettably the squadron leader, also in bathing trunks, ended off his bicycle in the monsoon ditch and I ended up in uniform in front of his boss. No one was quite sure what jurisdiction the RAF had over me, indeed what my actual crime was, but a barrister friend in Army Legal Services, also billeted in Seedaseer Lines, suggested that from what he had heard on his 'net', the safest thing for me to do was to leave the colony. Now!

The great secret in life is to have friends in low places, and so with some help from a sympathetic movements clerk, I was booked, under an assumed name, onto a flight the next day to Bahrein. I spent that night as a moving target flitting from one farewell party to another just ahead of the RAF police. There was a further snag. My father was flying in on an official visit the day I was flying out, and was due to stay with the Governor and Commander in Chief, Admiral Sir Michael Le Fanu. I was invited to the formal, welcoming dinner that night, but a discreet word with the Flag Lieutenant sorted that out, while ensuring that father did not know the reason for my absence. Ironically, though, my plane was on the taxiway waiting for father's plane to land when ours – in naval parlance – 'threw a prop'. The propeller didn't actually come off, but we had to return to the hanger to have it changed and where I was forced to sweat out a few more hours as I imagined the net tightening. My loyal friends gave nothing away and eventually I left Aden for the last time – but again under a small cloud.

It was a relief to leave the heat, humidity and grenade attacks (some of which were particularly unpleasant) of the colony, for the dry heat of Nizwa in northern Oman after passing through the SAF headquarters at Bait al Falaj (outside Muscat town) for joining procedures and the issue of my uniform. This last duty was a brief affair and consisted mostly of replacing my Royal Marine badges of rank with those of the Northern Frontier Regiment (NFR), learning how to wear the *shemagh,* and stitching an embroidered cap badge onto my green beret, replacing the Royal Marines' Globe and Laurel. The NFR wore commando green berets, the Muscat regiment a bright red, Scottish-style glengarry, and the Desert regiment a sand-coloured beret. Uniform it was anything but. Most of us wore some variation of a stone-coloured flannel shirt above corduroy style, fawn trousers made by the numerous tailors in Aden or Bahrain. Footwear was the ubiquitous desert boot. Few wore socks. This was our dress whether on ceremonial parade – a rare occurrence – desert patrol or night ambush.

In the 1960s there were three types of British officer in the SAF, totalling about sixty men. The bulk of these were on lengthy contracts after retiring from the army, police or some other military organisation such as the Sudan Camel Corps or the Hadhramaut Bedouin Legion. These officers tended to be older than the others and were more usually employed in quarter-mastering duties, training and administration tasks.

The British army seconded officers from various regiments and arms depending on what skills at command level were needed at the time. The third grade of officer (and the occasional senior NCO) were known as 'junior leaders'. They were lent from British forces serving in the Middle East command for periods of two or three months, usually to help the contract officers with modern training skills and procedures. Unlike the others, they did not leave their parent service as far as pay and conditions were concerned, retained their British uniforms, were not allowed into combat, or thus, able to receive Omani campaign medals.

The SAF consisted of three infantry battalions, one gendarmerie regiment, a navy of two dhows (one operational and one for training), a number of de Havilland Beaver aircraft for communications and rudimentary air supply, plus a number of piston-driven Proctor Provosts for fighter ground attack. The great advantage was that we all wore the same cap badge – just the hat itself changed with the organisation – and so petty rivalries and stupidities, as can be found in more sophisticated armed forces, did not exist. We had no artillery to speak of, although there was always talk of some ancient large calibre guns somewhere but I never saw them. We had no armour at all and no Special Forces – which, at that stage most of us considered a good thing! The infantry was equipped with Second World War .303 Lee Enfield, bolt-action rifles, 2-inch mortars with a choice of high explosive or smoke bombs, and a few elderly, medium-calibre mortars. Machine-gun support was supplied by the trusty Bren. Transport was either by donkey, Land Rover or Bedford 3-tonner. Communications relied heavily on a variety of civilian sets and acquired ex-RAF air-sea rescue hand-held walkie talkies.

On arrival at the battalion HQ of the NFR on the outskirts of Nizwa, the ancient northern capital of Oman, I was met by the commanding officer, Lieutenant Colonel Hugh Sanders, and immediately appointed as second-in-command of A Company under Major Colin MacLean. As a sideline I was also appointed animal transport officer in charge of a gaggle of donkeys. Just before my arrival, a British Army veterinary officer had removed all the donkeys' voice boxes so they could not bray while on patrol and thus alert the enemy. The unforeseen consequence was that they now made a most distinctive guttural croak that immediately identified them as NFR donkeys – army donkeys rather than civilian beasts!

I was lucky enough to have joined just before the periodical change round of locations and so enjoyed an interesting first few months with the reserve company at Battalion Headquarters before taking my company to Ibri under a new and effete company commander known throughout, rather unfortunately, as the 'cream puff'. It had also been useful, as a new boy, to meet and work with the headquarters' officers and particularly the Adjutant, Patrick Hibbert-Foy, a 16th/5th Lancers officer, and the OC Recce Platoon, Paddy Bell, a Scots Guards officer. Both shared my love of shooting and whisky although we tried not to combine the two.

Also at Nizwa was Richard Murphy of the Queen's Regiment with whom I had attended the language course, and Sandy Dawson, late of the Clackmackan police force – a wonderful contract officer who had joined with no military experience at all, and who was to end up holding a number of senior appointments throughout SAF. We were a happy team, kept in check when necessary, by Patrick, whose duties were not made easy by the commanding officer's predilection for sex and drink. The first was unobtainable; the second was available in large quantities. Nor was the CO helped by the irreverence of his junior officers, for whom, quite wrongly, he was considered fair game. There is no doubt that in the south at Salalah, when an attempted coup had been staged, the CO had been superb. Interrupted during his post-dinner drinks by the duty officer informing him that there was 'trouble' he instantly put down his glass and gave the clearest orders anyone in the battalion could recall. Once he was satisfied that all was understood, the CO returned to his brandy and the embryo insurrection was quelled. In the more peaceful north, though, he was not the same and missed his wife, with what might have been a touching form of home-sickness if it had not manifested itself in some strange ways.

One night, the colonel turned out the whole camp convinced that songs from the musical *My Fair Lady* were being played to annoy him through the air-conditioning unit of his *beyt* (mud hut). Rather more seriously, the officers were woken up during another night by the sound of pistol shots coming from the CO's *beyt*. The Adjutant was the first to reach his door with the others cautiously looking over his shoulders. Lying naked on his bed was the CO, a smoking 9mm Browning pistol in his hand. 'Ah,' he said quite calmly. 'I woke up to find I was being given oral sex by this girl and as I have forbidden women in the camp I decided to shoot her.' Of course there was no one there and he had narrowly missed his toes.

He had been wounded in the hands during the Second World War and could only lift a glass to his lips by placing his straight fingers vertically inside and gripping the glass between them and his thumb. Each time it was empty, he would raise it to the sky and shout for Ghoul, the Baluchi mess orderly. During particularly heavy sessions, his gin and tonics would be filled not only with the standard ingredients, but with a number of tiny fish that inhabited the *falaj* system (waterways not dissimilar to the Dartmoor leats), that irrigate the villages fringing the Empty Quarter. The end came during a lunch with all the battalion officers present except the second in command, Major John Clark, who was standing in for C Company's OC, down from Saiq camp on the top of the Jebel Akhdar, and the quartermaster, who was standing in for me at Ibri. Suddenly the CO, at the head of the table, put down his knife and fork, placed his thumbs to his temples with his fingers outstretched in the manner of some Martian antennae and announced that he was suddenly in contact with John, at Saiq, and instructing him not to waste a Beaver flight the next day, but to come down on foot with the weekly donkey patrol.

This conversation continued at spasmodic intervals throughout the meal with the rest of us trying very hard to keep straight faces. Maybe we had overdone the *falaj* fish, maybe the CO was right and he really was speaking to John, but we never knew, for the next week he was taken to Muscat and was not seen by the battalion again. A delightful man but one who could not come to terms with the loneliness of command in a lonely location and the absence of female company. Maybe too, the officers were much to blame for failing to help, but those were hard days of serious and difficult soldering while there was much heavy drinking when back in camp. Any stragglers, be they commanding officers or not, were left to their own devices.

I have to admit that I, too, had earlier been party to a cruel joke on our colonel.

At Ibri, a previous company commander had imported a life-size cardboard cut-out of a slinky girl bearing a tray of drinks. Using a borrowed Polaroid camera, the adjutant took a photograph of me with my arms around the girl's shoulders, framing the shot so that the tray did not feature. He then left the picture lying on a table in Nizwa's officers' mess, so that the CO was bound to see it. Desperate that an officer of his was secretly and illegally (although I never remember any actual rules) harbouring a girlfriend, the CO summoned a Beaver aircraft the next day and flew unannounced to introduce himself to the girl, and, for all we knew, confiscate her back to Nizwa. He was not amused but after the statutory gin and tonic – without *falaj* fish – he returned in a better humour.

Ibri. Now there was soldiering as one had dreamt it; thirteen thousand square miles of sand, gravel plains and foothills; 150 Arab soldiers and for much of the time only one British officer, myself – a 26-year-old Royal Marines lieutenant, acting captain. Each company also had a local officer, usually a second lieutenant, which, in the case of A Coy NFR was Aziz Sullemein. Local officers lived in their own mess – Aziz's was a separate mud hut – to avoid them from the temptations of alcohol which was tolerated only in the British messes. Nevertheless considerably more beer was drunk in Aziz's mess than in mine!

There were many incidents in this northern command, mostly related to gun running, gold smuggling and the flexing of the occasional muscle by the leftovers from the Imam's abortive attempt to impose his rule on the interior. However it was the escalating war in the south that drew most of our attention. The ambition of every company commander was to lead his personally trained men into battle against the rising threat of communism, but until that moment, my life was spent patrolling the Jebel Akhdar foothills, the gravel plains and the edges of the Empty Quarter.

My regiment was due to take over from the Desert Regiment (DR) in the spring of 1968, but in late 1967, it was decided that the western border of Dhofar needed strengthening in advance of the British leaving Aden. As it was not possible to take any of the DR companies away from their already over-stretched operational duties for this task, a much-enhanced A Company NFR was ordered south. As a supernumerary, Major John Edward-Collins was attached in overall command of this small task force. In practice, the division of duties was muddled and as there were only two of us, he in effect took administrative command of A Company which left me with the practicalities. As John was approaching forty and I was still only half way through my twenties, this suited us both fine. We got on very well indeed, sharing the same sense of humour, a love of shooting, soldiering and whisky.

On 4 November 1967, we left our home base, the mud-hutted camp on the outskirts of Ibri's date plantations, for the 550-mile drive across some of the most barren country in that barren land. Though there were no tracks through the foothills and along the eastern edge of the Empty Quarter (and those that were made were soon obliterated by the wind), it had been traversed many times before, but that was no reason to take the journey lightly. We travelled in overloaded Bedford three-ton lorries and long-wheel based Land Rovers. Without recovery vehicles (nor communications in case of difficulty), we took food and water for twice the journey's expected length, live goats, sacks of spices, dried fish, lentils, floor, salt and fire-wood. We towed one-ton water bowsers to refill the 'chuggels' (canvas bags containing water kept cool by the wind-chill effect as it seeped through to the outside) slung on the vehicles' sides to keep the water refreshing.

By the standards of those days, it was a reasonably trouble-free journey with only two night-stops in the desert: the first at the deserted oil rig of Saih Rawl and the second at the non-existent village of Mugshin. As with our desert patrols, each day we started at 0300 in order to get the best 'trafficability' from dew on the sand, which meant also that we could cover a good distance before the vehicles and their passengers had to rest from the heat. 140°F was the highest daytime temperature, with 120°F being about normal, yet with no vehicle canopies under which we could hide from the direct sun. In the cool of the evening, when it dropped to a pleasant 90°F we would put on woollen pullovers and sit cross-legged in the sand to play Bedu games as old as civilisation itself; most with dried donkey or camel droppings as counters placed in scoops in the sand, the aim being, as so often, to capture as many of your opponent's pieces as possible.

It was a dry, dusty, bone-jarring ride and although we entered the war zone at Midway on the southern edge of 'the Sands' we were glad of the mountain coolness after the burning heat of the desert, and pitied any Adoo that dared get between us and the cold showers and beer that waited at Salalah on the coast south of the jebel. We were met at the deserted oil village and airstrip at Midway by a DR patrol led by Philip Carte, to escort us along the rough track that was then the only pass through the Qara Mountains. It was frequently ambushed throughout its 50-mile length and was to become a familiar journey for me. At that time, almost all the resident company could do with its limited resources and firepower was to keep the road passable by providing armed escorts. It was never in a position to fight any encounter battle with an Adoo who chose when and where to attack. Indeed to have done so would have played into the enemies' hands and left the road wide open to mining or further ambush.

After two glorious nights (including careful briefings and two wonderful evenings of duck flighting on the *khors* (freshwater lagoons behind the beaches), we remounted our long suffering Bedfords and Land Rovers for the difficult journey back to Midway, before turning west through the foothills, then south along the border wadi that divided the Sultanate of Oman from the Hadramaut, or Eastern Aden Protectorate.

November was the month chosen by the British to complete the handover of the colony to the PDRSY and therefore the deadline for the building of our new border fort. Up to 1967, this physical marking of the border had not been necessary, but with the impending departure of a friendly neighbour, it was now an urgent requirement. On the Hadramaut side of the border was already a traditional, white-painted Beau Geste-style fort on the edge of the low escarpment that formed the wadi's edge. On the Oman side there was nothing, with the unmarked frontier running down the centre of the dried water course. A Company's task was to guard the civilian Arab workmen, mostly of the *khadim* or slave stock, originally from Zanzibar, under the command of a British civil engineer. While they built a border fort of mud and stone that had to be just that little bit higher, wider, taller and whiter than the one opposite, we were their protection.

Time was short. PDRSY troops, in support of the terrorists, were expected at any moment. Priorities were set: Wells were dug, not only for drinking water but for mixing the mud and locally produced cement; an airstrip on our side of the wadi was cleared, and the whole area was staked out and picketed with all-round defensive positions on the surrounding high ground. Although we were on the border, all the fighting up to that time had taken place to our rear, in the east.

Wadi Habrut is a wide, gravel-floored, dried-up river bed that runs from the Qara hills in the south, north into the Empty Quarter. It was an ideal convoy route for arms and supplies to enter the Oman from the Yemen by way of the desert, for although there were no tracks, the small stones and boulders on the wadi floor made it good going for camels and four-wheel-drive vehicles. Not only was it the legal border that needed marking and defending but it was also a main supply route that had to be blocked.

This was a fascinating period for a young officer in a sensitive and very lonely outpost. We came under fire regularly, patrolled every day in an attempt to keep the Adoo at arm's length, lived under a palm tree for an officers' mess, and ate locally shot sand grouse and duck, plus, inevitably, the standard, army-issue live goat and curried rice. The only surface water for duck was on the Adoo side of the wadi, but I'm glad to say this did not put either of us off from waiting for the evening flights. An example of the incongruity of it all was the method by which we ranged-in the 3-inch mortars. After dark our Arab mortar sergeant paced out the distance from the baseplates to the walls of the Adoo fort and returned to dial 440 yards on the sights. Life was as simple as that.

We cleared a football pitch area of stones on the wadi floor, though accepting that the south-west corner was legally, in Yemen territory. Nevertheless we played each day, more in an effort to impress those on the other side of the wadi that we were a friendly sort of people. Unfortunately the Sultan himself decreed that no soldier was to enter that corner of the pitch, which slightly curtailed the game and made refereeing rather awkward.

Those three months of total isolation was an amazing period of tension, coupled with long lazy days spent ignoring the considerable threat to our small force – by gazelle hunting, changing for dinner beneath the palm tree, and even building a bathroom, with bath, in the reeds by our wells. Food was often fresh game, baked in an ammunition box over a smouldering fire, supplemented with tinned, smoked oysters and whisky.

In mid-January 1968, with the citadel all but complete, A Company left Habrut feeling that the fort, then occupied by a Desert Regiment company was a fine testimony to our staunch defence of the project. Sadly, for it had become a very personal project, it was razed to the ground in a vicious and successful attack by the Adoo a few months later.

Before my company was due back to Ibri at the end of our fort-building days, orders were received for the move of the NFR to the Dhofar War. A Company would take over from 3 Company, Desert Regiment, at the notorious Ambush Corner on the Midway road in the new year. As an expedient, and as I was already in the south, I asked to be lent for a fortnight to that company in order to get to know the tasks and country that lay ahead of us. To ensure that I would take my company to the war, I had applied to the Royal Marines for a further nine-month extension of my tour. This had been accepted by the Corps and the commander of the SAF. I was thrilled.

On 3 January 1968, I left A Company at Habrut in a small convoy of vehicles for 3 Company's position at Ambush Corner. I knew of the importance of this post for without it the road could not be kept open. Every week in the situation reports sent to the north from the resident battalion in Dhofar, Ambush Corner featured in some way. I felt honoured that my company was to be given the most difficult, and possibly the most dangerous, position in the growing war. My men had earned this privilege through sheer hard work in training before acquitting themselves equally as well on the border.

I night-stopped with the small convoy at Midway's deserted oil camp in the vastness of the gravel plain, spending a comparatively luxurious sleep in an abandoned caravan, but it was a strange place. Stores were still on the racks in the sheds; food, rotting away, was still in the kitchens while oil drums, drilling-bits and pipes lay in neat lines ready for use. The only thing absent was any form of transport for when the camp was closed, with little notice, the oil rig workers drove their wagons to the internationally-sized airstrip and left them facing into the desert with weights on the accelerators. For miles around the camp there were abandoned vehicles that had run out of fuel in their driverless journeys.

I joined 3 Company and met the company commander, Major Jonathan Nason, a seconded officer from the Queens Own Highlanders (QOH). We had much in common especially as I had one favourite uncle in the Seaforth Highlanders and another in the Cameron Highlanders before these two Scottish regiments amalgamated into the QOH. However, there was not much time for reminiscing as my first night was spent creeping into a dawn cordon and search position around a village to the west, well into the mountains. We achieved our aim of surprise but found no known terrorists. The second night we moved into a position even further west and well into the heartland of the Adoo. The aim was to conduct a night approach through the wild country to a village on the edge of a steep valley which, in the space of a few vertical feet, changed from barren dusty moonscape into lush, almost impassable jungle.

The Adoo knew this country backwards and for the army to move undetected, even in the dark, was nigh impossible. The opposition travelled in small groups, had the population in their grasp and could attack on ground and at times of their own choosing: we seldom if ever made contact unless it was on their terms – classical Mao Tse-tung teaching. There was, therefore, a great deal of 'coat-trailing' by the Oman army, so our greatest training efforts in those days went into anti-ambush drills. It was dangerous stuff but the only way to force the Adoo into a battle of our choosing: it didn't always work to our advantage.

My duty for this patrol was to bring up the rear with one of two ex-Adoo we took with us as guides but before we had covered a mile it was clear that we had missed the next man ahead in the stealthy crocodile of soldiers. Maps were almost non-existent and those that did exist were very vague over topographical features.

I had a rough idea of the contours that had been outlined on a blackboard during the briefing but it was clear that following the wrong spur would mean an error of some magnitude by dawn with a deep, Adoo-held valley bottom between us and the remainder of the company. It was not a happy prospect but I trusted in my navigation, a subject I had practiced (admittedly at sea) since before I could hardly read or write. I decided, much to the horror of my two companions, that we would continue with the aim of making the dawn rendezvous. The ex-Adoo was, if anything, more apprehensive than I and the SAF soldier (a Baluchi).

At one stage in the night we came across a water hole and here I decided to set up an impromptu ambush more in self-defence than with a sense of aggression for we would undoubtedly have been outgunned and outnumbered. An Adoo patrol did slide past us in the dark, no more than a few feet away but wisely we decided to let them continue as I sat there with my pistol cocked, prepared, if necessary, to shoot first the ex-Adoo alongside me if he dared move a finger. Dawn did not come as a relief as we were open to observation but it did make navigation easier. It was, therefore, with great satisfaction, and rather by luck than fortune, that we saw the rest of the company on the same spur a mile or two ahead. They too had seen us and took up fire positions believing us to be the Adoo. At that precise moment a leopard appeared running towards us causing a brief clash of priorities in my tired mind. Do I shoot the leopard in self-defence and risk missing, allowing the round to hit our patrol beyond thereby confirming their opinion that we are Adoo, or do I allow the leopard to do the damage instead? I decided to shoot the leopard which our own men could not see from their distant positions, but luckily at the last moment he, or she, lolloped off into the undergrowth. The three of us breathed slowly and deeply as, risking the real Adoo, we stood in the open to identify ourselves to the distant company commander.

The search was a partial success, one man was identified as a rebel and the other, the one we actually wanted, escaped. We eventually returned to Ambush Corner without incident only to be told by our desert intelligence officer that there had been considerable Adoo interest in our patrol and that we had walked through two perfect ambush positions but they had chosen not to spring them. I believe that my unplanned diversion had confused them into thinking we had more men in the area than was so.

We were more successful a few days later on 11 January when we were ambushed three times in one afternoon. 3 Company had been ordered to patrol to the east of the Midway road and carry out a series of hasty cordon and searches in order to keep the Adoo on the move or, with any luck, catch him at rest. It was to have been very much a coat-trailing operation on the return journey although the way out was conducted as covertly as possible.

The approach to the Jebel Darbat area was begun from Ravens Roost, a position on the Midway road alongside a rough airstrip cleared out of the scrub and bush. From this point eastwards there was no track but our convoy of three, 3-ton Bedfords and two Land Rovers made good going for about 15 miles. Eventually we laagered up in a wadi bottom with good all round defence from pickets on the higher ground before moving off on foot, and in tactical bounds for the first of the suspect villages.

The houses in these villages were low, round dwellings made of mud and stone with, suspiciously, not one man present. That night we lay in ambush outside our second set of targets but detected no movement to or from them. It was clear that something was amiss and we prayed that it meant an encounter battle. On that morning (11 January) our searching again produced no young men but did include a cup of thick, black, sour but welcome, coffee with the Sultan's wife's brother – ironically the only male we met.

As we had been foot-borne for twenty-four hours our supply of water was running low (men can consume 4 gallons a day in the desert) and it was necessary to rejoin the transport. For my part all I carried were three water bottles, two days' worth of marmite sandwiches, (actually dried flat, unleavened bread) a Walther P38 and the issued No.5 .303 rifle. The No.5 rifle differed slightly from the more common No.4 rifle carried by the soldiers, being shorter-barrelled with a conical muzzle flash hider. For shelter I had stuffed into a thigh pocket a 'space blanket', silver on one side and bright red on the other: it occasionally doubled as an air panel. Medical evacuation was usually on the back of a donkey with only a faint chance of survival. The company's medical support was one Baluchi lance corporal whose medical knowledge relied heavily on enthusiasm for first field dressings and sticky tape rather than a deep knowledge of the human anatomy.

At 1630, a sudden, but partially expected, burst of machine-gun fire halted our leading vehicle-borne troops who swiftly debussed into their anti-ambush positions. In accordance with normal procedures the heights had been picketed with a rolling system that allowed the main body to keep moving along the low ridge in the wadi bottom. As we passed a picketed height, the men would descend as others in the front moved ahead to new positions. It was a well-practised routine which allowed slow but steady progress for the main body; it also relied heavily on superb mountain fitness from the infantryman.

I was driving the rear vehicle, a Land Rover, and responsible for bringing in the piquets while ensuring that we left no one behind. The Arab company sergeant major, by sad chance wearing my distinctive Canadian army combat jacket, was in the passenger seat with two soldiers in the rear. All three jumped out and ran forwards to a low crest 200 yards to our right while I threw the vehicle into a convenient acacia bush as camouflage. This delay probably saved my life, for a further burst of automatic fire swept the crest some seconds before I reached it. This burst came from our rear and seemed to precede me up the low hill, although a number of rounds smacked into the ground either side, uncomfortably close.

I reached the CSM and knelt down beside him to his right, behind a small but nevertheless convenient rock. Then, just as he began his initial assessment, a single shot removed the whole of the right side of his neck. As he sank to the ground it was clear he would not survive but I administered morphine – in truth, an overdose for he was beyond help and, tragic thought it might sound, other priorities beckoned. While injecting a second ampoule – a third might have been involved but such details are hazy now – I shouted for reports from those troops further forward and sent hurried fire control orders to the 81mm mortar team, already preparing for action. The company commander was somewhere ahead, beyond the crest, preparing the counter attack against the Adoo positions to the right, unaware that we, in the rear of the column, had been engaged from all quarters.

By ambushing us in the position they did, the Adoo had divided the company into two separate killing zones. To communicate between them I had to run a gauntlet along the dividing low ridge. This could have been an advantage to us if the Adoo had only opened fire from one flank or ahead or behind but by dominating both halves of the company and covering us with fire from 360 degrees, they showed a remarkable sophistication. Although this made us suspicious at the time little did we realise the full consequences of this forty-five minute battle. Jonathan and I believed that it was about to change for ever the Sultan's, and his army's perception of the war.

It was immediately clear that this was a battle of a size then unknown to SAF and was being conducted in a manner with which we were not familiar. For instance, the Adoo had prepared false sangars below the hill tops and then dug themselves into real fire positions. Our pickets had discovered the false fire trenches as they moved into position, but as they were empty assumed that any Adoo had left. These false positions drew our fire before we realised we were wasting ammunition.

The sergeant major died quickly. There was nothing any of us could have done except make his passing as painless and as swift as possible. On the track ahead of the parked Land Rover, as it crested the rise dividing the company, a lone signaller had set up his HF set and was even then laying out a dipole antenna in full view of the Adoo on all sides. By the time I reached him he was already establishing contact with Battalion Headquarters in Salalah. I wrote a Flash signal asking for immediate air support and ran back to the sergeant major's position which by then was in the middle of the rear defensive position. The corporal in charge was directing covering fire for what he hoped was the leading platoon's counter attack and, on seeing me, shouted helpfully in what he thought to be English.

'Left blanket or right blanket Sahib?'

As I spoke marginally better Arabic than he spoke my language, it took me a moment or two to recognise that he was anxious to know whether it was to be a left flanking or right flanking attack that needed supporting. One of his Bren gunners then stood on the crest and continued to fire his gun from the hip, again in full view of the Adoo. This attracted much return machine-gun fire but the Baluchi soldier insisted on flicking his fingers for replacement magazines until he had to be stopped and told to lie down. Although it was probably demoralising for the Adoo to be treated with such disdain it was actually a waste of precious ammunition. Another of the soldiers, a young man shortly out of training, lay beside his empty rifle with his forearm raised vertically in the air. On the training ranges this was the signal that he had expended one magazine and was awaiting orders to 'change magazines!'. He received the order and continued to engage the Adoo, such was the state-of-the art of the Oman army in those days. An increasingly sophisticated opposition, with Kalashnikovs, foreign training, 61mm mortars and on ground of their own choosing, was attacking an army that could boast of little except immense reserves of enthusiasm and courage.

Within eleven minutes, a single piston-engined Provost aircraft appeared above with the pilot demanding a target over the SARBE (sea, air rescue beacon) set that we used for air to ground communications. Conversations were conducted despite competing with the emergency beacon's bleeps. Time was short if we were to hit the Adoo. I had received no orders from the company commander. Indeed I had no idea where he was or what he was doing but assumed, from the lie of the ground in front of me and a vague idea of some of the Adoo positions, that he would be attacking in a certain direction. Identifying myself to the Provost's pilot by waving a red-spotted pocket handkerchief, the following conversation took place between me and the aviator above:

'Top cover this is Sand Hat. I'm standing by a 3-tonner and waving a red-spotted handkerchief. Line of my arm. 250 yards. Enemy positions. Rockets please. Beware of advancing own troops. Over.'

'Top cover. Roger. Out.'

This method of forward air controlling was conducted for ten minutes or so, by which time the aircraft had almost expended its load of one 250 pound fragmentation bomb, rockets and machine gun ammunition. The last dive had to be aborted while the aircraft was in the final stage of a machine-gunning run, for I had spotted the sand-coloured *shemaghs* of the Desert Regiment arriving on the Adoo's position. Luckily the pilot pulled up and out in time.

As the Adoo were pushed back into the scrub which fell away into the wadi bottom of near-jungle the battle faded to a halt. For forty-five minutes there had been non-stop fire from all directions and varying ranges by both sides. I lit a cigarette (I didn't normally smoke then but there was no beer in my Land Rover!) and ordered the re-grouping. The company commander joined me from the left flank and sent orders for the sergeant major to deliver the ammunition and casualty reports. I told him the sad news.

Ignoring the risk of further attacks on a lone vehicle Jonathan decided to take his Land Rover ahead before dark with our four wounded to the rough airstrip at Ravens Roost. The Adoo had never attacked twice in one day before and any delay might have been even more perilous for the casualties. I had applied a tourniquet to the upper thigh of one of our soldiers, others had received similar emergency first aid.

The company commander, having left, ammunition was redistributed, new orders were issued, and after allowing the wounded to get well clear we set off with the pickets re-briefed on the likelihood of future Adoo positions. The refuelled and rearmed Provost flew top-cover outside small arms range. I was now travelling in the back of a 3-tonner with a section of assault troops ready to execute our hastily revamped anti-ambush drills. After just two miles of rough track we again came under fierce fire, this time only from the right. The driver of the vehicle I was in was killed instantly while we debussed straight into an assaulting posture with bayonets fixed. The Adoo ran off into the scrub and were chased by the Provost dropping everything on them as they went, this time without guidance from me and my red handkerchief.

Realising that this was the only way to get to grips with the Adoo we continued our journey walking ahead of the transport, believing that they would probably not attack us if we were on foot. We kept a strong element of guides and patrols scouting out to the front and flanks. Nevertheless I was wrong for, sure enough, at dusk and almost immediately after the aircraft had left us (having completed a total of twelve airstrikes) we were again attacked: now from the left. The leading vehicle was hit several times but without casualties. I personally engaged the Adoo instantly with 2-inch mortar high explosive bombs. We used this weapon as a superb anti-ambush reply, for what it lacked in accuracy it made up with morale-sapping explosions in the general area seconds after the springing of any ambush.

As it was then dark we continued the rest of our journey, still on foot, using prophylactic fire against any likely Adoo position, for we were anxious not to have to fight a full-scale battle again as ammunition was low. Suddenly in a long low line of bushes ahead, a white light blinked from the centre of our Bren gun's beaten zone. The Morse message was unmistakably English in content. We ceased firing and the company commander's distinctive voice demanded to know what all the fuss was about. I went forward and told him of the two later ambushes. It was clear that he had been allowed to pass through the killing grounds by the wily Adoo who were waiting for the bigger target. We reached Ambush Corner with one further shooting incident not worthy of the accolade 'ambush' after a tiring, trying, but professionally satisfying 24-mile journey.

We had suffered two dead and just four wounded: remarkably light losses considering the weight of Adoo fire, and the reported fact that the Adoo now had 120mm mortars. It spoke volumes for the field craft and determination of the young Omani and Baluchi soldiers and we were immensely proud of them.

The following morning I took the dead down to Salalah and debriefed the Desert Regiment's command team. Reports were already coming in confirming what we feared. The first ambush had been laid by between forty and sixty Adoo and the second and third ambushes by fifteen to twenty each. This made a total of anything between seventy and one hundred Adoo prepared to take on a company-strength patrol operating in an 'advance to contact' role with air cover. This was unusual and disturbing enough but the last piece of news was astounding. The Adoo had lost six dead and ten wounded with the expectation that this was only half the figure. Among the dead were Chinese. We knew the war would never be the same again, for something had taken place that was altogether different and more sinister. From this day onward the SAF faced a new threat which brought its internal battle into international eyes – not only for the fact that foreign nationals were actively involved but that the communists were prepared, quite openly, to back the local revolution within this most crucial of Gulf nations.

I returned to Ibri with my company in order to prepare for our tour at Ambush Corner but my sojourn back in the north was shortlived as amoebic hepatitis had taken its toll as surely as any enemy action. I was destined to spend many of the next nine months in and out of hospital in Bahrain and London, during which time, and in subsequent relapses over the next five years, my Royal Marines career also hung in the balance. For a brief period I had thought I was better and attempted to take over my command again (including a return to the jebel to accompany the Desert Regiment's CO, Brian Barnes, on a number of post-ambush, follow-up operations). I was even offered command of the Oman Navy (two dhows – one operational and one in reserve for training), but a dramatic and embarrassing deterioration during a lunch with the Senior Naval Officer, Persian Gulf, finally convinced me the doctors were correct. I was evacuated to England the next day on a stretcher. Very sadly I have never returned.

Chapter 5

Beachmaster, HMS *Fearless*

My next ship after HMS *Anzio* in the Persian Gulf during the early 1960s, was to be HMS *Fearless*, which I joined in Liverpool in 1972 as the Officer Commanding the Amphibious Detachment. One of my duties was as beachmaster in charge of beach landings during an amphibious operation. Quite a complicated task, as a beach is a very busy and occasionally dangerous place with the coming and going of all manner of craft and helicopters, delivering all manner of vehicles and logistics while back loading the same. And then there is the weather, the sea state and occasionally, an enemy. All this at a meeting place, a melting pot, of three services (the aviators always managed to get in on the act!), each demanding priority for their own needs.

In April 1972, 3 Commando Brigade took part in NATO's annual southern flank amphibious exercise, which that year was held in Greece. I had only just joined the ship and was, as yet, unversed in the minutiae of beach work, other than the abundant 'theories'. Although I had been a landing craft officer for ten years I had never been a beachmaster, so I was about to learn very quickly, although as the following account suggests, I did not get off to a conventional start. But one that did my reputation no harm. This is an extract from my biography of HMS *Fearless*:

Fearless arrived in Gibraltar on 20 April, landed the commander in chief's band, loaded the balance of the Commando Brigade's headquarters and sailed that same day for Exercise Double Bass, the preliminary in-house rehearsal for the major NATO 100-ship exercise Dawn Patrol. Off Cyprus, *Fearless* met the commando carrier HMS *Albion* with 42 Commando and 848 Naval Air Squadron on board, to conduct an administrative landing at Dhekelia (Cyprus), before re-embarking their respective units and sailing for the first of Dawn Patrol's full-scale amphibious landings – deterrent operations close to the Kavala village in Greek Thrace. These landings were the beachmaster's first since joining *Fearless* and having listened to his predecessor's tales of the myriad problems that always occur on the beach, he was anxious to get off to a good start; not only in the eyes of the landing force and its commander, but also in the eyes of his own amphibious beach unit, plus of course, his own captain. Beginner's luck prevailed for the dawn weather was excellent, the gradients as expected, the water gap and the beach exits unmined and undefended. The Commando Brigade was transferred ashore without one drowned vehicle or wet foot. Things were to get even better, for as the sun brought clarity to the surroundings, two large camper vans were spotted parked among the neighbouring sand dunes, each with 'Adventuretrek' painted in large letters down their sides. A jovial, fit-looking gentleman eventually appeared rubbing his eyes and asking how many men were in the beach unit and for how long would they be staying. The curt reply from the Beach Unit's colour sergeant – a man of immense beach experience, was: 'Twenty, for two nights and this is a NATO exercise for which we have clearance'. We need not have been so on our guard for part of the subsequent conversation went something like this:

'You are not going to believe this but I am an ex-Royal Marines colour sergeant who now runs an adventure company which usually caters for middle-aged London couples who want to get away from it all on organised camping holidays. If you look towards Kavala you will see all my permanent tents. This week is different. Eighteen of the twenty places have been bulk-booked by a group of single Australian girls from Earls Court hell-bent on a massive hen party. They fly in this evening but there is a delay to their flight so they will arrive too late for dinner in the taverna.'

This was too good to be true – indeed a Greek version of the fictitious 'coach-load of nurses from Larnaca that never turns up' – and so bets were soon laid among the marines on who would achieve a first strike and how quickly. An air of disbelief enveloped the beach unit, for such things do not, in reality, happen. But this was about to, and it did. As the girls (plus one elderly married couple) arrived, the Army Catering Corps sergeant-cook began preparing government-issue Chicken Supreme on his hydro-cooker. This unlikely scene was lit, un-tactically, by the Beach Armoured Recovery Vehicle's (BARV, a converted Centurion tank!) searchlight. Pudding was inevitably, peaches in syrup and sweetened condensed milk, all eaten out of borrowed mess tins. It might not have been very military but even the most curmudgeonly of critics would understand the beach unit's predicament!

It was not the first meal in Greece that the 'sheilas' had been expecting – nor for which they had paid – but it was more memorable for that. A veil must still be drawn over the rest of the night, except to say that with all the embarked force vehicles and personnel up in the hills, and not expected to return for 48 hours, a run ashore was organised using the 50-ton BARV as transport. A simple recall system had been agreed should exercise plans change.

In the morning I held my first and only parade on a beach. Everyone was present, (there was one black eye), bets were honoured, and even the most optimistic expectations seem to have been achieved. Luckily a film crew from Telstar Productions that had joined the ship at Gibraltar to make a film about an assault ship's activities were shooting elsewhere.

HMS *Fearless*'s beach unit possessed the BARV. Because the United States Navy had no such vehicle it amused us to 'arm' our beast with a length of drain pipe to tease the Americans. They then formally complained that we had a weapon system undeclared to NATO. They never saw the joke. Nor did *Fearless*'s gunnery officer, who assumed we must have been keeping illegal ammunition not in his magazines!

Chapter 6

Amphibious Warfare – An Analysis

Written in 1998 for *Jane's Amphibious and Special and Forces*

No country with responsibility to protect dependencies and trade routes, no matter how far away or how close, or with a commitment to preserving international, political stability, the reduction of piracy and drug/arms running, can ignore the advantages of possessing an up-to-date amphibious capability. No government, which possesses amphibious ships and equipment, can ignore their value at a time of manmade or natural disaster. Over 70 per cent of the world's population, 80 per cent of countries and almost all centres of international trade and military power are in the littoral regions of the world. Trade routes and most oil, gas and mineral reserves tend to be found in the adjacent waters. Five per cent of the world's coastline is manmade where ships, landing craft and hovercraft can unload with ease. About 25 per cent have beaches suitable for landing craft, 75 per cent of these coastlines can be crossed by hovercraft, 95 per cent can accept landings by small assault craft, sometimes putting ashore cliff and rock climbing specialists, while less than 1 per cent is unsuitable for any form of landing. In the United States, amphibious warfare – littoral warfare – is considered feasible up to 650 miles from the coast. Rather obviously this distance, for most if not all other countries, will be considerably shorter, nevertheless the point is well made. Therefore, governments with maritime and amphibious forces have a unique political, diplomatic and strategic tool that can be brought to bear close to the bulk of the world's population. A maritime force can sail, project influence ashore without landing, withdraw and redeploy by exercising freedom of navigation in adjacent international waters. It was ever thus.

An amphibious operation projects power, support, or medical and humanitarian relief inland from the sea, rivers or lakes without using formal ports, slipways, roll-on/roll-off terminals, formal beaching sites or airfields. It can be militarily offensive or defensive, be conducted by search and rescue organisations, customs, drug enforcement or by disaster relief agencies.

Attributes

An amphibious operation's primary assets are flexibility and surprise, and this is not only in the planning, but also in the choice of operational areas and equipment available. Political, military and climatic circumstances can change rapidly so, if those twin assets of flexibility and surprise are not exploited, an amphibious operation will deserve to fail.

Pitfalls

Compared with a commander based inland or one defending the littoral, amphibious commanders at sea, both naval and military, have the advantages of choice and surprise to outwit an enemy. But, by working simultaneously in the four physical dimensions of land, sea, sub-surface and air, not to mention now, space and cyberspace, they also face a number of pitfalls. They must be aware that a prime disadvantage is the ease with which an amphibious operation can be disrupted or even prevented by a determined, amphibiously-aware enemy. The amphibious commanders must guard against over complicating already difficult events and remain flexible enough to chop and change by using all the assets available. The initiative, which should always rest with the amphibious commanders, must never be lost because surprise and flexibility, once denied, are unlikely to be regained on the beaches and among the shoals. Unless the commanders are fortunate, any such loss can only be reversed by a withdrawal and rethink.

Range

At one extreme, an amphibious operation is concerned with the littoral in its fullest depth and specifically those areas that straddle the boundary between land and sea. Amphibious operations on the largest scale achieve, sometimes by forcible entry, a stepping stone for the deployment and support of conventional, longer-term forces moving deeper inland. Amphibious operations may also include the covert insertion of, say, two men in a submarine-launched or parachuted canoe, for direct action or intelligence gathering purposes.

Four viewpoints

The Duke of Wellington said of his land successes in the Peninsula War at the beginning of the 19th century: 'If anyone wishes to know the history of this war,

I will tell them that it is our maritime superiority gives me the power of maintaining my army while the enemy are unable to do so'. Admiral Sir Bertram Ramsay (General Eisenhower's naval commander for Operation Overlord – Normandy, 6 June, 1944) wrote: 'A combined operation is but the opening under particular circumstances of a purely army battle. It is the function of the navy and the air to help the army establish a base, or bases, on the hostile coast, from which the military plan to gain an objective must be developed. It is upon the army to plan for the fulfilment of its objective that the combined plan must depend... Once the army has decided how to fight the land battle, it is necessary to examine how the troops can be put ashore to give effect to the army plan. In general, it is the responsibility of the navy to land the army as they require but, as the plan develops, naval considerations will arise, which must be discussed and agreed upon.'

Admiral of the Fleet, Lord Fisher, delivered the same message but perhaps more succinctly: 'The British Army should be a projectile to be fired by the Navy.' With the post-Cold War philosophy of expeditionary warfare among the larger nations, exercising the principles of Ship-to-Objective-Manoeuvre (STOM) and Operational Manoeuvre from the Sea (OMTS), these views stand as strong as ever. It might also be as well to remember another of Admiral Fisher's dicta: 'The essence of war is violence and moderation in war is imbecility.'

Violence to ensure success implies risk taking, a course of action well known to successful navies. At the end of the amphibious landings at San Carlos, during the Falklands campaign in 1982, Captain (later Rear Admiral) Kit Layman wrote: 'If the history of the Royal Navy is a good guide, ships are there to be used and therefore to be risked. The Royal Navy has never minded losing a few ships in the knowledge that warfare is a risk-taking business. Hitler, Mussolini and Anaya (Commander, Argentine Navy in 1982) hated losing ships and withdrew them – and in extreme cases, scuttled them – rather than have them sunk. The amphibious assessment was that the job could be done. It was done and the losses acceptable.'

The message being, that if neither politicians nor military commanders are prepared to use violence (implying a risk of losses and casualties to achieve the aim), then no phase of war, and especially not an amphibious phase, should be entered into. The opening phases of peacekeeping operations may, under certain circumstances, be an exception to this unwritten principle of war.

History of amphibious operations

Marines, sea soldiers or naval infantry, trained in the tactics of assault landings, have a long history in amphibious raiding, boarding at sea or establishing footholds ashore for future land-based operations. The earliest account of this comes from 1000 BC when Egyptian 'sea peoples' fought in ship-to-ship actions. The first recorded amphibious operations were Persian landings at Marathon in 490 BC, followed by the Romans, who employed amphibious tactics to help build their empire in the Mediterranean and then England in 55 BC.

The specialist role of the 'sea soldier' was given a more modern impetus when Spain formed her marine infantry in 1537. But some things have never (and will never) change. In 1905 the military author and tactician, Colonel C.E. Callwell, wrote during an age when steam power was thought by some to have solved the landing problem that:

The actual landing of troops and stores from transport is, unless the disembarkation takes place in some well-sheltered harbour, just as liable to interruption by bad weather as it was in the sailing era.

The beaching of boats is as difficult and dangerous nowadays if the sea gets up as it ever was, and it always will be, as General Eisenhower discovered 39 years later at Normandy. The Greeks and Romans recognised the many difficulties of putting men and equipment ashore, as did the Spanish in 1588, the French in 1805, the Allies at Gallipoli in 1915 and the Germans in 1940. Nor were the US-sponsored landings in Cuba's Bay of Pigs and the USMC landings on Somalia's beaches unqualified successes. Although in these last instances, public opinion, a sceptical press corps and faulty intelligence, were also to blame.

Nor is it a simple matter of having the right equipment, the right weather and techniques, the appropriate intelligence, control and public support. Amphibious landings tend to take place across an area where just one man and a machine gun can seriously hamper an enterprise. Of crucial significance, confusion can reign at a time of change in command and control, when a botched or simply muddled transition can easily herald disaster.

The UK expedition against the French coastal town of Rochefort in 1757 is an example of a breakdown in control (if not of command) where the admiral, Sir Edward Hawke commanding the fleet, did everything in his power to aid the general, Sir John Mordaunt who was commanding the landing force. There was no question of co-operation being absent, but the resolute and fiery Hawke had little sympathy with, as he viewed it, the indecision and lack of enterprise displayed by the army under conditions which were difficult. At Mordaunt's court martial, Hawke is quoted as saying:

I always looked upon it as my duty to convey the troops to the road of Basque and there, if possible, to find out a landing place for them and in the case of their landing to give them all assistance in my power for that purpose, but with respect to the question: Whither should they land or not? I thought it was the part of the Generals to determine that question by themselves. I considered it a matter of judgement which merely related to them and that the sea had nothing to do with it.

By modern convention it was the admiral who might be considered to have been at fault.

Good lessons were learned from that expedition, for at the end of the Seven Years War (1756–63), the historian John MacIntire was able to report that once the decision to land had been made and the landing points chosen, 'the whole command of the army is (now) given to a sea officer who conducts them to the place of landing. The (military) officer has little to do until the men are out of the boats for then is the time for him to show his judgement.' Therein lies the basic maxim which, with some streamlining, still exists today, although it would be a foolish admiral who chose a landing place without military (and unfortunately these days, political) approval. Nevertheless, the practicalities of crossing the water gap and the support of those ashore will always remain the naval commander's responsibility.

Throughout history there has been a tendency on the part of ground troops to misunderstand the difficulties of naval forces. Not so the Duke of Wellington, who when summing up his Peninsula Campaign successes, paid tribute to the part played by the Royal Navy. A fact that moved Colonel Calwell to write before the First World War:

In all disembarkation, whether they are opposed or not, naval assistance is indispensable. That is a principle which is universally accepted in the UK service. Where landings have to take place on slippery rocks, where in fact the process of getting out of the boats on to the shore presents special difficulties, it is preferable to detail naval personnel to gain a footing on land to start with and prior to the troops approaching. The soldier is not best at this sort of work. The bluejacket and marine are accustomed to it, and they are not prone to the perils and confusions of landing at an awkward place under fire, by falling into the water out of sheer clumsiness. Naval history provides a number of instances of small landing parties despatched from ships of war performing brilliant exploits on shore. Undertakings of this class are scarcely the soldiers' business.

Change 'boats' for 'helicopters' and the scene remains much the same. The British army's Special Forces (SAS) landing by helicopter on to a South Georgian glacier, against Royal Marines' advice, very nearly brought the Falklands campaign to a very premature close in Argentina's favour.

History is littered with examples of when armies have not wanted to be part of amphibious campaigns. The second battle of Narvik in Norway in 1941, is one where the admiral and rather more junior general disagreed on almost every point. The general was relieved of his command, but still no UK infantry took part in the assault on that city, a task left to the French Foreign Legion, once they and their armour had been put ashore by UK landing craft commanded and manned by Royal Marines and sailors.

The British army was also reluctant to help Admiral Nelson in his ill-fated expedition to capture Santa Cruz on Tenerife in 1797, and as recently as 1982, the British army and air force were hesitant to commit forces to what they deemed would be a certain humiliating defeat for the Royal Navy in the South Atlantic. The then UK Secretary of State for Defence, John Nott, summed up their joint feelings with the memorably defeatist prediction that the Falklands 'once taken could not be retaken.'

Luckily for the UK, the British prime minister took the First Sea Lord's contrary view and despatched a task force within days – on the insistence of the Royal Marines' Commando Brigade that the force also included two army parachute regiments. These decisions helped the Royal Navy win the day. Eventually, the army did send an amphibiously inexperienced brigade, a move that was in truth, made too late and which was to cause much confusion.

Modern philosophies and facts

To paraphrase the final paragraphs from *British Maritime Doctrine*, a Naval Staff Directorate dated 1997:

In the new strategic circumstances, the use of military force based on the philosophy of manoeuvre warfare is appropriate. This use of force must be four dimensional, integrating air, land, sea and political aims. Maritime force has to be regarded in a joint context in which naval assets are the servants of purposes which will be executed frequently and ultimately on shore and by land forces.

> *Maritime power allows the projection of force to be carried out at minimum risk,
> reducing financial and diplomatic cost, concentrating and easing the protection
> problem. It allows the maintenance in theatre and convenient re-supply of all
> that make up logistic sustainability and allows considerable in-theatre tactical
> manoeuvrability at any stage in a campaign.*

Naval power projection, of which amphibious operations are a part, comes in
many guises including Non-combatant Evacuation Operations (NEO), maritime
air support, land attack from surface and subsurface units and maritime counter
insurgency.

In the US, manoeuvre warfare is defined as the employment of forces on
the battlefield through movement in combination with fire, or fire potential, to
achieve advantage over the enemy to accomplish a mission. Manoeuvre warfare
depends on the skill of commanders rather than the sheer force of the units
under command. It depends on out manoeuvring an enemy by rapidly exploiting
weak points, the aim being to throw the enemy off balance by attacking where
least expected, rather than physically destroying him and by cutting lines of
communication, information and supply. Thus the enemy is prevented from
using his own forces in a decisive manner.

Much is being made of manoeuvre warfare in this confused post-Cold War
era where expeditionary and not positional warfare is the cry. Yet the manoeuvre
warfare definition describes what good armed forces should always strive to
achieve, and is precisely what the German army and air force did achieve during
their successful Blitzkrieg assaults across mainland Europe in 1939 and 1940.

In a recent presentation to the Royal United Services Institute, the UK's then
First Sea Lord said: 'Maritime forces provide the quickest means of deploying
a logistically self-sustaining and tactically coherent force over long distances,
providing an invaluable capacity for timely presence and the ability to nip trouble
in the bud. If this fails they can resource to demonstration, coercion and war
fighting; they can shape the joint operational environment in advance of heavier
forces and play a role in support of them, once established in theatre. Above all
else, it is this range and subtlety of choice within a single campaign that is the
key contribution which maritime forces will make to the complex, insidious and
demanding operational environment we now face.'

Some now argue that the recent operations in Afghanistan conducted from
the Bagram Airbase were, if not amphibious, littoral in that they were supplied
and supported mainly from ships in the Gulf. Certainly this was true to a certain

extent perhaps but this is to forget that most supplies arrived in heavy transport aircraft that needed secure airfields from which to take off. If Bagram was not, in effect, an airhead and one far from the prime objective, then it is difficult to imagine what is. Those who argue that, with Ship-to-Objective Manoeuvre, beaches are passé, forget that not all objectives are easily defined and those in the mountains of Afghanistan prove that point. It was necessary to establish a base ashore from which to operate and while that may have been established from the sea it became a land base in its own right, that was itself supplied by air.

Amphibious forces
Over forty countries possess dedicated amphibious infantry units in the guise of marines or naval infantry. There is an even greater number of countries with no such organisations but which retain the means to land men and equipment across unprepared beaches. Some of these military units are further trained as commandos, while others are trained as attack swimmers (frogmen) with the UK's Royal Marines' Special Boat Service (SBS) a prime example. In other countries naval underwater forces supply specialists to assist the infantry in amphibious operations: the US Navy's SEALs, the French Navy's *combatants nageur* within Commando Hubert, and Argentina's *Buzo Tacticos* (Tactical Divers Group) are examples.

A number of countries have small forces with inshore or riverine roles which often support the navy, in for instance, anti-narcotics operations. Uniquely, Bolivia with 2,000 men and Paraguay with 900 men have no seaboards, but deploy marines on inland waterways. In Austria and Switzerland the army man craft on the rivers and lakes, while in Bulgaria and Romania, naval infantry patrol and police the Danube. The tactical area of operations for Italy's Lagunari Regiment includes the lagoons around Venice and this force, part of the army, is equipped with amphibious vehicles.

Some marine corps such as those of Brazil, Thailand, the US and the Republic of Korea are as large as national armies with their own aircraft, armour and artillery. Others may only have battalion or company strength units operating with craft and support weapons thirty or more years old.

Many countries possess very modest amphibious capabilities with just a few landing craft, patrol boats or Rigid Inflatable Boats (RIB), and with no troops trained in beach assaults and landings. If a landing operation is required, infantry soldiers receive practical training. In this context it is worth remembering that many of the major landings in both world wars were undertaken by infantry not trained in living aboard ship, crossing water gaps or being supplied from the sea.

Nor does the status of a major maritime power necessarily indicate a political will to backup political rhetoric. The UK had until recently just one operational, 35-year-old Landing Platform Dock (LPD), one Landing Platform Helicopter (LPH) and five Landing Ship Logistics (LSL). Until 1999, the country had had no dedicated LPH for nearly twenty years, and never one built for the purpose. The fact that the Royal Navy was the major contributor to victory in the expeditionary, Falklands campaign was due to inventiveness, ingenuity, courage and certainly not to the superiority of the ships at sea, with the possible exception of nuclear submarines.

Of course, neither size nor age of equipment necessarily counts, for it is the level of training, dedication and professional commitment of the officers and men that matter most and is perhaps the truest test of a country's international standing and ability.

While expeditionary amphibious operations are generally accepted to be at the scholarship level of the military art and conducted only by the most sophisticated militaries, they are also being used by an increasing number of countries to meet expanding contingency plans undreamed of a few years ago.

Amphibious operations can be tailor-made to suit every level of operation provided it is accepted that they are not a stand-alone discipline but an adjunct to a nation's maritime power projection philosophy – whether it is a state-on-state operation or the cross-border, hot pursuit of drug smugglers.

Finally, amphibious forces (naval and military), regardless of any wider, expeditionary aim with which they might be faced, should also embrace within their remit the time-honoured practice of raiding from the sea. This might be to achieve a limited objective such as intelligence gathering, diversion, sabotage, demonstration of intent, the taking of prisoners, the insertion or retraction of agents or, simply the gaining of experience under operational conditions. Raiding though does require careful, specialist training to a level in excess of that obtained by standard infantry units.

Beaches – are they still in vogue?
Few military campaigns have not involved an amphibious operation across a beach or through a captured port, whether it be the prelude to a major land operation, an exploratory raid to test enemy morale, to rehearse command procedures or, as with Dieppe in 1942, to test equipment and gain experience for a larger enterprise in the future. The final destruction of the Nazi regime began with a series of amphibious operations in the Mediterranean and the English Channel.

After the Normandy landings of June 1944, the combined allied armies had to be supplied by sea. As they advanced eastwards they continued to be supported by amphibious operations that turned the enemy's sea flank one of the most useful was that at Walcheran in November 1945.

'Amphibious operations,' said Winston Churchill prior to Operation Torch in November 1942, 'have to fit together like a jewelled bracelet,' and that includes preparation, planning and making allowances for weather and surf conditions. Little has changed in this respect for exposed beaches are still expanses across which men may have to fight while struggling with heavy equipment, probably soft sand and with no natural cover from fire. Beach gradients and the necessary draught of troop-carrying vessels still ensure a wade, as they have done since man first began his territorial expansion over the sea.

Although future large-scale and expeditionary operations will depend increasingly on sea-based logistics, when the time comes for men and equipment to be moved forward they will do so, largely across a captured beach or through a previously secured port. Gaining these first footholds ashore will seldom be the prime mission but they will be major amphibious objectives – or prizes – without which no inland campaign can take place.

Some now argue that the phrase 'amphibious warfare' should not appear in the context of operational manoeuvre from the sea, itself an ancient philosophy redesigned to meet the 21st century's perceived threats. But why not? What other words will do to describe the complicated business of crossing the water gap and consolidating ashore. Especially on the assumption that not everything can be airlifted in, even by the USMC's tilt-wing Osprey aircraft, to a secured landing site, and even less likely, be flown to a handy, previously secured airfield. I suggest that it is the word 'warfare' that should never have been allowed to creep in, for it implies that amphibious operations are a war on their own. They never were and modern strategists will find much in common with the Persians, the Greeks and the Romans.

Relinquish the word 'warfare' if we must, but never 'amphibious', for many campaigns, expeditionary and otherwise, have relied on their amphibious experts to gain that first foothold and they will continue to do so. Once the options open to a self-contained, maritime force have been exhausted, and ignored by the potential enemy, there will be a need for an access point, by direct action if necessary. Although recognising that no amphibious operation should be an end in itself, men and materiel will have to be put ashore, preferably where an enemy is least expecting it. Airfields, whether in enemy hands or not, are static, rather obvious and usually defended areas, so there can be little element of surprise and that requires specialist men and craft to expedite this initial phase of a campaign.

There is nothing new in this. Think about William the Conqueror at Hastings, Admiral Nelson at Tenerife, the Duke of Wellington and the Peninsula campaign, General Eisenhower and the first weeks of his Normandy campaign, General MacArthur and the west coast of Korea and Brigadier Julian Thompson during the advance on Stanley from San Carlos in the Falklands. All these commanders needed secure beaches for their eventual success but none regarded the amphibious phase as an end in itself because greater objectives lay beyond the water's edge. The one thing these men had in common was the need to rely on an amphibious phase before the real business could begin.

It is interesting to note that although the Kosovo campaign had no amphibious element, ports, even 'friendly' ports, still had to be secured before their use could be guaranteed. Only one quarter of front line vehicles and logistics went by air, incidentally, costing five times more than that of the sea lift.

In fact, aircraft carried under 8,000 linear metres of supplies for a cost of £23 million compared with shipping which carried 13,800 linear metres for a mere £4.2 million. Of note, too, is that 95 per cent of everything needed for the earlier Gulf War of 1990–1991 went by sea. In both cases there were safe ports available but that will not always be so, an amphibious fact that must permanently be uppermost in contingency planning.

Beaches and ports may be mere stepping stones, conduits to greater things, but they are often the most difficult targets to capture. An amphibious battle to secure a beachhead may be a minor opening phase of a land war but it can be the bloodiest, the most vital to win and deserves the utmost attention to detail.

To emphasise these points, the United States Marine Corps (USMC) describes the key to expeditionary operations as being the ability to sustain combat and non–combat operations without host nation assistance and that, in my view, means gaining a foothold across unprepared beaches or through ports that first have to be captured. Of course it also means keeping the logistic tail at sea until required and then lifting it to where it is needed. But there will still be much that has to cross a beach, or land at a seized airfield.

Marines and naval infantry

Lest it be misunderstood, amphibious operations are not the sole prerogative of marines, naval infantry or the slightly misnamed coastal artillery, as they are known in some countries. But because of the complexity and dangers of crossing a water gap and consolidating ashore (usually under trying tactical and topographical conditions), plus the need to depend on the sea for support, the amphibious art does require specialists. Naval, marine, army, air and merchant navy forces have to be trained and continually exercised together in the various interlocking skills that make up the whole.

Ground forces may be required to live afloat during protracted periods without a degradation in morale, physical fitness or sense of purpose. Experience shows that this requires troops well practised in the art. It is equally important that military commanders at all levels are regularly trained with their sea-based counterparts. Nor does the work of amphibious-trained troops end at the back of the beach, for the maintenance of momentum will almost certainly ensure that a move inland takes place.

Most marines are trained in standard infantry tactics for conventional warfare and some are further trained (in the UK for instance they are further 'commando' qualified) for special tasks, including that of raiding. Depending on the circumstances, all but the largest corps may need to rely on extra support from outside their ranks, such as main battle tanks and heavy artillery from the army.

Marine corps throughout the world set high standards for their officers and men, regarding themselves as elite. Thus when they recruit from within their own ranks for further specialisation, such as combat swimmers or amphibious Special Forces, they are recruiting from an already highly trained pool of volunteers. Maritime Special Forces play a vital role in intelligence gathering, beach reconnaissance and preparation prior to an amphibious assault, as well as attacking enemy shipping and port facilities.

In some countries, coastal guns and missiles are the responsibility of naval infantry or marines. In Sweden for example, its coastal artillery (*Kustartilleriet*, KA) is an elite formation with its own amphibious capability.

A final thought, a few governments, mainly in South America and Asia seem to favour possessing a marine corps for reasons other than their amphibious prowess. Marines are seen as a naval counterbalance to the political ambitions of elite forces within armies. If senior army officers use airborne, paramilitary or police forces to attempt a coup d'état, marines can then be deployed to restore the government – or of course vice versa.

Composition of amphibious forces

The size and composition of the amphibious force a country needs to meet a threat should take into account the following factors:

- The nation's foreign, defence, disaster relief and fiscal policies are not always compatible.
- The size and composition of ground forces to match those policies and to meet the perceived threats and problem. They seldom do.
- The distance and time-scale over which any amphibious force will need to be transported, landed and supported.
- The relevant international treaties, bilateral agreements and memoranda of understanding.

Ground forces

Once these points have been considered, the size and component parts of the ground element of an amphibious force can then be judged. Ideally it will be a dedicated, all-arms formation which can be changed to match any operational scene, requiring anything from a section of troops supported by mortars to a division with its own air force. However, a sizeable force is likely to contain some or all of the following specialisations, headed by the appropriate command team. Any permutation for a lesser force can be made as appropriate for the task, from this list:

- Anti-tank tasks
- Armed reconnaissance – waterproofed
- Armour – waterproofed
- Artillery
- Catering
- Combat engineers
- Forward air control parties
- Helicopter command and control parties
- Infantry – preferably amphibious-trained troops
- Light air support for artillery spotting, communications, reconnaissance, small scale raids and
- Intelligence
- Military port control
- Medical and nursing
- Military police
- Naval gunfire support
- Post and courier service
- Religious support – if appropriate

- Signals and electronic warfare
- Special Forces
- Support engineers
- Troop transport – waterproofed.

Sea lift

Ideally the amphibious fleet, variously known as an Amphibious Readiness Group (ARG) or Amphibious Task Group (ATG), should be tailored to fit the military lift. This can be an assortment of ships containing all or some of the following:

- Amphibious beach units for command, control, preparation, terminal guidance, recovery and repair at the beachhead
- Assault ships with embarked, medium-lift support helicopters
- Canoes
- Command ship
- Host-nation docking facilities
- Fast, long-range insertion and raiding craft
- Infantry landing craft or ships
- Logistic landing craft or ships
- Mexeflotes: powered rafts (manned by the Royal Logisitic Corps) for the moving of large and heavy loads from ship to shore
- Host nation (when appropriate and available) landing and hovercraft for ship-to-shore movement and independent amphibious operations
- Tank landing craft or ship.

It is of note that fewer and fewer heavy-lift ships are being procured that can land their cargoes directly onto the beach. While this may be a function of basing logistics at sea, coupled with heavy-lift helicopters and the V-22 Osprey in the near future, when the time comes for cargo and heavy vehicles to move ashore, this logistic and materiel back-up needs to be double or even triple-handled via smaller aircraft. This is a time-wasting series of manoeuvres during the critical consolidation period immediately following an assault.

A new addition to the above stems from the Australian army's use of a very fast catamaran for the resupply of forces in East Timor in 1999. This successful operation was watched closely by amongst others, the US, which in 2002 took delivery of a 330ft (101m) high-speed Theatre Support Vessel from Austal Ships, which secured a 3-year contract with the US Military Sealift Command to use WestPac Express High-Speed Vessels.

Enhancements

The amphibious fleet will need to be enhanced by the following:

Aircraft carriers for fixed-wing air defence, Airborne Early Warning (AEW), fighter ground-attack support and anti-submarine warfare (ASW) defence.

AEW helicopters.

Escorts: frigates and destroyers for surface defence, ASW, air defence, naval gunfire support, advance-force and special forces operations.

Heavy repair ships.

Hospital ship/s.

Mine countermeasure vessels.

Ships taken up from trade (STUFT) once the military sea lift has been filled.

Submarines for subsurface defence, intelligence gathering, advance-force and Special Forces operations.

Support and heavy transport ships.

Order of events

Once the parameters have been established for the shape, size and use of an amphibious force, the likely order of events for an operation divide into clearly defined phases:

1. The issue of the initiating directive and selection of the Amphibious Objective Area (AOA).
2. Embarkation: the loading out of the men and equipment in the available ships, including those 'taken up from trade'. Ideally the outline plan for the initial phase of the operation will already have been decided, so that the ships can be loaded in the correct, usually reverse, sequence.
3. Transit: including poising over the horizon, deception, demonstration and rehearsal landings if necessary.
4. Advance force operations: to gain intelligence, survey or check the likely landing and beaching sites, to deceive the enemy and thwart pre-emptive or counter attacks.
5. Mine countermeasure operations assault support.

6. Tactical withdrawal: often the most complicated of all the phases, which needs to be planned as meticulously as the initial landings. Added complications will be the removal of damaged and unusable equipment, prisoners of war (if they are not to be left in situ) and the need for speed, possibly politically motivated. The withdrawal may be made in the face of continuing or even escalating hostilities. Command and control will not be easy. The re-embarkation will need to be conducted tactically so the landing force is immediately available for future operations.

Vocabulary

Amphibious warfare has its own language and terminology. The following four phrases are the most often misunderstood terms:

The Amphibious Operating Area (AOA) is a geographical area drawn up for purposes of command and control within which lies the objective to be secured by the amphibious task force. This area will be of sufficient size to ensure the accomplishment of the amphibious task force's mission and will provide a sufficient area for conducting the necessary sea, air and land operations. It is usual for the AOA to be dis-established on 'chop of command' from the naval force commander to the land force commander, once the amphibious objectives have been achieved.

The amphibious naval force commander, who up to then will have been *primus inter pares*, reverts to a supporting role, reacting to the operational demands of the land force commander. With emphasis on Operational Manoeuvre from the Sea (OMFTS), this definition may need to be redefined. This to reflect that the establishment of a beachhead will no longer be the prime objective and that command and logistic support will probably remain afloat. It remains to be seen how military commanders, who prefer to lead from the front, will meet these ideas.

Amphibious raids require troops of the highest calibre. They are limited by time and space and best described as the swift incursion into, or temporary occupation of, an objective. Amphibious raids end with a planned withdrawal. From the UK's perspective, it was for this precise form of warfare that the British Commandos were originally formed during the Second World War.

An amphibious demonstration: Conducted to deceive an enemy into making unfavourable decisions, as *British Maritime Doctrine* describes it: 'The demonstration is perhaps the most elegant expression of amphibious capability. The limited liability offered by poising at sea, both in a military and political context, provide a unique form of leverage which can easily and rapidly be converted into combat action ashore.'

Littoral, in the context of modern manoeuvre warfare, is taken to mean the area of the open ocean, which must be controlled to support operations ashore, and the area inland from that shore that can be supported directly from the sea. To each country with OMFTS capability, this littoral area will mean different things depending on the range of weapons and transport available. For the USMC, for instance, the littoral may one day extend as far as 650 miles from the sea, which is the operating radius of its new tilt-wing, troop-transport aircraft.

Advantages

Why, now that the positional concept (so apt, but not pre-eminent during the Cold War) has been discarded, is maritime power and especially the amphibious component of it, so important in the new philosophy of expeditionary warfare? The following list of advantages will answer the question:

Amphibious operations are an effective method of deploying balanced forces to prevent a hostile landing, to remove an aggressive force or to support a vulnerable neighbour without actually doing anything, unless required or asked. By poising in international waters off a potential trouble spot, amphibious forces provide a calming influence, or benign but powerful military to put political pressure on potential aggressors.

Maritime power does not usurp international law nor cause loss of political or diplomatic face, yet it can, when required or if asked, strike swiftly with surprise and devastating power. Army divisional commanders regard enviously the ability to move with impunity, a large force 400 miles in every 24 hours.

Not only is an amphibious force fully integrated and balanced but it can land at a time of its own choosing. It can select or alter its objectives at the last moment and it can advance or retire without taking or losing ground.

Amphibious commanders, from the sanctity of international waters, can be flexible in the size and composition of their responses and their choice of aims, timing and operating areas. An amphibious response to a problem is a joint service graduated response, instantly tailored to meet any objective. Unlike other forms of warfare, operations can take place and be supported long distances from their home base.

Maritime power needs no host nation support nor overflying rights.

Although amphibious forces are costly to train and equip, once in place they more than prove their worth. For instance, within one simple ship which equals the cost of a handful of fighter aircraft, there is a mobile barracks, an airfield, fire support, logistics support, command and control, a hospital and an evacuee reception area.

A ship, even a single frigate, is able to exercise political influence without infringing sovereignty and, frequently, with complete invulnerability. Nor is it a trite point to suggest that a timely cocktail party or sporting event for local factions, hosted by a warship, can defuse small-scale dramas before they get out of hand. (Was it not Lord Palmerston, Prime Minister of Great Britain between 1855 and 1858 and between 1859 and 1865, who said: 'If I want a thing done well in a distant part of the world I always send a captain of the Royal Navy'.)

Amphibious operations can offer relief and humanitarian aid when the facilities for landing or unloading are unavailable or destroyed.

Disadvantages

There are of course disadvantages inherent in amphibious operations:

Any amphibious force is at its most physically vulnerable during the transition from being seaborne to becoming land-borne. This is also a time when confusion over the change of command can jeopardise an entire operation

The greatest obstacle to amphibious operations, whether in times of military conflict or natural disaster, is the water gap – that area between the point of departure and the beach or landing point. It could be between, say, a transport ship at anchor and the beach or the distance a man has to wade from the ramps of his landing craft to the comparative safety among cover (if he is lucky) at the back of the beach. It could be between the banks of a river. This transit, be it in open water or along a coast, demands the utmost protection, for it is here that any amphibious force is at its most vulnerable. Apart from the enemy and the weather, successful completion of this phase depends on a number of changing and changeable factors. Unlike his army counterpart, an amphibious commander has to face threats from all quarters: the sea, the land, the air, possibly space and certainly underwater, as well as from electronic countermeasures and increasingly from cyberspace.

Shipping capable of carrying men, stores and equipment across an ocean cannot always beach with ease, safety or surprise. This makes the double-handling of follow-up materiel by helicopter and landing craft necessary, which leads inevitably to delays and frustrations.

Tide times, phases of the moon, beach gradients and surf all need to be dovetailed carefully with the military plan to ensure the minimum of disruption and the maximum of assistance.

Specialist craft must be designed to match all expected conditions and this is expensive. For instance Minor Landing Craft (MLC) carrying tanks need to be able to beach, unload and retract on gradients as flat as 1:120. These craft need to be designed to give plunge depths (especially for unwaterproofed, wheeled vehicles) of no more than 1.1m (3.5ft). Propulsion and steering systems should not be proud of the bottom of any landing craft. MLC need to be able to winch themselves into deeper water by using kedge anchors. The reason for this is because the stern wash can dig a hole in a sandy beach of 9m x 3m and 1m (29.5ft x 9.75ft x 3.25ft) deep in thirty seconds – an unseen trap for the next wave of offloading vehicles. The Landing Craft Vehicle Personnel (LCVP) range of vessels need to be designed so that personnel on a flat beach wade no deeper than 0.7 metres (2.25ft). The argument over slow armoured landing craft versus fast un-armoured landing craft will continue. MLC need to be simple but utterly robust. A guide is that all but the most serious damage and maintenance must be carried out on the beach, in one tide and by the crew alone.

Hovercraft may need to be deployed to the flanks and across beaches that the enemy might assume to be unusable. This increases the chances of an unopposed landing but adds to the planning matrix.

Specialist vehicles and equipment are required and everything (from radios and electronic weapon systems to aircraft) needs to be waterproofed or 'marinised', yet remain operational. Being small, slow, lightly armed and sparsely armoured, MLC and their cargoes are vulnerable to small arms fire.

No active aids to navigation can be used when crossing the final stages of the water gap. For this critical period the success or failure of the whole enterprise will rest in the hands of junior commanders and even younger coxswains, while the politicians, admirals and generals have to wait to take charge again. Charts may not be available nor up to date, while unexpectedly severe weather can change beach and approach gradients immediately.

Special Forces need to be deployed in advance of a landing. This can lead to loss of surprise if compromised.

Some of the disadvantages can be overcome by the use of subterfuge, deception and sophisticated equipment that an enemy may not understand. Many of these apparent problems can be turned to an advantage, provided the enemy is unwary or amphibiously naive.

Over the horizon

The desire to possess an Over-the-Horizon (OTH) capability is, at first glance, an attractive one, especially for those countries powerful enough to deploy such equipment. Yet it is a philosophy which needs careful thought as it is possible that the disadvantages might outweigh the more obvious advantage of surprise. It does not necessarily indicate a quicker deployment and build up ashore despite the speed of individual ships, craft and aircraft.

The first question has to be, how far is the horizon? Once it was line of sight, say thirty miles from a hilltop, but now with radar and submarine or satellite surveillance, it might be argued that there is no horizon at all. In practice an unsophisticated target country is unlikely to possess such equipment but many do or have allies who do.

Although each operation must be conducted to meet a specific threat, the following could be considered a checklist of advantages and disadvantages when comparing an OTH assault with an inshore assault for any given situation.

OTH operations

The advantages of conducting an OTH assault might include:

- An assumption that submarine and air superiority exists
- Flexibility of response
- Surprise
- A reduced mine threat
- A reduced threat from underwater combat swimmers and fast attack craft (FAC)
- The ability to disperse shipping
- Enhanced early warning of air attack
- A greater area needing protection from all quarters and from subsurface, surface and air forces
- A reduced threat from land-based weapons
- Greater security from land-based visual sensors or observers
- The operation is conducted from outside territorial waters until the executive command is given.

Disadvantages might include:
- A greater submarine threat
- Air defence and sea defence needed over a wide area
- Assault craft (for instance LCAC) and vehicles (AAAV) need to operate at full speed in ocean swells
- During the run in towards the beach assault vessels need protection and risk loss of surprise
- Lengthy build up of armour ashore
- Inshore operations.

The advantages of an amphibious operation conducted from close inshore may include:

- A reduced submarine threat
- Easier control
- Less chance of an attack by sea-launched anti-ship missiles
- Quicker build-up of forces ashore
- More difficult for enemy aircraft to acquire a target in good time
- Calmer sea conditions
- Amphibious fleet closed up for easier protection
- Easier to protect assault craft immediate control of events on the beach.

Disadvantages of a closer inshore operation may include:

- A greater chance of an air threat and attack without warning
- A greater chance of combat swimmer attack
- Mines
- The early loss of surprise
- The threat from land-based weapons
- Loss of secrecy due to land-based sensors or observers
- The possibility that the task force will need to enter territorial waters before the executive order is given.

Further observations on OTH operations

Heavy-lift hovercraft, Advanced Amphibious Assault Vehicles (AAAV), and the Osprey, ensure that the USMC has an OTH capability to enhance the element of surprise. Does this OTH philosophy actually increase the pace of an assault and especially the landing of MBTs from 40 miles further offshore?

Currently, the USMC's OTH capability is based around the 40kts Landing Craft Air Cushion (LCAC capacity of one MBT or just twenty-four troops) with seven classes of ships capable of operating between one and four from enlarged docks. Wasp-class ships can carry three LCACs; Tarawa-class – one; Anchorage-class – three; Austin-class – two; Whidbey-class – four; modified (cargo) Whidbey-class – two or three; and San Antonio-class – two.

In 1988, the commanding officer of the Anchorage-class LSD, *Pensacola*, commented publicly that as the result of converting his ship to carry three, pre-loaded LCACs, she had lost the tank deck capacity for a second wave of LCM-embarked tanks. Thus his 13,700-ton landing ship was only capable of delivering three M60 MBTs across the Atlantic and upon delivery there would be no further work until the end of the operation or exercise. His point may have been over dramatised but the thrust of his argument was well made. A corollary to his OTH debate was that supposing he had had room for a second LCAC wave of three MBTs they would not be delivered to the beach until more than two hours after the first wave.

There are other factors that make the element of surprise from OTH less easy to sustain, such as advance-force operations and the initial taking of the beachhead by troops. This makes an interesting balance when compared with the slower speed but quicker turnaround times across a water gap that might be less than one mile in length from the heavy-lift shipping to the shore. Because ships without LCACs tend to have more internal cargo space, they can carry, as did the British LPDs, a squadron of sixteen MBTs (Main Battle Tanks) and by landing four in each wave of 10kts, these organic LCUs can put more ashore more quickly, and immediately behind the initial waves of personnel-carrying landing craft (thirty-five troops at plus 18kts) and helicopters.

Currently the UK has no offensive amphibious capability either over or under the horizon. It is hoped (without much optimism it has to be said) that the future Multi-Role Support Ships (MRSS), planned for the 2030s will address this capability gap.

Operations other than war

Non-combatant Evacuation Operations (NEOs) are now familiar tasks for amphibious forces when internal security has made ports and airfields unavailable. An amphibious operation becomes essential at such times. Additional to any military consideration, amphibious forces are most effective in times of natural or manmade disaster. They can operate from a sea base or from makeshift ports and with the correct craft, they can cross uncharted waters (especially after an earthquake or flood) and when the surface is littered with flotsam. They are able to deliver bulk food and medical supplies and establish emergency medical centres close to or within, a disaster area, rather than forcing casualties to be moved before their conditions can be stabilised.

If it is not accepted that operations other than war have anything to do with expeditionary warfare or operational manoeuvre from the sea, then perhaps it is worth considering a USMC document from the early 2000s which tabulates the order of events that are likely to attract an expeditionary force. The list moves up from humanitarian assistance, through disaster relief, evacuation operations, small-scale contingencies to, inevitably, a major theatre of war. The USMC's three-block war philosophy starts with humanitarian assistance that degenerates into a peace keeping or peace enforcement phase, and finally to intensive combat.

Collaboration

New weapons, organisations and equipment can make national amphibious forces more effective, but multi-national force groupings are a pointer to the future. In the Mediterranean in 1995, the Combined Amphibious Force Mediterranean (CAFMED) was authorised by Supreme Allied Commander Europe (SACEUR) and came into operation that year. This allows Striking and Supporting Forces Southern Europe (STRIKFORSOUTH) to bring together the amphibious forces of Greece, Italy, Spain and Turkey. The Netherlands and UK forces (and possibly French forces) will be available as add-on reinforcements.

CAFMED staff, consisting of five marine and three naval officers from the seven participating countries, established a database which allows planning staff to know immediately which units and equipment are available and interoperable.

In November 1998, a Spanish-Italian Amphibious Force (SIAF) was established which may be regarded as the Mediterranean equivalent of the UK-Netherlands joint amphibious force.

In the UK, 3 Commando Brigade Royal Marines is linked with the Royal Netherlands Marine Corps to form the UK/Netherlands Landing Force (UKNLF), which is assigned to SACLANT. In turn SACLANT may offer this force to SACEUR, Maritime Control Force Atlantic (MARCONFORLANT) and STRIKFORSOUTH. The UKNLF is also earmarked for inclusion in the NATO Allied Command Europe (ACE) Rapid Reaction Corps (ARRC), and may form part of a Multinational Maritime Force (MMF) or a Multinational Amphibious Task Force (MNATF).

A twinning agreement was signed in 1995 between 3 Commando Brigade and the French *9eme Division d'Infantrie de Marine* (9e DIMA) – the amphibious, light-armoured element of the French *Force d'Action Rapide* (FAR) rapid reaction force.

While these European bilateral and multi-lateral agreements (including the ARRC) sound good, they tend to be politically rather than militarily inspired. In practice a common European defence policy will be unrealistic and unworkable for it will be little more than a smokescreen behind which individual countries can hide their weaknesses, parsimony and differing foreign and defence policies from public scrutiny.

(The Serbian example should be proof enough of Europe's joint military and political ineffectiveness without significant US assistance). The truest tests of loyalty will come (and be found wanting) in times of genuine conflict. This is perhaps why (according to General Klaus Maumann in March 2000) it will take a further ten years (the original deadline was 2003) before a European Rapid Reaction force becomes a reality, if then. European politicians know this and know too that they can always fall back on assistance from the long-suffering and patient United States. Perhaps it is this very reliance that prevents European nations (not so subconsciously) from facing their individual dilemmas head on.

Bolivia, Guatemala and Colombia placed reliance on US forces to help in riverine and coastal, anti-drug operations, while The Netherlands agreed to US use of the Dutch naval air station on their Antilles island of Curacao. Whether or not these arrangements still exist in 2025 is uncertain.

Summary

The changed military and political world is one for which the flexibility of maritime power might have been designed. However, it is important to stress that maritime power does not mean naval power per se. It means the use of specialist ships, craft and equipment to deliver sea, land and air power to where it can most usefully be deployed. Amphibious forces will be an integral component of maritime power. It is a joint contribution to a joint endeavour. The Duke of Wellington, Sir Bertram Ramsay and Lord Fisher were right. Some countries though may never accept Lord Fisher's dictum that 'the essence of war is violence and moderation in war is imbecility'. Nevertheless if they want to be on the winning side, they would do well to adopt this view and steer clear of those nations whose politicians refuse to take risks.

Chapter 7

My 1982 in a Nutshell

That Argentina invaded the Falkland Islands did not come as a surprise to anyone who had lived there before 1982. Then, the near-constant topic at private parties and public meetings in Government House, across the settlements and in the pubs, had never been 'if' but 'when and where'.

I had been appointed to command Naval Party 8901 between 1978 and 1979, in preparation for which I attended meetings in the MoD, the FCO, GCHQ and at Fort Monkton. This Naval Party of forty Royal Marines, sponsored by the FCO, was to act as a trip wire in an attempt to avert an Argentine invasion. The unrealistic aim being 'to buy three weeks bargaining time in the United Nations'. My orders were clear. During 'our year' we were to disregard the previous plan, which, on invasion, had us rushing into the bare countryside to conduct guerrilla warfare. We were now to propose and if agreed at Cabinet level, to practice a staunch defence of Stanley and especially Government House. For this we began planning and training but there were two snags. First, we had no defence stores or weapons and, second, Governor Jim Parker, was being briefed by a different department within the FCO and one that supported his view that any invasion force should be 'met with cups of tea'.

Thus, much of our training had to be conducted without the governor knowing – and when he did get to know he forbade it. Bizarrely, these prohibitions also restricted me, my wife Patricia, and our two young children, Hamish and Hermione from mixing with most of Stanley society. Clearly this was impossible and culminated in a signal to the Secretary of State for Foreign affairs from the governor, complaining about my military and social disobedience. Luckily we had an ally in Rear Admiral William Staveley, then Chief of Staff to the Commander in Chief Fleet, who wrote a personal and strongly worded letter to me offering full and total support for both my military and 'social' actions.

One of my many requirements was the selection of a beach on to which a SBS reconnaissance patrol could be landed by submarine, in advance of any (possible) re-invasion by the British. I could not choose this in isolation, so needed to visit as many beaches as possible, not only to allay suspicion of what I was really up to. This ensured that I had the widest selection from which to choose the best (eventually, Campa Menta Bay) from both the hydrographic point of view and the military perspective.

Using our 150-ton MV *Forrest*, under the command of the redoubtable Jack Sollis – and one visiting yacht – I instituted a series of patrols that, in addition to our duty to train the Settlement Volunteers, allowed me to survey as much of the coastline as possible. I could not risk anyone, especially the governor knowing the secondary reason for these visits and so was obliged to state that I was compiling a yachtsmen's guide for the various clubs of which I was a member. Of course, this did not amuse the Governor either, although the kelpers thoroughly approved. At the end of the year I had amassed over 1,000 photographs and filled a 120-page A4 notebook with hand-drawn charts, notes and sketches of the coastline. I had also annotated the eight Admiralty charts I had, almost all of which were dated 1833!

On my return to the United Kingdom I offered this work to the chief hydrographer of the Navy who commented: 'These are the amateur jottings of an itinerant yachtsman and are of no interest to this department. And there the matter lay until the morning of 2 April 1982 when I was summoned to Headquarters 3 Commando Brigade and a very busy Brigadier Julian Thompson.

'Tell me all you know about the Falkland Islands', he said.

'I won't tell you a thing unless you take me with you!' I replied. We were long-standing friends.

'You're coming. Now prepare a lecture for my HQ first thing tomorrow morning.' I did and homed in on San Carlos, among one or two other locations, as a 'place of interest'.

On joining HMS *Fearless* four days later, I had not been expected so I was obliged set up my office and cabin in a senior officers' bathroom. The next morning I pondered over how I was to play the immediate future for this needed careful handling to prevent my love affair with the islands clouding my advice.

Eventually I explained to the Brigadier and Commodore Amphibious Warfare, Michael Clapp, that I would only offer facts – and never (my very subjective) opinions. They agreed, and from then onwards I was on call throughout every twenty-four hours, often summoned at 0300 to watch a big toe point to a section of a large map spread across the brigadier's cabin carpet. 'There, Ewen! What's that place like?' I would give a five minute synopsis and if they thought the place needed further discussion I would return with a slide-show and comprehensive brief. Added to this routine were my instructions to lecture every military formation in the Task Force as it headed south, requiring numerous flights and night-stops across the fleet.

Only twice did I let my personal feelings creep into my advice. On one occasion I wanted to prevent a landing onto the only King Penguin colony (Volunteer Bay) and, on another, I needed to thwart the destruction of one of the most beautiful islands (Carcass Island) with a vast concrete runway. The commanders saw through each subterfuge and quietly, pretended to ignore me – but I am glad to say that neither locations were used.

Having sailed from Ascension Island I briefed many ships' captains and military commanding officers, including those of the SBS and the SAS; the latter two for a number of 'advance force' operations prior to the main landings. Subsequently it became clear that while the SBS took my advice on local conditions and planned accordingly, the SAS 'knew better'. Hence the raid on the Pebble Island airstrip was inexcusably delayed for, against my guidance, the reconnaissance party was landed to the east of the notorious Tamar passage – with a tidal stream of up to 10 knots – which they then decided to cross in canoes: the most inappropriate method of travel across the whole archipelago. I had advised them to land across a beach at the north of Pebble Island in inflatable craft launched from a frigate. This would have led to an unhindered approach to the airstrip and not one that was obliged to by-pass not only the settlement with its dogs but, crucially, the Argentine garrison. As a result the SAS asked Rear Admiral 'Sandy' Woodward – the Battle Group Commander – for a delay which would have meant the raid taking place after the San Carlos landings. Thankfully, Woodward ordered them to 'get on with it'.

Finally, on 13 May, yet with no final confirmation from Northwood but with an original list of eleven possible assault areas reduced to three, and on the assumption that San Carlo would be the chosen one of those three, the brigade commander gave his 'Orders Group'. The commodore's pre-landing conference would follow.

Immediately prior to this O Group, I was for the first time, asked for my personal opinion of San Carlos as our amphibious objective. Up to then, I had not been privy to the differing needs of the sea and land forces and could only comment as far as the topography was concerned. Now I could state that it was certainly the best anchorage that I knew of – land-locked, surrounded by hills and with useful beaches – from which to conduct further operations once the Commando Brigade had been established ashore. I played no part in choosing San

Carlos other than extolling its virtues: that final judgement was for those more senior than me to make with all the facts and intelligence available to which I was not (totally) privy. Considerations ranged from the comparative strengths and capabilities of ours and the Argentine forces (afloat, ashore, and in the air) together with the topography, weather and sea states, distances to Stanley, distances from the closest enemy airfields, logistic support areas, transport availability (mainly helicopters) and the rest.

I suppose it was inevitable that, as the senior landing craft officer in the Task Force and as one who knew the area well, I was tasked with leading the initial sea-borne amphibious assault onto the chosen beaches within San Carlos Waters on 21 May. Then, in theory, my part in the saga ended, but I remained on call for future tasks, one of which was the landing of the Scots Guards into Bluff Cove from HMS *Intrepid*. However, on this occasion, the ship did not launch its four, laden landing craft in the position ordered by the commodore.

This unforgivable and cowardly action by a Royal Navy captain led to a lengthy, open-sea journey with no charts, in the dark and in fast deteriorating weather, during which the small, unarmed convoy was star-shelled, targeted by high explosives and frightened by the sudden appearance out of the darkness of two (friendly?) warships. It also led indirectly to the loss of a large number of Welsh Guardsmen (and others) in RFA *Sir Galahad*. This is covered in my book *Reasons in Writing* and needs no retelling here, other than to reiterate my continued disgust at the unprofessionalism of two Welsh Guards officers who, a few hours before their ship was bombed, refused to allow me to transport their men ashore to Fitzroy Settlement, from where they would be lifted to their destination, Bluff Cove, after dark.

When the fighting ceased on 14 June I was detached to HMS *Avenger* and, with her helicopter, was to scout the western shores and islands for any enemy who may not have known that the war was over. I was also a member of the tiny team that took the surrender, to the settlement's enormous relief of Pebble Island (Argentine commanding officer: 'Oh good. My men will be pleased'). Our major task, though, was to search for any downed pilots. Sadly, I found a number of dead aircrew and tabulated their positions meticulously for recovery prior to formal military burials. We also conducted a day-long, but fruitless, search for *Fearless*'s lost landing craft *Foxtrot Four*.

With the frigate's enthusiastic commanding officer, Captain Hugo White, we took an hour off to visit Jason West Cay – the nearest island to Argentina – to see if vague rumours of an Elizabethan wreck were true. They were, partially so, for there was indeed a wreck high and dry in the very middle of the island – but none of the rumoured skeletons. Eventually I sent samples of her wooden hull and iron fastenings to the National Maritime Museum who confirmed, as I expected, that the ship, the *Lady Dufferin*, was comparatively modern and had been wrecked in 1882 with all her crew saved.

On our return to Stanley, I spent a riotous 36 hours visiting as many old Falkland friends as possible before it was time to leave. As I was determined to reach the United Kingdom in time for that year's Two Handed Round Britain and Ireland Yacht Race, in which I was skippering a 36-foot sloop, I reckoned that SS *Canberra* would reach Plymouth before HMS *Fearless* and so hitched a lift to the 'Great White Whale' in a Wessex. My plan nearly ended in disaster for we crashed enroute onto Stanley's race course with some injuries but, thankfully, no fatalities. A second helicopter dropped me at my destination yet, as before, I 'belonged' to nobody and so the senior embarked naval officer tried to send me back. Luckily the commanding officer of 42 Commando, Lieutenant Colonel Nick Vaux, an old friend, successfully argued my case.

Because I had not been in command of anyone, my only duty on board *Canberra* was to write my Report of Proceedings of Landing Craft Operations for Major General Jeremy Moore. This was an easy task. All our years of training among Norway's arctic fjords had paid off. Thus there were few lessons to be learned other than that of command and control should the long-proposed, 3 Commando Brigade's independent landing craft squadron become a permanent reality – which it did two years later as 539 Assault Squadron.

The long cruise home in a luxury liner was unforgettable with non-stop concerts, SODS operas (Ships Operatic and Dramatic Society) and impromptu parties. In the end I was two days late for the Round Britain Race but not for anything would I have missed the reception in the Solent by thousands of water-borne well-wishers, then finally at Southampton's Ocean Terminal, by families and friends. For me it had been a very personal crusade.

Chapter 8

The Falklands Conundrum 30 Years On

The following chapter was written in 2012 for tourists on a 'Captains Choice' luxury flight around South America that included the Falkland Islands.

In 2023, Javier Milei was elected President of Argentina and although his government continues to claim sovereignty over the islands, his declared aim is to pursue this through diplomacy and not through military action. It is also of note that from 2025 the United Kingdom has no blue-water amphibious capability, apart from a handful of Royal Fleet Auxiliary civilian ships with which to counter any second attempt to take the islands.

Also in 2025, Cristina de Kirchner (Argentina's president from 2007 to 2015) – a staunch Peronista and vociferous advocate for Argentina's sovereignty over the islandsdelete parenthesis/bracket – had her appeal against imprisonment refused, and so will remain under house arrest for another six years – much to the satisfaction of the Falkland Islanders.

Thirty years ago, Argentina, ruled by a military junta, began invading British sovereign territory in the south Atlantic via an initial, unsubtle subterfuge, camouflage even, of a load of scrap metal workers landing on South Georgia. Then, exploiting a spurious claim to ownership of the Falklands themselves, the junta purposefully misinterpreted an event of 149 years before to back up their actions. After many brief but bloody battles at sea (and beneath it), on land and in the air, the British Task Force emerged the convincing victors Once more the Falkland Islands were 'under the government desired by their inhabitants' and so, in due course, was Argentina. There, after 390 years since they were discovered, matters should finally have been allowed to rest. Thirty years on the problem still simmers.

Why? Because no Argentine president is ever going to admit that the Falklands are not on the agenda, for that way lies instant removal. No British prime minister will do the same although, in law, they have the easier task for the UN's declaration of self-determination – regardless of any other factor – is on his or her side.

Argentina has always threatened the Falklands, which, on the face of it should be considered odd, as no Argentinean wishes to live there, with the possible exception of the inhabitants of Patagonia. Walk into any bar in Puerto Madryn then in Welsh, ask for a drink, the chances are high that you will be sold precisely what you asked for! One senior member of Buenos Aires society recently told me that the islands are a mere 'trophy for the ruling classes and nothing more'. 'The war,' she declared, 'was lost and that is that. We must move on. Including our president.' Similar sentiments have been expressed to me by many retired Argentine servicemen. They have 'no stomach for a renewed fight with the British. Our friends.' So why the current Argentine rhetoric and the equally vociferous commentaries from our side of the Atlantic?

Before I enter this quagmire it is well to remember that pre-1982, the greatest threat to the Islands' sovereignty was from the British government itself, and now, (in 2025), the greatest threat is still from the British government, through its wilful inability to offer a credible defence. If the Argentine government takes advantage of this appalling state of affairs who can blame it.

I must too, at this stage mention an earlier Russian position. The USSR was interested in the Islands – economically and militarily – prior to 1982, for they possessed, and still possess, the finest sheltered anchorages closest to that part of Antarctica most likely to contain recoverable minerals while also being, then, the geographical key to any Soviet dreams of expansion into the Pacific. The Islands now possess the largest military base in the area and this comes with the added attraction of the possibility of oil – 20 to 60 million barrels of it. In 1978 it was estimated that had Argentina invaded, and neither the United States nor the United Kingdom lifted a finger, then the USSR would have been in possession within three weeks! A sobering thought that should remain in the back of the mind, rather than being ignored as fanciful, in these post-Cold War days.

Those British politicians and diplomats who huff and puff now might care to remember that their own government made an offer to President Peron in 1974, to turn the Falklands into a condominium, with both governments 'sharing' the islands. An Argentine diplomat, Carlos de Rozas, reported that Peron commented to his foreign minister: 'If we put a foot on the Islands, nobody will ever get us out again, and soon sovereignty will be entirely ours.' Peron died shortly afterwards and well before this British offer could be accepted. It was a close run thing: an expression that remains apt when describing most of the political, diplomatic and military shenanigans that have embraced this peaceful, non-belligerent community for far too many years.

De Rozas had also declared that even earlier, in the mid-1960s, that he had met in London with the then British Under Secretary for South America, Henry Hohler. At this meeting de Rozas was told, confidentially, that the Falklands were no longer of any strategic value to the United Kingdom and would become Argentine sooner or later. Hohler's advice to de Rozas was to do everything possible to win over the hearts and minds of the Islanders well in advance. The Argentines did just that through sweet talk and practical help. If ever there was a case of Greeks bearing gifts this was a prime example.

Those with long memories, aided by a copy of the relevant Hansard, will recall that on 28 March 1968 in the House of Commons, it was admitted that sovereignty of the Falkland Islands was being discussed with Argentina. During August the Foreign Office stated that it 'would accept Argentine sovereignty of the islands from a date to be determined as soon as Her Majesty's Government was satisfied that the Islanders' wellbeing would be taken into consideration by the Argentines'. In November of that year, Lord Chalfont, on a visit to the Islands, stated that it was Her Majesty's Government's responsibility 'to look ahead and see what their best interests would be in the next generation or after'. One kelper was understandably moved to comment that had Chalfont uttered such a remark in an African colony he would have been shot.

Other early signs of Britain's waning interest came in December 1971, with the unexpected, and certainly inexplicable withdrawal of the 700-ton, 15-year-old, still seaworthy MV *Darwin* – the islanders only link with 'the outside world' as she plied her monthly trade of passengers and the wool clip between Stanley and Montevideo. All the Islanders lacked, they had argued at the time, was a runway for civilian aircraft. This bombshell forced the Islanders – as intended by the duplicitous British government – into accepting Argentina's offer of an air link based on a temporary airstrip they would build at Hookers Point, prior to a more permanent runway at Cape Pembroke.

If this essay was to include details of all the nefarious goings-on behind the scenes – and certainly behind the Islanders' backs – it would be three times as long. Let me just say that the Islanders' best interests were not being served by ministers such as Chalfont, Rowlands and Owen. Yet it was certainly not only socialists that were involved in these various deceits. In July 1979, the new Conservative Secretary of State, Nicholas Ridley, during a visit to Stanley, assured the Islanders that no action – no agreements with Argentina – would be taken without their concurrence. Unknown in the Islands was that Lord Carrington in September was to agree, in a private conversation with the Argentine Foreign Minister in the United Nations, to proceed with negotiations over sovereignty.

More openly now, Ridley returned to the islands in November 1980 to place three proposals before the Falkland Islanders: a form of condominium or joint administration; a moratorium freezing the status quo for a set number of years; and thirdly, the handing over of sovereignty to Argentina, with the United Kingdom then taking out a long lease of perhaps two or three generations – the lease-back option. The first two were clearly a smokescreen through which the wily kelpers saw with ease, while the last – the government's favoured choice – was even worse. The hapless Ridley's departure was a personal embarrassment with a cynical rendering of Rule Britannia being sung amid jeers and taunts!

Bilateral talks, mostly without any Falkland Islanders present and euphemistically referred to as 'communication discussions', lingered on but the many delays were becoming an irritant to the Argentine government – a military junta since July 1976 – as it felt it had become close to achieving its objective.

This situation, from the Islanders' point of view, was further exacerbated by the British Conservative government's proposed reduction in the United Kingdom's amphibious warfare capability – then complete with its own aircraft carriers, plus commando and logistic ships – the only form of warfare able to address a problem so far away from home waters should the worse happen. If that was not bad enough, militarily, the removal of the ice patrol ship, HMS *Endurance*, was a clear diplomatic pointer that there was no longer any British interest in the South Atlantic.

Before continuing, let me dispel one myth perpetuated by people this side of the Atlantic who had never heard of the archipelago until 2 April 1982. Before that date – that watershed – and contrary to British tabloid belief, not every small child in Argentina was brought up to believe that *Las Malvinas* were theirs – for the taking or even for the asking. The Buenos Aires intelligentsia, if they discussed the islands at all, would do so with a wry shake of the head. They were not worth the worry, and while their children in the more enlightened academies may well have been shown where they were on the map, ownership was of as little concern to them as that of Calais to a British child. Yes, one or two hotheads had landed various aircraft and planted their blue and white national flags before endeavouring to take off again. A departure that was usually unsuccessful for their intelligence never covered such a vital detail as the load-bearing capacity of Stanley's peaty racecourse – the preferred landing site before the aluminium-planked airstrip was laid down by Argentina at Hookers Point in 1972.

Those were the days when the wool from 600,000 sheep, a mixture of Corriedale, Polwarth and Merino, was the staple of the gross national product, with each 'woolly' bringing in five pounds per year; although 47 per cent of the land was owned by the Falkland Islands Company whose loyalties (and financial investments) lay outside the islands. Stamps produced about £150,000 and tourism as good as nothing. The cunning kelper still keeps roughly the same number of sheep, just in case! They were also the days when all domestic oil was imported to the islands by courtesy of the Argentine oil giant YPF, and some tertiary education was conducted on the mainland. Serious medical cases were transferred to Argentina by their seaplanes, otherwise the only way in and out of the colony was in the *Darwin* – until she was removed. Fresh vegetables, sugar, rice and flour also came from the mainland, as did the delicious wine, all at a high price. While there was always a perceived threat there was certainly a considerable amount of live and let live.

This was also the era when there could be as many as thirty fishing vessels in the surrounding seas (mostly Polish) for it was estimated that two thirds of the world's protein requirements could be caught (krill, a tiny shrimp-like crustacean) as well as twice the world's white fish needs – both sustainably. By 1978, oil was known to exist and possibly in commercially viable quantities. The expectation was that it would be drilled by international consortia and then piped ashore to the huge refinery at Comodoro Rivadavia before being sold by Argentina on the world's markets. The oil companies and the Islanders would take a cut of the profits, thus everybody would be a winner. I am told that behind very closed doors, this arrangement could still be extant, providing Argentina can come to terms with the sovereignty issue.

Now the gross national product is upwards of £70 million, with more than 50 per cent coming from the sale of fishing licenses – figures that are helped, ashore, by an 'absence of the absentee landlords' who seldom ploughed back their profits into the place where they had been earned.

With the Hookers Point runway and subsequently with the 'new' airport at Cape Pembroke, operational, Argentine established an air link. The airline, *Lineas Aeras del Estol* (LADE), was little more than the civilian arm of the Argentine Air force. This service from Buenos Aires via Comodore Rivadavia saw the introduction of the hated 'White Card', the *Certificado Provisorio*, a form of visa that all travelling to and from the Falklands were required to carry, and that could only be issued by the Argentine authorities in the capital. Although the islanders quite rightly, and quite legally, objected to this loose assumption that they were part of Argentina, it did ensure that someone else with more authority was able to keep out those that were clearly undesirable. It might be interesting to note that, should the current president have her way and cancel the current twice weekly LanChile flights from Santiago via Punta Arenas, in favour of thrice weekly *Aerolineas Argentinas* flights direct from Buenos Aires, then this 'visa' may well be re-introduced. Clearly this would be as unacceptable to the Falkland Islanders as the flights themselves, for they would both form the thin edge of a very long wedge. Kirchner knows that too or she would not be suggesting this course of action. As I discuss shortly, the regular arrival of *Aerolineas Argentinas* airliners could have serious security implications for the British garrison.

With the junta in power, the Sword of Damocles was real rather than imagined. Argentina was too, exercised by her problems with Chile and in 1978, so nearly invaded the Falklands purely to have an airbase outside the range of enemy aircraft. The 'new' 2,800 feet runway at Cape Pembroke had by then been built and was considered by Argentina to be a superb site from which to operate fighters against her old and far more traditional enemy. The then British Labour government saved the day by a pre-emptive and very public deployment of, among other vessels, a nuclear submarine. Would that Mrs Thatcher had done the same in March 1982. It would have saved us all, on both sides a great deal of heartache – and lives.

Argentina's greatest mistake then, was four years later, to embark on a military solution that pre-empted the diplomatic battle they appeared to be winning. At the time it was widely commented by those with no sympathy for the junta, that the reality of permanent Argentine ownership had been put back indefinitely. That is what the British and the Falkland Islanders, even thirty years on, should have every cause to continue to believe – and yet ?

One aspect that is now certain, from the United Kingdom's point of view, is that there will be no alteration to the status quo – sovereignty – unless specifically sought by the Islanders themselves. So far so good, but diplomats, politicians and economists are not concerned with the status quo if it does not suit their long-term plans. Did not both the socialist and Conservative British governments offer the electorate a referendum on something so fundamental to their way of life, as continuing membership of a wayward, even corrupt, potentially bankrupt European Union?

In 2012, Argentina's President Cristina de Kirchner, re-elected in December 2011, declared her country's determination to own the Falklands by diplomatic means alone, while the British government stated, equally as robustly, that it would not yield unless the Islanders wish it to. Meanwhile, in February 2012 a number of Argentina's leading intelligentsia, joined by historians, constitutional experts and politicians, published an open letter calling on their own government to rethink policy towards the Islands. The seventeen signatories censured their government for being absurd, accusing it of needlessly harassing the Falkland Islanders.

Again, so far so good on paper. Full stop? No. Stalemate – because Kirchner needed to impose her will on her people. Nothing – addressing the economy, smoothing social divisions, solving teachers' strikes, decreasing the national debt, reducing the growing rate of poverty, allowing imports (many are forced to travel to Montevideo merely to buy medicines), lowering inflation (currently at 25 per cent) – could unite her subjects better, than xenophobic comments centred around *Las Malvinas*, and she knew that only too well.

It was ever thus, as we saw with chilling results when General Leopold Galtieri, heading the junta between December 1981 and June 1982, decided that he needed to appease his naval chief of staff, to whom he owed a debt of personal gratitude, while shifting Argentine thoughts away from the 'Dirty War'. This was waged in Argentina from 1974 to 1983 and was a period of state terrorism orchestrated by the military junta during which political dissidents and those suspected of leftist affiliations were hunted down.

A swift amphibious operation that, his intelligence suggested, would earn him little more than a 'rap over the knuckles' in the United Nations, was his flawed solution. Kirchner may not have had a 'Dirty War' on her hands that needed masking, but she did have her problems – not least of all a dramatic loss of popularity, particularly with the leading Buenos Aires newspapers the *Clarin* and *La Nación,* who regularly attacked her domestic policies.

Both Britain and Argentina have agreed that only peaceful solutions are the way ahead yet, in truth, neither country has the means to do otherwise except though unconventional warfare.

So let me compare what is possible and what is not possible in 2012 (and now in 2025), with what was achieved by both the United Kingdom and Argentina in 1982. In 1977, during my pre-embarkation training to take over command of Naval Party 8901 – the Falkland Islands garrison – I was briefed by the Ministry of Defence and the Foreign and Commonwealth Office in London that, unlike our predecessors over the previous twenty years, whose orders were, on invasion, to take to the hills and play at guerrilla warfare, my tiny detachment of just forty Royal Marines was to defend Stanley – with no extra men nor an increase in arms, equipment and communications.

How we planned to do that is now irrelevant, other than that the main thrust of my 'new' orders were to 'buy three weeks bargaining time' in the United Nations: as pointless a gesture as the 'guerrilla option' and one that could only have been thought up by a civil servant in King Charles Street! Those orders still puzzle me, coming as they did from a Foreign Office intent on allowing the Falkland Islands to slip quietly into Argentine ownership. The governor at the time was probably being realistic (he was certainly being briefed by a different department within the Foreign Office) when he told me that instead of fighting the invaders it would be best if I ignored London and met them with a cup of tea!

When Galtieri ordered the invasion – *Operacion Rosario* – on 2 April 1982, his advisers knew that, at the best from his point of view, the Falklands were only defended by forty Royal Marines, and at the worst eighty, if he invaded during the changeover of command. He did. He knew too, that the defenders had no heavy weapons, no mortars, no mines, no defence stores and only basic communications. Thus it was decided to land just 500 marines of 5 Marine Infantry Brigade across Yorke Bay beach from the one tank landing ship that the Argentine navy possessed. This 8,000-ton (fully laden) amphibious ship – all that was needed – disgorged her load using amphibious tracked landing vehicles. The town and therefore the colony was soon taken. Once Britain's unexpected reaction became clear, most of the Argentine marines were replaced by up to 15,000 army personnel, mainly made up of conscripts, some of whom thought they were in Patagonia facing the Chileans.

It is popularly assumed, that if this was to happen in 2012, the United Kingdom would not have the amphibious capability to carry out a repeat re-invasion. Apart from one glaring absence this is not true. The United Kingdom's current capability includes far better, and more, amphibious ships than existed in 1982. Then the amphibious task force centred around two 12,000-ton assault ships – HMS *Fearless* and HMS *Intrepid,* but both were elderly and with out-of-date communication systems. *Intrepid,* in refit, was swiftly returned to front line service. There were no helicopter carriers (known sometimes as 'commando ships') as HMS *Hermes* had been converted back to operate Harriers and the earlier stalwarts of the amphibious fleet, the original 'commando ships', HMSs *Bulwark* and *Albion* had long gone. Six 5,000-ton Royal Fleet Auxiliary logistic landing ships of the Sir Lancelot class also carried marines and stores. Each had one helicopter spot.

In other words, as far as 'helicopter spots at sea' were concerned (a must for commando, heli-borne, ship-to-shore operations) there were just fourteen spots spread across eight ships: a planning nightmare, and why the initial landings had to be conducted by slow, unarmed and vulnerable landing craft. The old *Bulwark* and *Albion* had had nine spots each with each ship able to carry 900 marines. In support, there was a second aircraft carrier HMS *Invincible* with her embarked Harrier squadron and that was that as far as the country's amphibious capability was concerned. In due course a number of Royal Fleet Auxiliary and merchant ships, including the cruise liner SS *Canberra*, were added to the fleet.

In 2012, an amphibious task force could have consisted of (counting those in refit for, as was demonstrated in 1982, when the need is there, these can be made operational in a remarkably short time) two modern 20,000-ton assault ships, HMSs *Bulwark* and *Albion* each with four, roll on-roll off landing craft and one helicopter carrier or commando ship, the 22,000-ton HMS *Ocean* which, unlike earlier conversions from aircraft carriers, is the only such ship to have been designed for purpose from a blank piece of paper onwards. An additional helicopter carrier, 'commando ship', is the 21,000-ton HMS *Illustrious,* while 539 Assault Squadron with its modern hovercraft and potent, heavily armed and fast offshore raiding craft is a new addition to 3 Commando Brigade's order of battle.

Supporting this nucleus of the amphibious fleet is the Royal Fleet Auxiliary *Argus* capable of transporting six medium-lift helicopters. Her role now is as a 'primary casualty receiving ship' but as she is not declared as a hospital ship she still has a military role to play. Further logistic support comes from six 26,000-ton, civilian transport ships and, replacing the six logistic landing ships, are three 16,000-ton Bay-class landing ships (although they cannot actually 'beach' as their predecessors could) with their internal dock for unloading stores onto smaller landing craft and their ability to operate Chinook helicopters. That makes a possible twenty-one helicopter spots (depending slightly on configurations at the time) across six ships, all of which are designed to, or can at a pinch, carry Royal Marine commandos. A luxury compared with 1982. (By 2025, all amphibious shipping had been sold with no replacements in sight until, possibly, the early 2030s.)

Some have pointed to the tragic decimation of the British merchant fleet in recent years – without whose ships any such amphibious expedition would be pushed – but civilian ships can change flags and their nationality in a matter of hours, again as happened in 1982.

It will though be noticed, that there is a vital missing component to the overall amphibious task force of today: sea-based, fixed-wing aircraft for airborne early warning, air defence and ground attack. It is this absence that now renders any amphibious operation impotent if it is to be conducted more than, say, 300 miles from the United Kingdom, or a similar distance from a friendly country who will allow overflying rights and host nation support.

Such conveniences are becoming less and less likely in the Far East and certainly will not exist in the South Atlantic. Even host nation support comes at a price, as we saw in Libya where the Typhoons were only able to attack a single target, on a single mission on sorties that required air-to-air refuelling plus further, and vast expenses incurred for using a foreign air base. Attacking ground targets in Libya – often a single vehicle – could so easily have been undertaken by sea-based aircraft. Apache helicopters were deployed successfully but inevitably their range was limited compared to a Harrier, had we still had them.

It continues to beggar all military, financial (even to me who has yet to pass O level Maths) common sense that the Royal Navy – indeed our very country with its continuing world-wide obligations – had no sea-based, fixed wing aircraft to tide it over until the two Queen Elizabeth-class aircraft carriers became operational in 2020. (They did become operational but with only a fraction of the fixed-wing aircraft for which they were designed to operate.)

Thus, it must be concluded, that Great Britain had a far more potent amphibious capability than in 1982, and again, Kirchner knew that.

Although she said there will be no military intervention, is she to be trusted? Can we believe her? Currently we can, providing she means there will be no conventional attempt to regain the Islands by force for the simple reason that, unlike thirty years ago, Argentina has no amphibious capability at all. Argentina's one tank landing ship has been scrapped and although the country still possesses tracked amphibious vehicles (as used in 1982), there are now no vessels in which to transport them to the Islands. The four tiny and ancient landing craft she does still operate, are only of any use in confined, coastal waters. Recently there were plans to purchase two 12,000-ton French Foudre-class assault ships, similar in operation to the British Fearless-class, but the contract was cancelled due to lack of money. Had they been purchased and had they been used in an amphibious repeat of 1982, escorted by the current thirteen, Exocet-armed destroyers and frigates of the Armada Argentina, with up to eleven air-to-surface Exocet-armed Super Étendards in support, then the two British surface ships, currently HMS *Dauntless* and HMS *Clyde*, might have faced a problem.

But the *Foudre*-class landing ships were not acquired and so Argentina is, in 2012, unable to launch an amphibious assault against the Falkland Islands. That of course does not rule out the use of the highly capable Argentine Special Forces nor of some maverick expedition with little official approval. The Achilles heel in the Falklands Islands are no longer undefended beaches, but the well-defended air base at Mount Pleasant.

The British Prime Minister says that 'given time' reinforcements would be sent, but they would have to arrive via Mount Pleasant airbase. Yet supposing that was already in Argentine hands? It has been stated – and all who understand these things will agree – that if Mount Pleasant was to be lost, then the Islands would too be lost. Clearly the current senior officers in the Falklands (echoing those in the British Ministry of Defence) do not accept this hypothesis on the basis that the islands are 'so well protected' that no Argentine attack would succeed. To use an apt cliché, 'they would say that wouldn't they' to appease their political masters. Argentina no longer has, it is true, the conventional ships with which to take the Islands back, but the country does have a useful selection of highly trained and efficient, unconventional organisations and military units. While I trust that this form of assault has been well war-gamed we should remember that we are considering a land mass the size of Wales surrounded by at least 15,000 miles of coast line and over 900 islands.

Thus, the Argentine government still has the odds on its side for quite simply, the only defences of the Falklands at the moment, assuming no British reinforcements can reach the Islands in time, are minuscule. Cameron makes the assumption that the Argentines will post on Facebook precisely when, where and how any retaking might take place. The Argentines are not stupid, indeed very far from it, as the Prime Minister should have learned from a predecessor. Any re-invasion will be planned and rehearsed under covert or even clandestine conditions.

Four Typhoon aircraft, one Type 45 destroyer, one offshore patrol vessel, one infantry company, the Falkland Islands' efficient and professional Defence Force (now a far cry from the enthusiasts who served in this 'dad's army' prior to 1982), a detachment of the Royal Air Force Regiment plus Royal Artillery Rapier surface-to-air missile teams, is not a large enough defence force when one considers the juxtaposition and size of the potential enemy, as well as the area to be guarded. The fact is that it should be more than sufficient to deter any Argentine attempt to try for a second time, yet here lies the dreadful paradox. While Argentina's forces are in many respects a shadow of what they were in 1982, the United Kingdom's amphibious capability has increased considerably, and yet the threat to the Islands remains, due to lack of sea-based air power. It really is as simple as that.

One British commenter – a learned academician – has stated in a public letter that, if the Argentines land, then we could simply bomb Mount Pleasant runway yet we do not now have the wherewithal to do so. A glance at *Jane's World Air Forces* will reveal that the word 'bomber' is strikingly absent from the list of current RAF aircraft. Another learned, but also non-military gentlemen announced, that Argentina could never take Mount Pleasant, while failing to consider all the possibilities of unconventional warfare: hypothetical and probable. The word 'never' is not in common use among military planners, or it certainly should not be. The unexpected should always be expected.

In 1982, the Argentine naval air arm had five Super Étendard aircraft (one of which was cannibalised for spares following an arms export embargo imposed by the French President Mitterrand) and five air-launched Exocet missiles with which to confront a fleet containing a number of major warships, including the two carriers and the two amphibious headquarters ships. That they were not hit while others were is not relevant. Very serious damage was inflicted to morale and plans. Let us not forget that for Argentina, the 'Exocet war' of 1982 was a resounding success, waged against one of the most sophisticated (although not, now, one of the largest) navies in the world. Currently Argentina has – or will have when their up-grading is complete – ten (possibly eleven) Exocet-armed Super Étendards to launch against one destroyer – albeit one of the most modern and capable air defence ships in existence – and one patrol vessel. What would be the chances of at least one missile getting through from say, a mass attack of eight Super Étendards, coinciding with the landing of an innocent-seeming civilian airliner with *Aerolineas Argentinas* painted down its side, yet full of Special Forces?

Now let me consider a number of hypothetical scenes. There are periods when no Typhoon is in the air. There are times when HMS *Dauntless* (or her replacement) is 800 miles to the east patrolling South Georgia. While she can detect multiple aircraft from very far away and 'take them out' she is a few days sailing away against a gale-force westerly wind and heavy seas. A scheduled *Aerolineas Argentinas* airliner is inbound from Buenos Aires, heading for Mount Pleasant. Eight Exocet-armed Super Étendards are made ready at Rio Grande naval air base, as are four Hercules C-130 heavy-lift aircraft. Argentina's two 2,300-ton Santa Cruz-class submarines (described in *Jane's Fighting Ships* as 'capable for commando insertions') are returning from operations along the

Falklands' southern coasts. To allay suspicion, in a variety of naval bases and ports along the length of Argentina's coastline, six Exocet-armed Espora-class frigates are under sailing orders as are four, similarly-armed, Almirante Brown destroyers. Both classes are fully stored with ammunition for their OTO Melara guns capable of engaging land targets out to twelve-and-a-half nautical miles.

Let us assume that Kirchner had had her way and that this is a regular *Aerolineas Argentinas* airliner on a return trip to Mount Pleasant, a round journey it makes three times a week. Earlier the Argentine Navy's *Buzos Tácticos* had embarked in two of their three notoriously-difficult-to-locate (impossible to detect by HMS *Clyde* then the Islands' guard ship), conventional submarines. One team has landed south west of Mount Pleasant and begins reporting back aircraft and ship movements. Snipers and demolition experts are sent forward to watch the airbase. A second team was landed south of Stanley and begins to observe the Cable and Wireless complex, Government House and the Cape Pembroke control tower, ready, on orders, to assault all three.

The passengers on what appears to be the regular *Aerolineas Argentinas* flight are yet more Buzos Tácticos and Comandos Anfibios. No one will willingly – not even a Type 45 frigate's commanding officer, a Typhoon pilot or a Royal Artillery Rapier battery – shoot down a civilian airliner. The aircraft lands on the 8,500 foot main runway but stops at the intersection with the secondary cross-runway. Due to the crosswind strength the Typhoons may have difficulties taking off (it's a bit late anyway and they will have been targeted by Special Forces mortar fire) while the follow-on Argentine Hercules will be able to land and take off using the west-east runway. The 'passengers' disembark from their Boeing, rapidly and aggressively in a well-practiced routine using ropes from each escape exit, and supported by covering fire not only from the aircraft itself through instantly broken windows but from Special Forces already ashore from their submarines. The Argentines know well how to attack an airfield having studied the British attempts to do so at Rio Grande in May 1982.

Of course the above demands a number of failures on the British part. To start with, intelligence. If, as we must hope, British intelligence reports from South America are more acceptable to Whitehall than they were in 1982, then it is just possible that reinforcements could be flown in to Mount Pleasant in time. But I wouldn't bet on it.

For the Argentines to gain control other British failures would need to occur. The Type 45, if in the area, is capable of dealing with these hypothetical threats, but as we saw with HMS *Sheffield,* even the most modern of warships is only as good as it weakest link – the crew's vigilance. Another failure would be to allow the *Buzos Tácticos* to land from a submarine and observe but we are talking about a large area and superbly trained men. A major failure would be to allow the airliner to land yet that would, indeed, be a difficult decision to weigh up almost instantly.

With no air defence over the Falkland Islands, the Argentine navy's destroyers, frigates and forty-seven fighters (albeit now elderly but with no aerial opposition) could close on the islands long enough to bombard vital points, including the radar and Rapier installations, until the ships were forced away by the eventual arrival of a Royal Navy nuclear submarine.

So, let me end this hypothesis with a stark statement. Argentina now holds Mount Pleasant and Stanley airfields. She also has air superiority and (temporary) control of the surrounding sea. Britain's only possible military response (let us forget what might be debated in the United Nations) is to send a nuclear submarine. Now we have another stalemate situation. What does the United Kingdom do with that boat? Launch Tomahawk land-attack missiles onto mainland and Island targets or admit defeat? Cameron's promise that the Falklands can be reinforced quickly is seen to be a hollow, uneducated statement based on political hope rather than reality.

Thus, thirty years after John Nott's gloomy prognosis that the Islands 'once taken could not be regained', his defeatist attitude will finally have come true. It will have come true thanks to a Conservative government and the senior Ministry of Defence officers that briefed it – officers and politicians who were responsible for the loss of sea-based air power, plus the near one hundred years of harsh experience that came with it.

Is much of the above a truly fanciful hypothesis? Yes, I sincerely hope so, but despite promises and a lukewarm military, history shows that a South American president is a dangerous beast when cornered by events at home. This would be especially so if he, or she, is persuaded that the odds of success in the Falklands were worth the gamble in the sure knowledge that, if conducted swiftly enough, this time, there will be no retaliation.

Chapter 9

Stanley Runway and the Operation Black Buck Raids, 1982

A number of us were disturbed at the confusion over the success or otherwise of the bombing of Stanley airfield during the Falklands conflict. I was asked to research and then write a paper to be signed by many who were involved. Among the many responses, to save space, I have included just three illustrations.

BACKGROUND

On the 21 July, 2020, the *Daily Telegraph* published a letter by Dr M. Fopp, a member of the RAF Historical Society, which read in part:

> *I take issue with most of what Mark Campbell-Roddis says in defence of aircraft carriers and the Royal Air Force [Letters, July 20] As a historian, I object to his suggestion that the RAF raids on Port (sic) Stanley in the Falklands conflict were 'ineffectual'. As well as demonstrating the strategic ability of Britain to attack a target at a greater distance than had ever been achieved before, the 'BLACK BUCK' raids denied the airfield to the enemy's attacking fast jets... and cratered its runway. Royal Navy spin doctors gave little credit to the RAF's contribution, but it was key in 1982, as the proposed coordination of effort is meant to be today.*
>
> *Dr Michael A. Fopp*
> *Director General, RAF Museums, 1988-2010.*

This was followed by a response from Major General Julian Thompson, published on 25 July, which read in part:

> *The runway at Stanley in the Falklands was not damaged by the BLACK BUCK raids as Michael A. Fopp says — or not enough to prevent Argentine C-130s from using the airfield almost every night of the war. As we got closer,*

my artillery forward observers could see them, but my guns were just out of range.

Staff visiting the airfield just after the Argentine surrender reported no craters on the runway, but several on each side. The runway was too short for fast jets, and the Argentines failed to use the time before the British carriers arrived to extend it.

Major General Julian Thompson
Commander, 3 Commando Brigade in the Falklands, 1982.

Anxious to nip in the bud these apparent misconceptions by an RAF historian, Lieutenant Commander Lester May spoke and wrote to Dr Fopp on 29 July, 2020. This elicited a reply email on 30 July, which contained no text but just one photograph of Stanley runway showing a bomb crater precisely in the middle, and just short of halfway down the runway from the east. Dr Fopp offered no explanation and tellingly, no clue as to this photograph's origin. We now know, and are puzzled by, this photograph's provenance whereby a Fleet Air Arm-sourced (FAA) aerial photograph has appeared in RAF files in The National Archives showing a crater in a position that does not appear in any other known FAA photograph. Together with its RAF-centric caption, it was clear that this confusing affair needed to be studied in more detail.

Although this photograph is credited on its reverse to 101 Squadron RAF, at that time the only aircraft capable of aerial reconnaissance were the Sea Harriers of 801 and 800 Naval Air Squadrons.

Interestingly, the first three craters in this RAF photograph – one on the runway's centreline, one on the edge on packed grass and earth over peat, and the third also on packed earth – are all too similar. Commodore Michael Clapp (lately commanding officer 801 Naval Air Squadron flying Buccaneer Mk II bombers, and in 1982, Commander Amphibious Task Group) believes that they are suspiciously evenly spaced and in a dead straight line, unlike lines of craters in other photographs which tend to be slightly zig-zagged and not so evenly spaced.

INTRODUCTION

The RAF have long claimed to have hit Stanley runway dead centre with a Vulcan-launched 1,000 lb bomb during the first raid of Operation Black Buck (Black Buck 1), on the night of the 30 April/1 May 1982, while also claiming that this strike seriously restricted Argentine flying operations. The RAF also claim that their raid on Stanley airport forced the Argentine air force (AAF) to remove a significant number of aircraft to the north of the mainland to protect the major cities, and especially Buenos Aires, against British bombers, thus reducing the threat to the Task Force. After 38 years of assumptions, this paper has been written using all photographic, eyewitness and written evidence that can be obtained from Argentina, France, the United States, the Falkland Islands and the United Kingdom, in order to assess whether or not the RAF claims for the success of Black Buck 1 have any authenticity. Black Buck 2's bombs, dropped overnight 3 /4 May landed off the western end of the runway. Black Buck 3 was cancelled, and Black Buck 7's bombs missed in the same general area as Black Buck 2. The results of these latter three raids are not in contention

After the campaign, the same photograph that Dr Fopp sent to Lieutenant Commander May was circulated within the RAF and became accepted as fact. Commander Tim Gedge (CO of 809 Naval Air Squadron on HMS *Invincible* in 1982), has stated in an email to Major General Julian Thompson:

> *This photo shows the runway as it was after the second BLACK BUCK raid. In the photograph sent to Lieutenant Commander May by Dr Fopp, amazingly the runway has grown a new crater, this one dead centre of the runway. This photograph has however been widely circulated by the RAF and I assume it was released as an official photograph....*
>
> *This original photo [processed on board HMS* Invincible *within an hour] is un-doctored, unlike one I was shown at Cranwell some months later which showed the first bomb crater slap bang on the runway centreline – and which has appeared several times in published media since then. But your point about C-130s landing there is most relevant. We all know from numerous sources that the runway was never put out of action.*

A first exploratory paper on this subject was written on 17 August and distributed internally. Mindful of the broader implications of our findings, it was decided to alert the First Sea Lord, Admiral Radakin. This was a matter of courtesy that allowed him to hear firsthand of our concerns before they reached a wider readership. Commodore Clapp sent this email which reads in part:

> *Dear First Sea Lord,*
> *I am writing on behalf of General Thompson and several others to warn you that a Dr. Michael Fopp, who was once the Director General, RAF Museums,*

has been accusing some of the retired Naval Service of being spin-doctors over the subject of the Stanley airfield runway in the Falkland Islands in 1982. The matter is that the RAF by their BLACK BUCK raids have always claimed that their Vulcans managed to drop one bomb on the runway and so put it out of action. However, Lt. Col. Ewen Southby-Tailyour and others have evidence that no bomb was landed on [the centre of] the runway. This is supported by opinions from Argentine officers...including General Menéndez.

It is apparent that photos have been 'adjusted' and the spin doctors must have worn light blue. Dr Fopp was politely informed nearly a week ago but has so far failed to reply. [He replied on 12 August with a non-committal response and the e-correspondence was terminated.] We hope this matter will not boil over and hinder any relationship you have with the Chief of Air Staff or create too much acrimony. If you wish to see the evidence I will let Ewen know. Colonel Maynard suggested we hand it to the Naval Historical Branch and this will happen when Ewen returns and all known evidence is collected.

With my best wishes,
Michael Clapp, CB. Cdre. Ret'd.

The First Sea Lord's response (also writing as a barrister) states in part:

Dear Michael,

Very good to hear from you and thank you for the email. All that you say makes very good sense to me and bringing in the Naval Historical Branch strikes me as the best tactic. I have copied in Stephen Prince accordingly. And I hope that I am close enough to Mike Wigston [CAS] to dampen this down if it all starts to boil over.... Thank you to you and Julian and Ewen for highlighting this issue in The Telegraph and all the preparatory work that accompanies such efforts: history and truth are as important as ever.
Best wishes,
Tony

This second paper not only has a wider circulation list, outside the naval service, but it takes the discussion to a higher level. It will look at as much eyewitness, documentary and photographic evidence as possible in order to refute or verify Dr Fopp's photographic opinion that the Black Buck raids denied the runway to Argentine fast jets and cratered it on the centreline as shown in the original photograph. In doing so it will also conclude whether or not the Black Buck raids met the RAF's official aim which was to impede Argentine air operations.

HISTORY

Argentina invaded the Falkland Island overnight on 1 /2 April 1982.

While the Task Force was being made ready and despatched towards Ascension Island, the RAF was authorised to attack the only paved runway throughout the archipelago in order to prevent fast jets from operating out of Stanley airfield (had the Argentines lengthened the runway across the cleared ground to the west) and, secondly, to prevent transport aircraft from resupplying the Argentine occupying forces. As the (unextended) runway was just over 4,000 feet in length two craters would have been needed for this second aim to have been met. A single crater, halfway down the runway would allow C-130s to operate off either end. Using 'tactical take-off' speeds, and depending on its payload, a Hercules can become airborne in as little as 900 feet, although 2,000 feet is preferred. Most fast jets would have needed the full runway.

The RAF mounted seven Black Buck bombing raids from Ascension Island; the first three targeted the runway (the third raid of these was cancelled prior to take off because of the weather), and the seventh raid targeted airfield installations. The remaining three raids (4, 5 and 6) were aimed at radar installations and airfield facilities. According to Air Operation Order 3/82 271440 Z APR 82, the mission of the Black Buck raids was 'To impede Argentinian air operations from Stanley Airfield'.

In between the first and second Black Buck raids, the Argentine cruiser ARA *General Belgrano* was torpedoed and sunk, thus forcing the Argentine Navy and merchant fleet to remain in national coastal waters for the duration of hostilities.

The first AAF Hercules to land at Stanley following the second Black Buck raid did so in daylight on 6 May. The last took off during the night of 13 /14 June.

Hostilities ceased on 14 June. The Royal Engineers began their survey of Stanley runway on 17 June and started repairs two days later. The first British Hercules to land at Stanley did so on 24 June.

AIM

The aim of this paper is to establish whether or not British Vulcan bombers managed to impede Argentinian air operations from Stanley airfield during Operation Corporate in 1982.

SCOPE

This paper does not concern itself with the strategic aspects of the Black Buck raids, nor does it speculate on the effectiveness of naval gunfire support, Harrier GR3s or Sea Harrier operations against the runway.

This paper does not discuss Black Buck raids 4, 5 and 6 but does address the claim that Argentine aircraft were moved to the north as the direct result of the Black Buck raids.

It is important to state that we all would rather the RAF had put Stanley runway out of action, but sadly this was not the case, despite remarkable personal courage by the aircrew involved, and highly inventive staff planning. We would also like to emphasise strongly, that all of us involved 'down south', in the naval service and the army, retain our full admiration for a number of aspects of the RAF's involvement in 1982. We acknowledge the fine work of the Harrier GR3s in support of ground troops and we are full of praise for the gallant and invaluable efforts of the sole surviving Chinook's ground crew and pilots. We particularly admire the two Hercules crews who flew almost continual 24-hour sorties to supply the Task Force deep in the South Atlantic, with urgently needed spares and not least, mail.

What we cannot accept is the RAF's claim to have damaged Stanley runway to a significant extent, with a 1000lb bomb on the centreline and that Argentine air operations were impeded. This analysis will clarify why we hold this view. At this point it might be useful to highlight just one account by the Vulcan pilot of Black Buck 1 which explains why we are concerned at the falsification of history and the public's perception of the success of the Black Buck raids. Similar claims are made in various other websites and interviews.

The twenty-one 1,000lb bombs were released 2 miles out from Stanley – one hit the runway and the others hit the dispersal areas causing damage to aircraft and the fuel storage area. Mr Withers (Black Buck 1's Vulcan pilot) describes the raid as '100 per cent successful'. He said: 'We had one bomb right on the runway and as a result the runway was never used for the rest of the war by the Argentineans.'

Throughout, we have restricted ourselves to presenting only eyewitness, first-hand facts, plus accounts from official historical records both in the United Kingdom and Argentina, untainted we believe, by manipulation and personal hypotheses. For the majority of the archive research in Argentina we acknowledge the work on Argentine aviation matters by Santiago Rivas. For his research in the British National Archives at Kew – and his adroit application of the Freedom of Information Act – we are indebted to Dr. Alejandro Amendolara. We are also grateful to the military historian Mariano Sciaroni for researching various Argentine Air Force (AAF) documents concerning the repairs to the Stanley runway as well as the repositioning of fighter aircraft from the south to the north. Alejandro Pita was our link to his father, *Capitán de Navioe Infantería de Marina*, Miguel Pita, who commanded the initial Argentine amphibious assault, and later, the Rio Grande air base.

We have discounted all third-hand accounts and accounts from those who were not directly involved on the ground or in the air over Stanley runway. There are three major exceptions to this restriction: a published excerpt accompanied by one contemporaneous, annotated photograph from a respected French publishing house is included, as is evidence from Lieutenant Colonel Roger Blundell (an aviator), who was serving at Northwood in 1982 on the C-in-C's staff as the Fleet Royal Marines Officer and who was a member of the C-in-C's sea, land and air briefing team. The third example is a USMC staff paper dated 2 April 1984, headed *Offensive Air Operations of The Falklands War* (sic) by Major Walter de Houst.

This paper has been written with the help and input of considerably more people (at home and abroad) than those quoted or those whose signatures follow. For the sake of clarity all ranks stated are those held subsequently and not, necessarily, those held at the time.

Black Buck 1
Over the night of 30 April/1 May, one Vulcan bomber dropped twenty-one 1,000 lb bombs aimed at Stanley airfield's paved runway. During daylight hours of 1 May an aerial reconnaissance photograph was taken by a Sea Harrier from 801 Naval Air Squadron. This was then analysed on board HMS *Hermes* by Rear Admiral (later Admiral Sir John) Woodward's staff. No RAF aircraft were involved.

This AAF photograph was taken before the Argentines would have had time to muster the resources required to fill in or alter any crater. The first bomb to land hit the southern half of the runway, the second bomb crater clipped the runway as can be seen clearly. In a comparison with the RAF-sourced photograph also (apparently) taken on 1 May, a distinct difference is immediately obvious: in one photograph, whose origin is undoubted and whose clarity is obvious, the first crater is off the centreline, but in the original (which comes via the RAF's 101 Squadron and whose fuzziness is evident), the first crater is central and the photograph has been notated with an overlay.

The original Fleet Air Arm photograph shows clearly that the first bomb missed the centreline of the paved runway. There is no indication of any damage, or dummy crater or rubble on the centreline at this stage. We now know that the first bomb's crater was filled in before Black Buck 2. (See Commander Air Group Malvinas, Brigadier Luis Guillermo Castellano's comments on page 113.)

Having analysed the FAA photograph Admiral Woodward [CTG 317.8] sent a signal to Admiral Sir John Fieldhouse [CTF 317] in Northwood on 2 May which was then repeated by Admiral Fieldhouse to the MOD, with a description of the battle damage as far as could be ascertained from the photograph: First bomb made single crater halfway down the runway just south of the centre.

Interim summary

Although, presumably, the same photograph, the position of the first crater on the FAA photograph, whose origin is not in doubt, differs from the first crater on the 'RAF photograph', whose provenance is confused by the inscription on the reverse – and yet they are the same photograph.

Post Black Buck 1

After the first raid and before the second, ARA *General Belgrano* was sunk. This action, combined with the introduction by the British of a Maritime Exclusion Zone followed by a Total Exclusion Zone, influenced any intention to operate fast jets out of Stanley as the Argentine historians, Santiago Rivas, and Dr Alejandro Amendolara explain. Their accounts have been amalgamated.

Damaged or not, the runway was not affected on its operations until the end of the war. To operate fast jets from it didn't mean only to extend the runway, but to have enough fuel for them, a storage for air-to-air missiles, and the creation of dispersal areas, among other needs.

There was a ship, the 10,000-ton ELMA *Rio Cincel* under the command of Captain (Merchant Navy) Juan Carlos Trivelin, that sailed from Buenos Aires on 3 April with logistic supplies for the army and air force in the Falkland Islands. These consisted of six vehicles, eighty pallets of aluminium planks and 800 drums of JP1 fuel. She arrived on the 7 April and the AAF Construction Group No 1 was able to extend the 'parking' capacity of the airfield by 100 per cent. The aim was then to extend the runway, not to deploy fast jets to the islands, but to use the runway as a diversion or only to refuel after a sortie over the Islands before returning to the mainland.

A second merchant ship, ELMA *Córdoba* sailed from Buenos Aires on 8 April laden with further logistic supplies plus another 231 aluminium planks for the runway extension. However, she was delayed in Mar del Plata when the Maritime Exclusion Zone was enforced. Hoping still to make the journey to the Falkland Islands she moved to Puerto Deseado where she was detained by a collision with the dock. When she was ready to sail ARA *General Belgrano* had been sunk.

Interim summary

That the runway extension was never possible was nothing to do with the RAF and the Black Buck raids, rather the imposition of a Maritime Exclusion Zone by the Royal Navy on 12 April. This was followed by the sinking of ARA *General Belgrano* by HMS *Conqueror* on 2 May and the extension of the Total Exclusion Zone to 12 miles from the Argentine coast on 7 May, after which no Argentine ship, naval or merchant, left national coastal waters.

Black Buck 2

A second raid took place over the night of 3 /4 May, with all the bombs missing the western end of the runway. Within hours of this second bombing mission an aerial photograph was taken by Lieutenant Cantan in a Sea Harrier from 801 Naval Air Squadron. This not only shows the Black Buck 2 bombs that missed the runway, but also the Black Buck 1 bomb crater just off the south side of the paved runway and about halfway along. This photograph was processed and analysed within an hour or so of Cantan landing back on board HMS *Invincible*. Its origin and authenticity have never been queried. Yet this photograph also differs when compared with the photograph supplied by the RAF.

The bomb on the southern half of the paved runway in the original photographs has disappeared in subsequent photographs and in its place there would appear to be a faint white ring clipping but not straddling the centreline. Yet the bomb crater in the RAF-supplied photograph straddles the centreline. Thus it must be concluded that some manipulation of the RAF photograph has taken place.

The origin of the RAF photograph needs to be established. The only aircraft that were available to take such photographs in that time frame were the Sea Harriers, which retained an optical camera fit (F95) as standard for multi- role aircraft or satellites. No RAF aircraft were available to take other photographs.

Yet the photograph supplied by the RAF is also the photograph used by Wikipedia and which no one has seen fit to replace.

Another photograph is an enlarged version of the FAA photographs, from which it is even more clear that there is one crater clipping the southern edge of the paved runway and no other extant crater on the runway following Black Buck 1. The white circle towards, but not straddling, the centreline is hardly visible. This suggests that the crater had been filled in.

Interim summary

The disparity between the FAA-sourced photographs and the RAF photograph needs some explanation which we are unable to offer, short of concluding that it has in some way been altered. It has certainly become more fuzzy than the FAA original.

AN ARGENTINE PERSPECTIVE

That same day, 4 May, Brigadier General Mario Menéndez (the then Argentine military governor of the Falkland Islands) took his own ground-level photograph of the bomb crater that clipped the runway. In an email to Lieutenant Colonel Ewen Southby-Tailyour in 2013/14, he explained that this crater was very deep and shows no damaged concrete blocks, as it had exploded on the grass and hard-packed earth on the south side of the runway. Debris had, he explained, been strewn across the paved runway as far as the centreline – 'collateral damage' of a sort that was immediately exploited by the Argentine engineers.

In the photograph supplied by General Menéndez, the paved runway is beyond the vehicles. This north-facing photograph, coupled with General Menéndez's accompanying description, offers evidence that this crater is not on the paved section of the runway. The runway was constructed of twelve inches of crushed stone on a sand base, covered by four inches of concrete (then overlaid with asphalt, although this has to be confirmed). There is not much sign of that in Menéndez's photograph. Either side of the paved runway, the surface was hard-packed earth topped with rough grass. These two strips, each 180 feet wide along the runway's full length, were suitable for (although not constructed for) parking and the taxiing of light aircraft.

In an exchange of emails with Southby-Tailyour in 2013, the general confirmed that the photograph he had taken of the crater was just clipping the edge of the paved runway and was the first bomb to hit. He made no mention of bombs either side of the runway or in the middle, although he admitted that much rubble was spread unevenly across the paved area towards the centreline. His statement is though at odds with that of Brigadier Luis Guillermo Castellano, Commander Air Group Malvinas. As will be shown, this rubble was enhanced to fool the

British in an action described enigmatically by the general a : 'consecuently. much subterfuge'.

BATTLE DAMAGE ASSESSMENTS

On 12 May, a further photo-reconnaissance flight was conducted by a Sea Harrier, as result of which Admiral Woodward was obliged to send a signal on 13 May which suggested that he knew that the runway was still operational. He did though, as did the RAF MoD staff, believe initially that the runway was only operational over each end, and not down its full length. He too, underestimated the Argentine determination to keep flying. Interestingly he notes that no repair work had been carried out, despite subsequent Argentine insistence that it had.

Black Buck 3

The third Black Buck raid, due to have taken place on 13 May, was cancelled before take-off due to adverse weather conditions. Nevertheless. on 26 May, Woodward sent a signal clearly expressing his concern that the runway still remained fully operational despite what limited damage may have been inflicted.

Black Buck 7

The final operation order for Black Buck 7 was sent on 11 June giving the target as Stanley airfield's aircraft parking and storage areas. The fuses were to be set for air burst to avoid further damage to the runway in advance of British forces. On 12 June, a signal (No. 5) was sent from Ascension Island to the C-in-C at Northwood offering an optimistic crew assessment of the damage caused, and stating that all bombs had been seen to have detonated on target. This was followed on 12 June by a second signal from Admiral Woodward expressing his concern that all the bombs were only suspected to have missed the target.

Finally on 13 June, it was confirmed in a signal from Woodward that all bombs had missed the target, while expressing some doubt over how many might have actually detonated.

A ROYAL ENGINEER'S PERSPECTIVE

This ties in neatly with the view of Andrew Rastall, who in 1982, was serving with 49 EOD Squadron, Royal Engineers. He offers this narrative:

We conducted clearance work around the airport/runway area several times. Sometime in August '82 I was working near the runway and was using a very sensitive metal detector along with two pioneers were there to dig out anything I'd located. We were systematically searching the area at least several hundred yards to the north of the runway and west of the airport buildings. Towards the end of that day I got a very strong signal from a puddle. The water was dark brown and we couldn't see anything in it, at which point one of the pioneers pushed his spade into the water and hit something hard. Unless they've got a very high iron content, rocks don't generally register on metal detectors so I started to bail out the puddle with a discarded food can. As the water level dropped, the rock turned out to be a 1000 lb bomb. The tail of the bomb had broken off and the cylinder of the brass fuse was clearly visible. The brass itself had oxidised and was dull but there were two small bright grooves cut into the edge of the cylinder, presumably where the pioneer had struck the thing with his spade.

Normally, we'd blow the thing in situ but it was one of our own and the MOD boffins wanted the fuse to find out why it hadn't detonated. Incoming air traffic was put into holding patterns while the OC and myself went to deal with the bomb. Once the fuse was removed and the bomb made safe the decision was made to blow it in situ immediately because planes were waiting to land. We had to bring up plastic explosive, det cord, detonator and an electrical firing cable. Having prepared the bomb for detonation we took cover behind a rock. We got covered in lumps of peat and something hard hit the rock we were sheltering behind – it turned out to be a large piece of shrapnel that I took home for a souvenir.

I've studied the photographs in your paper and have tried to position the UXB I found relative to the craters from Black Buck 1. My thinking has been along the following lines: Basically, someone must have a record of the number of bombs dropped on that first raid. If the number of craters in the photograph supplied by the RAF can be seen to equal the number of bombs dropped then they've failed to account for the UXB I found. This would mean that one of those craters should not be on the photograph, i.e. too many craters for the number of bombs that actually detonated. Looking at the RAF photograph and counting from the 'crater' in the middle of the runway, there are four craters which appear to be relatively evenly spaced and then there's a longer gap between the fourth and fifth craters. The UXB I found was certainly to the north of the runway and to the west of the airport buildings and may well have been in the gap between the fourth and fifth craters on the RAF photograph.

It could be that the UXB I found was part of a stick dropped on that third raid – a line of 'duds'? Assuming the fuse we removed from the UXB was sent back to the MOD it may be possible to find out in which raid that particular bomb was dropped if records have been kept of bomb and fuse serial numbers? If it turns out that it was dropped in the first raid then the only position it could have been was between the fourth and fifth craters on the RAF photograph. Assuming the original aerial photograph is of sufficient quality, it would then be a case of counting the craters made by the bombs dropped on that first run. If the number of craters equals the number of bombs dropped then someone will probably have some explaining to do.

ARGENTINE EVIDENCE

The Argentine military historian, Mariano Sciaroni, has written:

BLACK BUCK 1 was an incredible story of planning and professionalism on the part of the RAF, but in my view, the only concrete effect was... publicity. The Argentine Air Force did not modify its logistics operations due to the single impact, but simply instructed the pilots to use only one side of the runway. Nothing else. In that sense, BLACK BUCK 1 did not meet its objective, not even partially.

Sciaroni explained that two AAF C-130 pilots had written books about the war. Alfredo A. Cano wrote in his book *Recuerdos Transporteros*:

Fortunately, the accuracy of our former 1981 International Air Tattoo Judge, Gordon Graham, [navigator in BLACK BUCK 1's Vulcan] was not as good as his host performance; only one of the 1,000-pound bombs dropped hit the southern side of the runway. That has been one more reason to continue remembering him with great affection....

Besides the joke, for the C-130 pilots (according to their histories, the crater was not an issue at all in the planning stage. Also, remember the crater was not enough to prevent the runway's use by MB-339 jets.

In the publication *Malvinas – Testimonio de su Gobernador* (Carlos M. Túrolo, Editorial Sudamericana; Buenos Aires, 1983), General Menéndez is quoted as saying:

The runway had a direct hit that at first it was believed to render it useless, but later we were able to verify that it had not. Later, the Air Force men, led by Commodore Destri, did an excellent job of trying to fool the English into believing that the runway was really disabled. They used stones, paint, etcetera.

This might explain the faint white circle in one of the photographs. It does not explain the centreline crater in the RAF photograph, the only photograph of dozens, aerial or low-oblique, to show a crater exactly on the runway's centreline.

If I remember correctly, it was that night when in Buenos Aires among the news that were broadcasted, one was that the runway had not been affected by the bombing and could continue to operate, which is why the British later bombed it again. The English were always in doubt, as they say, that according to aerial photographs, the runway could not be used, at least with large aircraft. On the other hand, the news that came from Argentina led them to the idea that maybe the runway was in good condition.

With the majors Buitrago and Doglioli to the airport area. It would be 1 or 1.30 pm. On the way, while we were crossing an isthmus [between the Canache and Surf Bay] from where the sea is very well controlled, we saw three white spots to the southeast. I commented to the majors: 'Those are three English ships that are approaching to complete the task of the airplanes, they come for naval bombing'. At the airport we could see the great destruction that was there: the planes, the sheds, the building... at that time there were no people to be seen anywhere, they were all in their foxholes or shelters, except for the defence personnel, not close to the place. We saw the holes left by the bombs; the one that hit the track [no precise position given] had made a large crater and you could see that it had left a gap intact, but [the runway] was still full of stones so it was not known if the track would be usable or not. There were unexploded bombs, so they had to be very concerned.

It had been determined already that the runway could be used and I already commented on the information that was released in Buenos Aires that the runway had not been damaged and was in good condition. This, related to the repetition of enemy air attacks on it, aroused a tremendous anger among the men, both from the Air Force and from all of us.

[It would appear that the Argentinian armed forces had the same problem with their national broadcaster as did the British with the BBC.]

The point is, that when the news that was given on the track on the continent broke, there was an explosion of anger. At the command post for example, where Brigadier Castellanos and the Air Force staff were, they said it was inconceivable…but the flights were restarted. This does not detract in any way from the effort of the Hercules pilots who arrived in Puerto Argentino [Stanley] or the naval Fokker pilots who also crossed, challenging the blockade, the weather conditions and the decrease in the runway operability.

This corroborates the above statement, for there is no crater straddling the centreline. The crater caused by the one bomb that did hit the runway is quite clear, suggesting that this photograph was taken before Black Buck 2 by when it had been filled in. The significance of the yellow circle is not known. It does though mark the area known to have been overlaid with rubble. It is thought that this area might have suffered superficial scarring made to look much worse with rubble, then eventually patched as shown.

In addition to General Menéndez's written description of the crater just clipping the runway sent to Southby-Tailyour, along with his photograph of the crater the following comes from Vicecomodoro Alberto Vianna in an email to Southby-Tailyour in 2013 and repeated in *Wings of the Malvinas. The Argentine Air War over the Falklands.* (Hikoki Publications, Manchester, 2012). The author, Santiago Rivas, corresponded for over two years with Southby-Tailyour on this and other aviation matters. Vianna, the first Argentine pilot to fly a Hercules to the Falkland Islands after Black Buck 2, says and wrote in part:

On 6 May the navigator had led me to the final approach to the runway. We saw the runway and went in to land, we saw there was a crater to one side of the runway so we landed on the other side and waited for the ambulances with our engines running… the engineer told me that the leading tyre of the right main gear had blown. We could take off but very carefully because the rubber was dangerous if it began to shred.

It is important to emphasise that his landing took place less than 48 hours after Black Buck 1 had been taken, yet no mention of a crater on the main runway. Vianna made it quite clear in a series of emails to Southby-Tailyour, that had he seen the slightest sign of damage to the main runway – or had the control tower warned him of a crater, which it did not – he would have aborted his landing for which he used the full runway. Laden with eight casualties, Vianna took off at

1625 and landed safely at Comodoro Rivadavia at 1835. This confirms that the crater on the runway had already been filled in before this flight and thus before Black Buck 2.

On 7 May another C-130 landed with a payload of 31,750lb (just under half the maximum payload – depending on the variant) and no mention of any crater by the pilot and so the air bridge continued to the end (although there were to be interruptions due to the presence of Sea Harriers and bad weather). Hercules daylight flights continued until the 20 May, after which they were all at night.

In the book *Guerra Aérea en las Malvinas*, (by Benito Héctor Andrada; Emecé Editores, Buenos Aires, 1983), the following information was supplied by the Argentine Air Force:

The Base Commanding Officer and his immediate collaborators were dedicated to verifying the effects of the attack, helping the wounded and taking them to the medical post. In a first impression, they had estimated that this could be a disaster. However, they immediately verified the opposite and all the staff regained their calm. The Vulcan's bombs had fallen on a trajectory oriented obliquely to the runway.

It was a kind of trail formed by impacts separated from each other by about thirty or forty meters and placed alternately, to the right and left, (i.e. in a zig-zag formation) of an imaginary line that was about a thousand meters long. Only one bomb, the first, had hit exactly the centre of the paved runway, but on one side. Of the thirty meters wide, it had disabled half with an impressive crater seven or eight meters deep and ten or twelve in diameter.

All the other bombs had 'gone long,' with respect to the target that was undoubtedly the runway itself. One of them, fallen in the middle of the bivouac formed by the tents where the soldiers slept, showed part of its body, which emerged more than a meter from the ground where it was buried. It was nailed at a slight angle, and in contact with the side panel of one of the tents. Rotating near the tail, grains of explosive matter were visible within.

There were sixteen impacts from the Vulcan bombs, but only fifteen craters. Only fifteen craters because there had been no more than fifteen explosions. The bomb dropped among the soldiers had not exploded.

The pilots prepared for landing in Puerto Argentino [Stanley]. They knew they could only use half the width of the runway, the fifteen meters on the north side, because the other half, on the south side, was disabled by the crater of a bomb dropped on 1 May. Its edges were dangerously close to the centreline of the track.

[According to Brigadier Castellano, it was considered sensible to fill in the runway to avoid aircraft landing too close to the northern edge.]

In *Malvinas – Otras Historias* (by Rubén Oscar Palazzi, Editorial Claridad; Buenos Aires, 2006) Brigadier Luis Guillermo Castellano, Commander Air Group Malvinas, states:

In the early morning of May 1, we were resting next to our command post, when a deafening thunder lifted us off balance. I immediately contacted Commodore Destri, who was the Commander of the Military Air Base Malvinas, and he laconically informed me that a Vulcan had probably bombarded the runway. The magnitude of the violence of this apocalyptic and surprising attack was consistent with the desired effect: neutralizing the airfield runway, a vital point of communication between the islands and the mainland. Its tremendous destructive power was such that it is enough to imagine that only one of the craters measured twelve meters in diameter by more than six meters deep. The assumption that we would be the enemy's first target had been met, but the intensity and shock of its effect was unimaginable.

After overcoming the initial surprise, still perceiving the acrid and penetrating smell of explosive that remained in the air, the men began to react positively and even recklessly, to the point that efforts had to be made to control the contagion of heroism in them, which were exposed in the dark, to help the wounded comrades and subordinates, being guided only by the laments and exposing themselves to the explosions by delay.

The enemy's intention to break the will of our forces to fight on that same day was very clear, but evidently, it did not succeed. We dominated the anxiety, until the first light of day, to allow us to verify that only one bomb had hit the track, thus maintaining its operability.

Then we found that twenty-one bombs of 1,000 pounds each (454 kilograms) had been used in the attack and that when they were dropped late they missed the track, but reaching the bivouac where the troops slept until the night before, miraculously only perishing the two soldiers on duty.

On May 1 at 0440 am, without any prior warning, an Avro Vulcan bomber plane, heading NE /SW, dropped a trail of twenty-one bombs weighing 1,000 pounds (454 kilograms) each, which exploded in less than ten seconds. The first hit the side of the runway, opened a crater twelve metres in diameter, and rendered useless fourteen metres of the thirty of width the runway had. Fifteen of the bombs fell in the area of the bivouac, causing great damage to the precarious facilities. The remaining bombs fell long and exploded in the waters of the bay.

[After the unsuccessful Black Buck 2 raid] *someone said: 'What if we help the English break the track?'. So we decided to build two simulated impacts on the track so that the Vulcan would stop shaking us and the result was successful.*

After the second Vulcan bombing, it was sought to make the enemy believe that had achieved his objective. For this, two craters were simulated similar to the real one already repaired. A later English aerial photographic reconnaissance (publicly released), revealed that the runway was affected with three bomb hits, for which they assumed that our Hercules were landing and taking off on the strip of land adjacent [packed earth, not the paved runway] to the runway, when in fact they did so in the remaining sixteen meters of width.

Lieutenant Carlos Centeno had served as a commando in the Argentine Forces. Later he established a company making TV documentaries on the wildlife of Argentina and the South Atlantic. On the invasion of the Falkland Islands, he offered his services as a war correspondent, and with a team of three volunteers from his TV company, spent the duration of the conflict recording the action on the Islands. Concerning the air war, he has provided the following information:

I did my job and 'with a little help of my friends' (three TV workers, also volunteers) recorded a three-hour documentary as war correspondents, that aired in 1983. It's also true that as I was a keen radio amateur, I was excited with an infantry radar 'Rasit' which had a 30k m range capacity. So every night I detected the warships that were firing from 14km away from shore and that was useful as early warning and helped save many lives. I tell you this in order for you to understand that because of my earlier service as an Argentine commando, I was free to move all around the defensive positions without asking anyone's permission.

The truth I can tell you about the airport runway, which not only I visited but also filmed and got photos, is that it was fully operational until the last day of the war. Air Force C-130 Hercules and Navy F28Fokkers normally operated every night, and did so until the early hours of June 14th.

I remember that night well. It was when my three TV workers were evacuated from the Island on the last Hercules flight around 3 am, taking with them all the recorded material and equipment. I remained as a POW until the people of the Red Cross and a very decent Parachute Regiment colonel let me go on June 18th.

Thanks to my ability to move freely in pursuit of recording the conflict, I spent many days and nights on the airfield. Before dawn, the military authorities would make use of bulldozers and other heavy equipment to create simulated big holes – craters – on the runway using earth and stone circles. The runway was fully operational all the time, except one or two times that Marine Corps engineers had to disable an unexploded, retarded, bomb [delivered by a Sea Harrier] that remained close to the runway. I think to be honest when I say that really the Vulcan's bombing on the runway did not significantly affect the actions.

I walked the full length of the runway a few days after the opening of hostilities with BLACK BUCK 1 and that there was no visible sign of any crater damage on the runway's centreline.

In forwarding the above extracts the Argentine military historian, Alejandro Amendolara, says:

I hope the extracts are helpful for the paper. What emerges clearly from them is that the runway was actually hit, not in the centre, but just to the south of the centre axis, in the runway. And that was the crater filled by the AAF personnel the next day and covered up with rocks and mud, for the aerial photo reconnaissance that followed over the next days and during the rest of the conflict. Also, it is interesting the Woodward's signal attached dated May 26, in which he 'urgently requires laser-guided bomb kits to ensure urgent neutralization of Stanley Airfield'. Evidently, he knew the airfield was still operative.

Argentine aviation historian, Santiago Rivas, wrote in August 2020:

Regarding the BLACK BUCK raids the runway was fully operational until the end of the war. I not only talked with Vianna a lot (and his entire crew, as we are writing their story), but also with Pucará and MB-339 pilots who flew from there until the end of the war, and they all talk about the simulated craters and a real one on the side that didn't affect the operations. In any case, they only used the northern side of the runway, which was wide enough for the operation of the Hercules, Fokker F28 and all the smaller aircraft, which flew until the last night of the war.

I had never seen any clear picture of a big crater inside the runway, but I have a couple of pictures, unfortunately of not good quality, which show what could be some damage to the runway. But the pictures are not clear enough to determine if they were real or fake craters. At least two fake ones were made, close to the taxiway, one on each side of it, being the darker areas on the picture.

In the photograph taken by the AAF, the crater that clipped the southern edge of the runway is clear. There is no hint of a crater straddling the centreline.

ALLEGED MOVEMENT OF ARGENTINE AIRCRAFT TO THE NORTH
It has been claimed that as a direct result of the Black Buck raids, Argentina moved a number of fighter aircraft north to protect their major cities, thus reducing the air threat to the Task Force. We now know that no such significant move took place. The aircraft assigned to the defence of Buenos Aires had already been designated by mid-April in Buenos Aires Defense Scheme (Order 1/82), dated April 15, 1982.

This was supplied by Mariano Sciaroni, who also states:

Only a handful of aircraft remained on alert in the vicinity of Buenos Aires, to face any incursion from the sea or from Chile: two Mirage III, two Dagger, two MS-760 and two Pucará. The order was not changed after May 1, so it cannot be thought that a number of aircraft would be tied up by a possible Vulcan bombing.

I don't know what they were going to do with the Pucará and the MS-760 (surely, not intercepting a Vulcan). One of those Pucará crashed during the war, apparently the pilot was doing unauthorized stunts.

Santiago Rivas confirms these facts in an email dated 18 October 2020:

The reality is that, as Alejandro and Mariano have detailed, there was not much concern of an air strike by Vulcans to Buenos Aires. The Mirages and Daggers that remained at their bases in Moreno and Tandil were the two seaters, so with less combat capacity and, in the case of the Mirage IIIs, no radar. Anyway, they performed CAPs over the city (I remember seeing them flying very high every day, despite being a kid). Also, the pilots that were at the bases were the less experienced ones, as all the others were deployed south.

As the Navy had also a couple of ships deployed on the mouth of the Rio de la Plata, any attempt to bomb Buenos Aires will be warned at least with enough time (not less than 30 minutes) to scramble a pair of Mirages (which were at less than five minutes of flight from Buenos Aires) and guide them to their target before the Vulcan reached Buenos Aires. Also, a night bombing of the city would cause more civil casualties than military ones (most probably, none), so should have been a big political setback for the UK and, most probably, a bigger support to the war and the military government by the Argentine population.

It may not have been known at the time of the first Black Buck raid that the Argentines had foreseen an attack on the Stanley runway and were standing-by to repair any damage. At the end of hostilities, Major Raul Oscar Maiorana, the commanding officer of the AAF's airfield construction unit, *Grupo I Construcciones*, wrote in his Report of Proceedings:

The bombing attack on 1st May 1982 affected the runway causing damage to the surrounding taxiways [presumably, according to AAF photographs which show two craters on the hard-packed earth either side of the main runway, this is the 'taxiway', used also for parking] producing a crater of 18m. diameter and 6–8m in depth [with damage/rubble] on the surface in the surrounds [to the runway]. Patched up so that repair of the runway could be carried out. 80 per cent of plant was used to clear the splinters. 20 per cent had been totally destroyed by the air attack – loss of heavy vehicles and a motor grader.

Three simulated craters were constructed on the main runway with the aim of deceiving the enemy before possible armed reconnaissance missions (took place).

Interestingly, no mention of a direct hit on the runway – except splinters – but only on the taxiways. Three dummies are mentioned whereas elsewhere, two and the 'real' crater are mentioned. We are inclined to believe the above, although we accept that there could be cause of confusion. Either way, the runway remained operational.

There can be no doubt from the evidence that the *Grupo I Construcciones* were extremely proficient and professional in their task: especially so considering the lack of equipment and building material. The ROP goes on to state:

Although the task of Group 1 of Constructions is clearly specific [the maintenance of] the execution of runways and platforms and everything inherent to the airport works, other non-specific tasks were carried out. The requirements [carried out] were satisfying. Regarding the suitability of the

*personnel, it was possible to detect that they were [ideal] in the handling of the
elements for their use.*

THE FRENCH EVIDENCE

Although this might be considered circumstantial evidence, a French report
published in the learned *La Guerre des Malouines* (Édition Larivière, Rennes,
2002), known its exceptional accuracy, clarity and research in all its titles), states:

> *The effect of the string of 21 bombs of 450kg had very questionable results.*

It goes on to display a photograph of unknown origin that shows a number of
damaged areas, none of which are on the main runway. The photograph has this
caption:

> *Aerial photos of the Falklands aerodrome in an attempt to take stock of the
> raids. Despite the tons of bombs the 'piste' remained usable until the end of the
> conflict.*

UNITED STATES EVIDENCE

Although the following is not a first-hand, eyewitness account, it is instructive and
was published just two years after Operation Corporate. Because the operation
was overall, a resounding amphibious success, the United States Marine Corps
took a very close look into the lessons learned.

On 2 April 1984, Major Walter de Houst, of the USMC Command and Staff
College wrote a paper headed *Offensive Air Operations of the Falklands War*. He
concluded:

> *The most critical judgement of the use of the Vulcan centres on the argument
> that their use was "...largely to prove (the air force) had some role to play
> and not to help the battle in the least." This illustrates the practice of armed
> services to actively seek a 'piece of the action' when a conflict arises, even if their
> capabilities or missions are not compatible with the circumstances of the conflict.
> Using BLACK BUCK as an example shows that the effects of this practice can
> be trivial and the results not worth the effort (nor the fuel) involved.*
>
> *However, the success of BLACK BUCK can be at best described as minimal.
> The seven attempted missions included three aborts, three of undetermined
> results and one of minimal success – the first. The runway was continually used*

by Argentine C-130 s until the end of the war. The Argentines would leave the runway covered with piles of dirt during the day causing British intelligence to surmise that repairs were still in progress. This deception misled the British as to the condition of the airfield and the success of their raids.

FALKLAND ISLANDS EVIDENCE

When the Argentine forces invaded the Islands and took over Stanley, Police Officer Fred Clark was serving as one of the four town police officers. He and his colleagues remained under close arrest in Stanley throughout the conflict. Although restricted in movement he was able to monitor all operations closely. His evidence concerning the bombing of the airfield is as follows:

The first raid did not do enough damage. They were still flying the next day, I remember that. Don't forget the Argies built moveable craters that were put on the runway when not in use and removed them only when flying operations required it.

BRITISH EVIDENCE

Commodore Clapp (Commander Amphibious Task Group in 1982) has written about witnessing the unease felt at the time among senior RAF personnel that all had not gone quite according to plan: [It is not clear which Black Buck raid this was.]

When we were in Ascension I sat with the Group Captain listening to one of the raids. He told me he was unimpressed by their aircrew as one raid failed to close their cockpit canopy and turned home while another screwed up on some other event which I cannot remember. Probably a navigation error. [Or, if Black Buck 7, the incorrect fusing of the bombs?]

    Air Marshal Sir John Curtiss, who was AOC Coastal Command and Air Component Commander for Operation Corporate in Northwood, also admitted there were failings from lack of training but hoped the Argies would accept the Vulcans could bomb their mainland if it came to that. They may have had a degree of deterrence, but how much is beyond me and, I suggest, Dr Fopp.

Captain Peter Hore, Royal Navy Joint Logistics Officer, Ascension Island in 1982, has added this vignette covering Black Buck 1 which suggests much the same as above:

My recall of the first bombing is sitting in the CBFI HQ tent on the afternoon afterwards, [1 May] when we had no Battle Damage Assessment of what the single Vulcan over the target had achieved. The senior RAF officer had briefed that the mission had been fully successful, but I gathered that that only meant a singleton a/c had reached the target area and all had returned.

Present in the tent were Group Captain J. Price RAF and myself. In came Don Coffey, the civilian Pan Am manager who ran the American facilities, and he was holding an envelope or something similar in his hand. He began to speak to Price and showed him something.

After a few minutes of hushed whispering at the top table, I heard Price raise his voice and start shouting. I don't remember the exact words, but Price first accused Coffey of being in possession of misleading propaganda, then of being in possession of classified information, and then he threatened to have him court-martialled.

However, I quickly gathered that Coffey had been sent from somewhere in the USA, a satellite (or U2?) photo of Stanley airfield, and Coffey had dutifully brought it in to show Price. Price's anger was based on his refusal to believe what it showed. On reflection, I don't think that Coffey knew how poor our (British) intelligence was and that we didn't already have this info. It was however the first visual intelligence we received on Ascension Island of BLACK BUCK. Shortly afterwards both men left the HQ tent, Don was red-faced and clearly very angry, Price in a squeal of tyres.

I learned that evening via Coffey's girlfriend, who was the headmistress of the Cable & Wireless school, that a friend of Coffey, maybe a brother-in-law, worked 'stateside' somewhere else in Pan Am or maybe NASA and he had obtained a satellite photo of the airfield clearly showing Beetham's one bomb and had sent this to Coffey – or maybe it was a deliberate leak by our friends?

It is quite feasible, indeed most likely bearing in mind Price's reaction, that the photograph Don Coffey had given Price, showed that no bombs had caused such damage that the runway was unusable.

At this time the RAF staff in the MoD appear to have been muddled over the Black Buck battle damage assessment. Nearly three weeks after Black Buck 1, a Group Captain Crwys-Williams (DI3 Air) wrote a 'secret' paper for Air Chief Marshal Sir Michael Beetham, the then Chief of the Air Staff (Reference: D13 (Air)/6/2, dated 19 May 1982). This followed an earlier briefing paper (dated 16 May) by the same author for the CAS, on the status of Stanley airfield.

HMS *Wizard*

Sir Anthony Eden (2nd left) author (2nd right) in white shorts

My tent at Dhala, looking north-west towards the Jebel Jihaf

Author on patrol, Dhala 1961

Haib fort on the edge of a 1,500 foot precipice! Very quick pen sketch made at the time

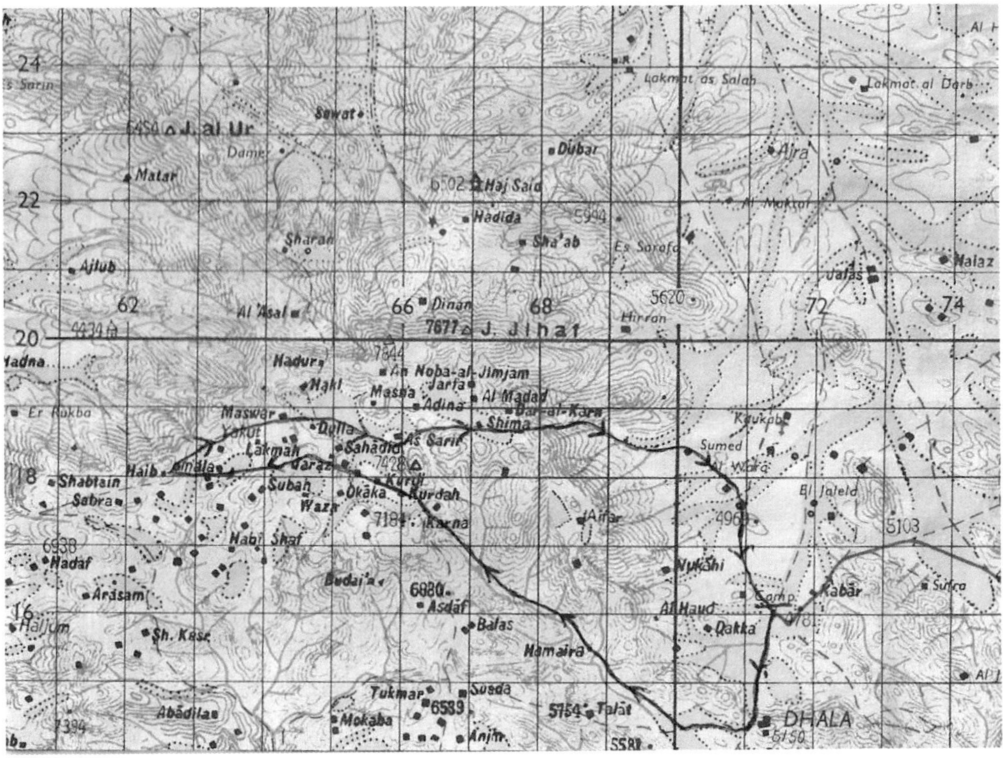

Map showing the Haib foot patrol from Dhala camp

The Kariba Pass

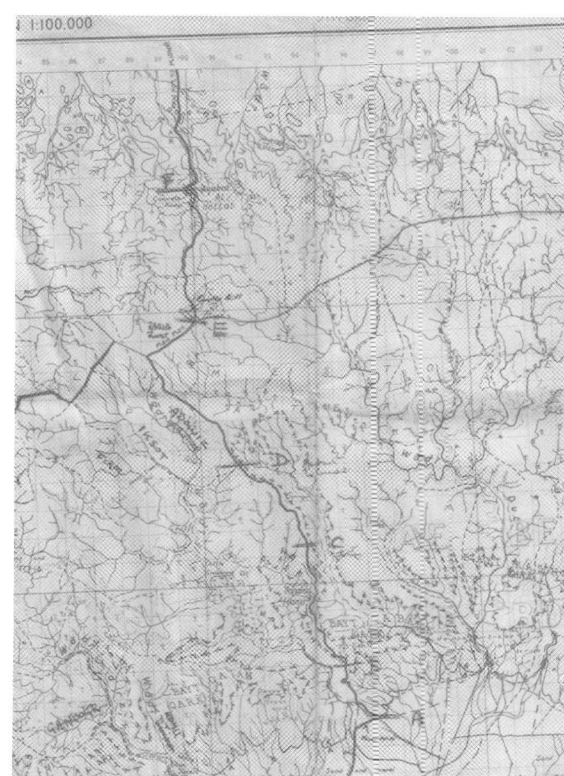

Various patrols in the Dhala area

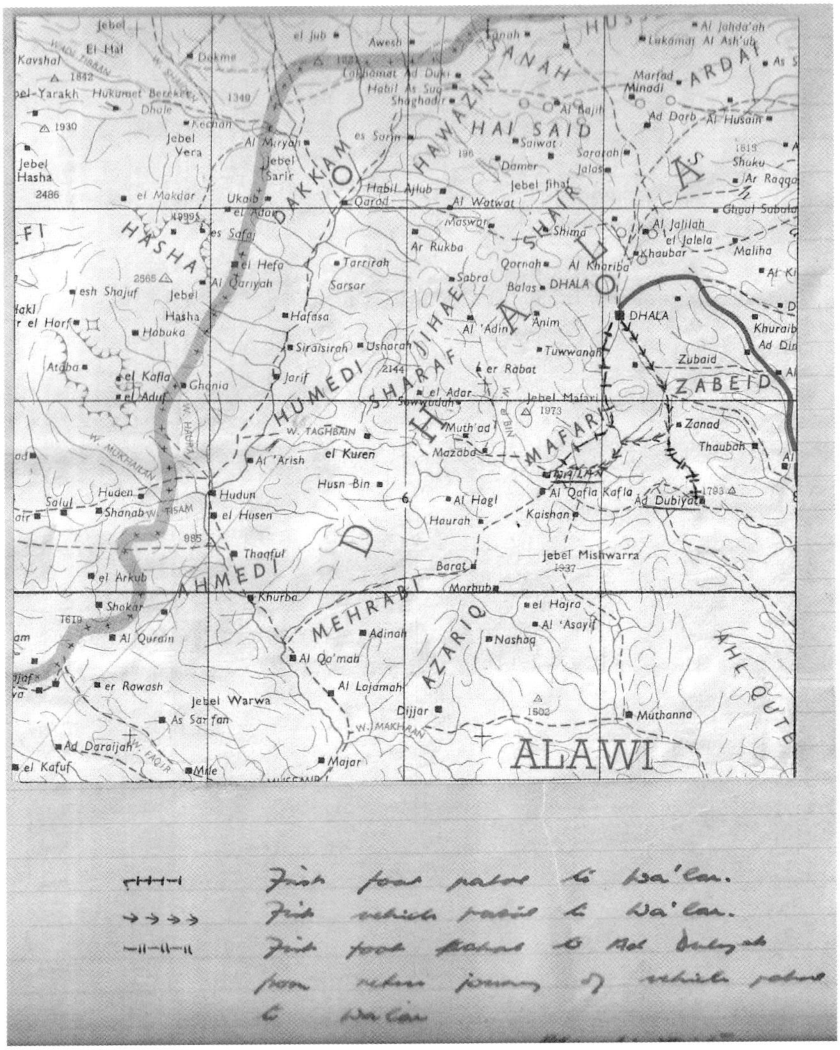

Typical weekly patrolling routine from Dhala

Ad Dubiyet. Very quick pen sketch made at the time

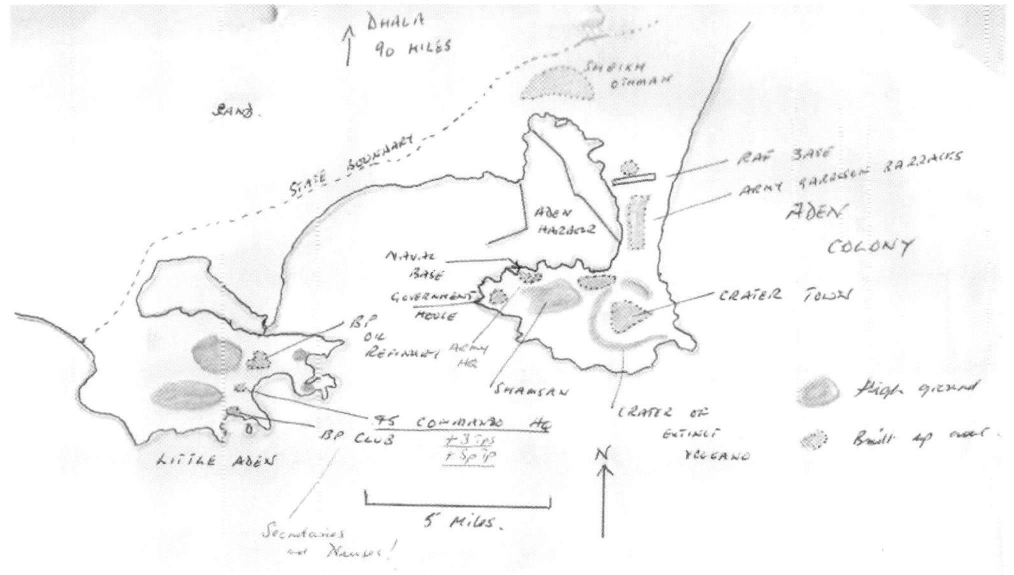

Aden and Little Aden

Les Commandos Marine cap badge with the Cross of Lorraine at top left

Author and Bruno de la Maisonneuve in Corsica

FS *Arromanches*' flight deck at dawn

Embarking in the Nord Atlas 17

Author in the Empty Quarter

The author with the Ibri 'lady'

Edge of the Empty Quarter

The enemy fort at Habrut on the west bank of the wadi, beyond our mortar position

Aqaba Camp, Habrut, taken from below the enemy fort. Our fort was being built on the high ground to the left of the picture

Talking to the Provost ground-attack aircraft flying 'top cover' for our move north the day after the main battle on 11th January 1968

The very sparse maps in use. The 1st, 2nd and 3rd ambushes marked. 11th January 1968 (Sultan's Armed Forces)

The BARV with 'gun'

Classic amphibious
infantry assault

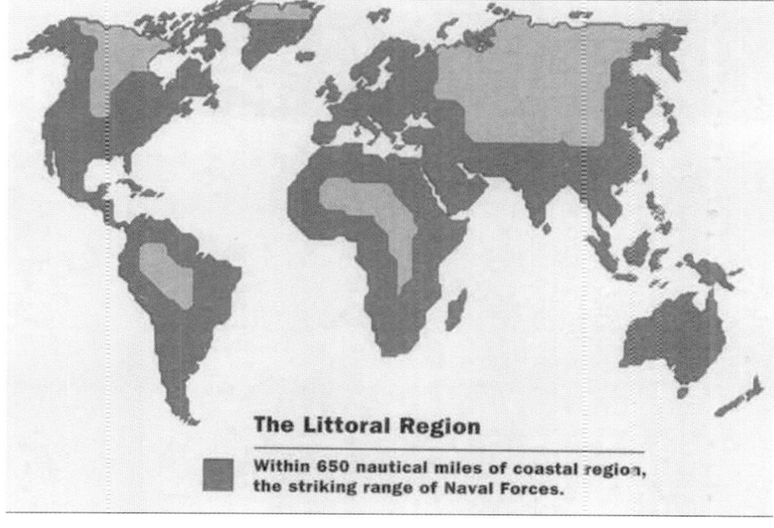

The Littoral Region
(Jane's Information
Group)

Recovering a Rigid Raiding Craft into a Chinook during maritime anti-terrorist exercises (MoD)

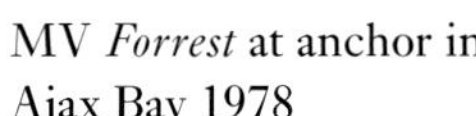

MV *Forrest* at anchor in Ajax Bay 1978

Falkland Islands wildlife. Commerson's Dolphin (the Puffing Pig), juvenile and adult Wandering Albatross, field sketches of a King Penguin

Beaver float 'plane sent by Governor Parker to drag me back to Stanley from SV *Capricornus* at Goose Green

Surveying Choiseul Sound on board SV *Capricorn*, 1979. Painting by David Cobb

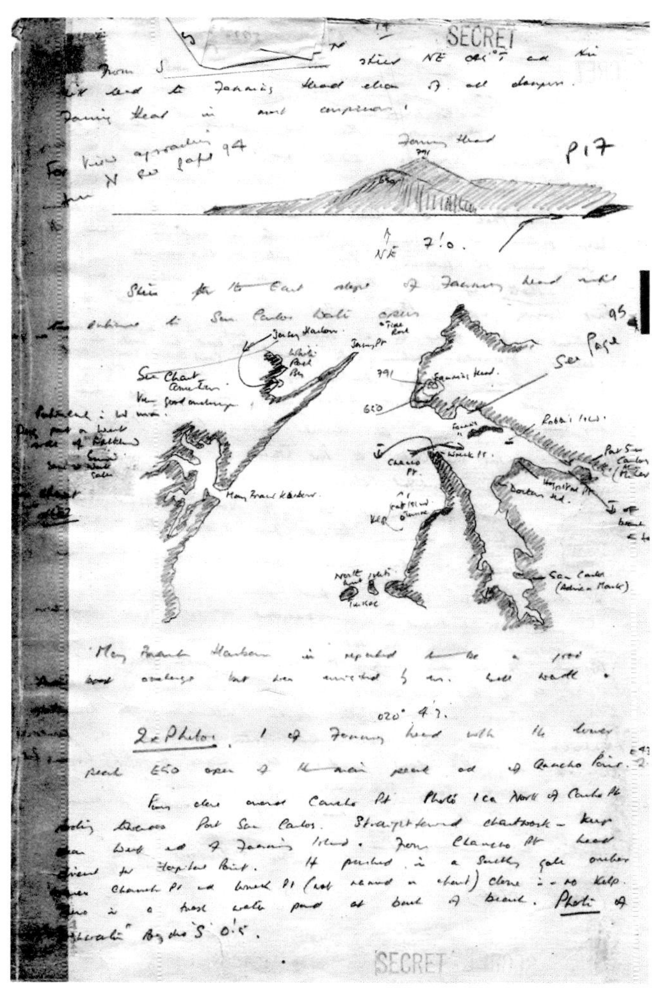

Page from my note book of San Carlos Water, drawn in 1978

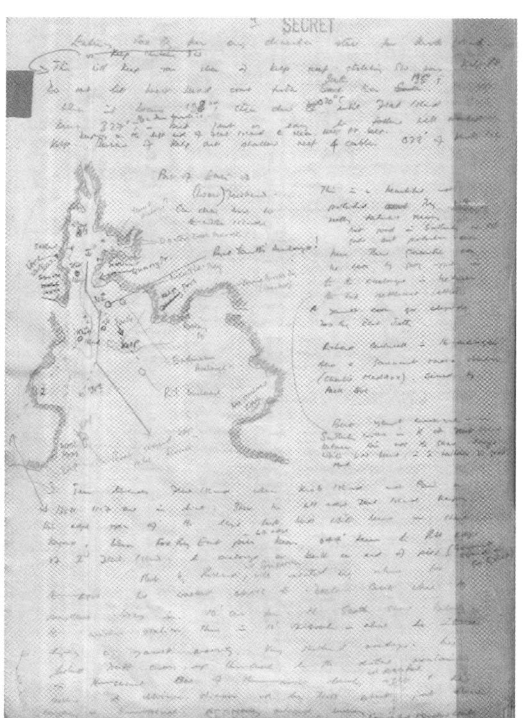

Page from my note book of Fox Bay, drawn in 1978

Argentine marines landing at Yorke Bay, 2nd April 1982 (Argentine Navy)

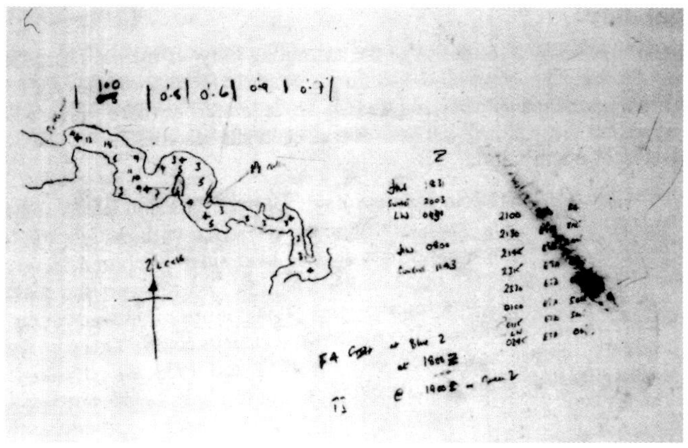

My rough chart of the San Carlos River used to extract 42 Commando. Original is just 4 inches by 3

HMS *Fearless* under air attack in San Carlos Water on D Day (MoD)

Route taken to Bluff Cove with the Scots Guards embarked in four LCUs

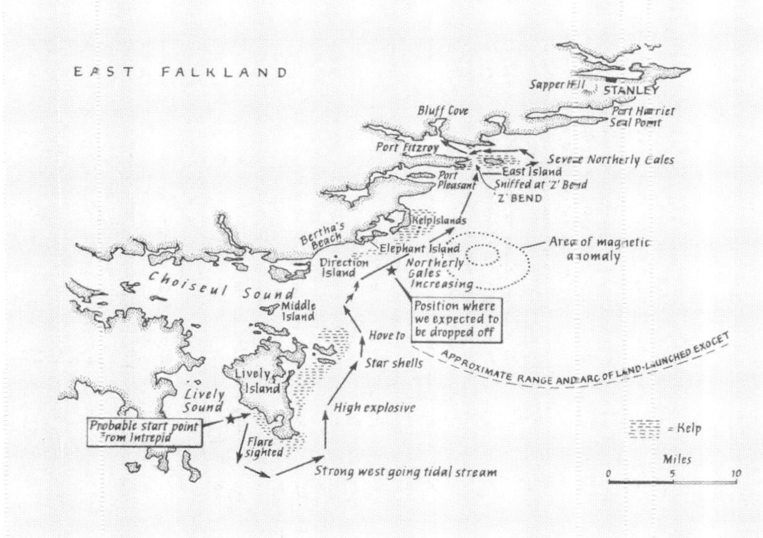

LCU with the Scots Guards embarked and heading for Bluff Cove having been dropped by HMS *Intrepid* 35 miles from our destination instead of just 15. Painting by David Cobb

Crashed *Wessex* on Stanley racecourse on my way from HMS *Fearless* to SS *Canberra*.

Home coming in SS *Canberra*. Painting by David Cobb

Return of HMS *Onyx* flying the Jolly Roger (MoD)

Argentine chart 23071 showing the complicated approaches to Puerto Deseado (Argentine Navy)

HMS *Onyx's* damaged bow and torpedo tubes (MoD 42)

Preparing Geminis for floating off

National Archives document AIR 27/3593. Although this photograph is 'attributed to 101 Squadron RAF (Falklands Conflict)' and is found in RAF Form 549 for 101 Squadron. In fact the original photograph was taken by a Fleet Air Arm Harrier from 801 Naval Air Squadron and shows the runway without the RAF's 'crater' on the centre line. (MoD/RAF)

Taken on 4th May by 801 Naval Air Squadron and showing the offset crater and the ring of white stones on the centre line where the RAF's photograph (actually taken by the FAA and then 'doctored') showed a 'crater' (MoD/RN)

Argentine Air Force photograph of the whole runway showing a pile of rubble on the near right and in the far distance, on the right, the crater that just clips the runway. (Argentine Air Force)

The ABS M-10 medium-lift hovercraft which, although never procured by the Royal Marines, paved the way for the future (ABS Hovercraft)

The Royal Engineers armoured and armed demolition bulldozer, one of four we landed on the west bank of the River Foyle during Operation Motorman on 31st July 1972 to destroy the barricades in the Bogside (MoD)

The Sleeping Beauty submersible canoe. A primitive forerunner of modern SDVs (HG Hasler)

Mk VIII Mod 1 SDV, Advanced Swimmer Delivery Vehicle (MoD)

Karen Plaza beach reconnaissance

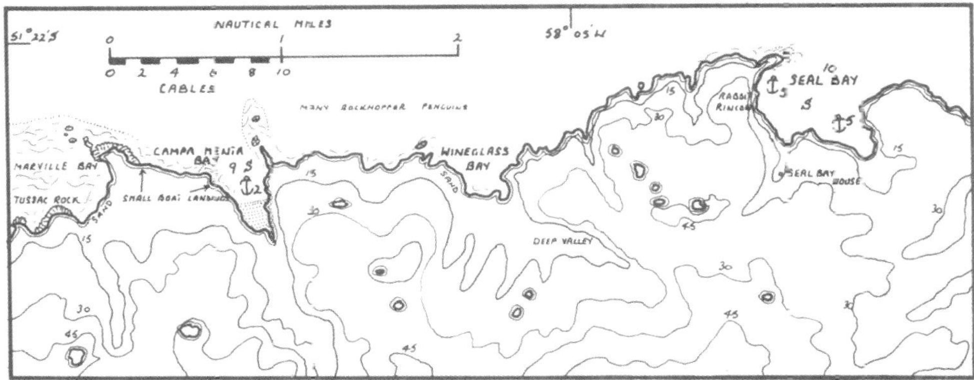

My final chart of Campa Menta Bay, original drawn in 1978

The self-proclaimed Republic of Serbian Krajina in dark grey (ECMM)

The yacht Eloise, chosen for our escape from Croatia to Italy

Ethnic cleansing of the Republic of Serbian Krajina by Croatia in August 1995 (ECMM)

Author with Captain Dragan dur_ng the 'official' (ECMM) visit

Šibenik Bridge

WORLD NEWS

Blitzkrieg in the Balkans

Serbs panic as rearmed Croats capture Knin

by Jon Swain

THE BALKANS had been holding their breath for days over whether there would be a wider war. As diplomacy floundered, the hints were ominous: mobilisation of tens of thousands of Croatian troops backed by tanks and artillery; appeals for blood; the call-up of men of fighting age.

From Zagreb, the Croatian capital where the UN is headquartered, to the coastal towns of Split and Zadar, the air was thick with talk that President Franjo Tudjman of Croatia had decided at last to take the momentous decision to invade the rebellious region of Krajina in a war to reunite his country.

He had — and yesterday, barely 36 hours after his troops had crossed the start line, they achieved their principal goal: the capture of Knin, the "capital" of the breakaway Croatian Serbs.

Knin commands key rail and road routes that connect the coastal and inland halves of Croatia. The town, crowned by a 13th-century castle, was the seat of medieval Croatian kings; but it was also the fount of the Serb revolt that started the violent disintegration of Croatian Serb enclave of Western Slavonia, also wrested by Serb rebels in the war of 1991. The army wrapped up this 200sq-mile piece of territory in a 72-hour blitzkrieg whose speed and ease encouraged the generals into believing themselves strong enough to reconquer Krajina itself. It was the Serbs' first big defeat since Yugoslavia's wars began, and they lost it despite rocket attacks on Zagreb that killed and wounded more than 200 people.

Despite the smart white uniform he has begun to wear, Tudjman is not a military leader but an elected, cautious politician. His original plan, openly known in Zagreb, was to wait until this autumn to fight a war in Krajina; he wanted to give a chance to the political process. But after performing so well in Western Slavonia, his army again performed brilliantly in western Bosnia 10 days ago. In a cross-border operation it captured two Serbian towns to relieve the Serbian pressure on the UN-protected, Bosnian government-controlled pocket of Bihac, which abuts the northeast side of Krajina. An unstoppable momentum had built up.

General Zvonimir Cervenko.

● The Croats attacked the rebellious region of Krajina at dawn on Friday. Their assault began with a massive artillery bombardment of the self-proclaimed Krajinan capital of Knin 125 miles south of Zagreb. Over the next hours thousands of Croatian troops, backed by tanks and artillery, were advancing on Krajina in one of the biggest military operations of the Balkan war. By nightfall the Croatian army was closing in on Knin from the east, southeast and southwest. Its outnumbered defenders were no match for the well-co-ordinated Croatian offensive. In the north of Krajina the Croatian army sought to neutralise Serbian rocket sites threatening Zagreb. The Croats shelled Petrinja and pushed into a valley where the rockets were believed to be hidden. Another main thrust of the Croatian offensive was from the town of Gospic. The overall strategy appeared to be to slice Krajina into pieces, thereby fatally weakening the Serbian defences, before moving to the second phase of the campaign — an advance into the rugged and forested heartland. But the swift collapse of Serbian defences at Knin changed the nature of the offensive and has made it probable that the Croatian army will overrun Krajina in six to 10 days. The fall of Knin is the biggest military defeat inflicted on the Serbs in four years of war. The Bosnian Serbs were unable to come to the rescue beyond a brief bombardment of the Croatian port of Dubrovnik. The Croatian victory will also relieve Croatia's Bosnian Muslim allies under siege in Bihac. The Serbian defeat almost certainly spells the end of the nationalist dream of a Greater Serbia, incorporating Krajina and Bosnia.

The *Sunday Times* report on Operation Storm 5th August 1995

The modern airport at Brač

The LPD HMS *Bulwark* now sold along with her sister ship HMS *Albion* leaving the UK with no amphibious capability (MoD)

Royal Marines' dog Anton
and the officers of 27 Royal
Marines Battalion

British power projection courtesy of amphibious operations. HMS *Bulwark* in the 1960s

In the latter paper, (Paragraph 5a under the heading DAMAGE ASSESSMENT, it is stated: '*There are 3 x apparent craters, one on each side, one on the runway*'.

Yet no photographs have ever shown craters from Black Buck 1 'on each side of the runway'. Even the RAF photograph shows no craters to the north of the runway. In Paragraph 6a of the same paper it is stated:

Vulcan – A single crater, with first bomb halfway down runway just south of centre. Remaining bombs to SW without further damage over 1000m run.

Yet in Paragraph 5a, Crwys-Williams talks of: '*One on each side of the runway*'. Which is it to be?

A diagram in the same RAF paper ties in with most Argentine statements. However, unaware of the Argentine determination to continue flying, it erroneously suggests that only half the runway in each direction was usable.

Soon after hostilities had ended, and before the Royal Engineers had started work, a number of interested parties inspected the runway with the express purpose of establishing any, or no, damage. Rear Admiral Sanders, (then a commander and Rear Admiral Woodward's Staff Officer, Operations), accompanied by Major General Moore and Rear Admiral Woodward, Commander Gedge (CO 809 Naval Air Squadron), Major Norman, (lately OC Naval Party 8901) and Lieutenant Colonel Southby-Tailyour, (OC NP 8901 1978-1979), all came to the same conclusion: there was no sign of any significant damage to the runway – which suggests that the Argentines had been highly successful in their repair work on the paved runway, or there never had been a crater on the runway.

Rear Admiral Jeremy Sanders:

I walked the runway on 17th June with General Moore and Sandy (Woodward) and my recollection matches Southby-Tailyour's.

Commander Gedge again:

The usable part of the runway is of course the centre part, just a foot or two wider than the white threshold markings (piano keys) at the ends: the first bomb of the stick of 21 (Black Buck 1) landed just off the very edge of the usable runway as we can plainly see and was easily filled in. I walked slowly down the entire length of the runway with the late (Commander) Mike Cudmore on 16 June 1982 and it was difficult to see any signs of the filled-in crater. There was, however, a dummy crater on the threshold of runway where debris had been shovelled onto the runway to make it look as though there was a crater. I prodded this with a stick to find a pristine surface beneath.

Later Commander Gedge was to write:

The runway was intact apart from the dummy crater at the western threshold, just in from the piano keys on the southern side. I was also at the airfield on 17 June but I think the runway inspection was on the first day.

I cannot recall any sign of the crater on the runway itself so, if it had been there, it must have been filled in very promptly after BB1 – and before the Cantan photo on 4 May. The 4 May photo does show some signs of discolouration closer to the runway centreline but we have always thought this was either fake or the result of one of the other (I understood to be 228) explosives that were thrown at the airfield by one means or another.

This ties in with the comments above by Commodoro Héctor Luis Destri, Commander Military Air Base Malvinas, as well as the historian Alejandro Amendolara, both of whom state that the crater was filled in immediately, and a false one constructed more towards the centreline, but not quite as central as the one in the official 'RAF photograph'.

Lieutenant Colonel Southby-Tailyour, who commanded Naval Party 8901 in the Falkland Islands 1978–1979, and who was with the Task Force in 1982, has written:

At the end of the campaign, on 23 June [the day the Royal Engineers had completed enough of their work to allow a Hercules to land the next day.] I drove the length and breadth of the runway with Ian Strange, a Falkland Islander and internationally acclaimed ornithologist who knew the runway well, in his Land Rover. Up and back. No sign but plenty of craters to the south and shallow scores either side and on the tarmac (Harriers?) filled in. One small hole that could have been a bomb crater. I had driven up and down the runway many times in 1978–1979 as I was then responsible for its security, thus I knew what the original surface looked like.

Major Mike Norman, OC NP 8901 in 1982, and subsequently, OC Juliet Company, 42 Commando during the campaign:

Later that day, the 15th June, [Prior to the Royal Engineers' recce.] having acquired an Argentinian Mercedes I drove to the airfield to see:

a. How the PoWs were progressing.

b. To view the damaged runway which I had last seen on 2 April.

The runway was undamaged apart from several small canon holes. There were a couple of large craters in the soft ground but absolutely no damage to the hardstanding or any sign of recent repair. The runway was exactly as I remembered it, but not so the airfield. I drove up and down the runway several times and then returned to my disarming duties.

Lieutenant Colonel Roger Blundell (an aviator) then a major, was the Fleet Royal Marines Officer on Admiral Sir John Fieldhouse's staff who worked closely with the three service commanders at Fleet Headquarters, Northwood, including Air Marshal Sir John Curtiss the Air Component Commander. Lieutenant Colonel Blundell's evidence corroborates that of Commodore Clapp who also spoke to Air Marshal Curtiss:

Having achieved the flight there was indeed only one hit on the runway and that on the edge and therefore did not in any way stop the Argentinians using the runway as they wished with aircraft types appropriate for the shortish length.

Not mentioned, so far, was that after BLACK BUCK, the Argentines put piles of mud not only around the one hit but also thoughtfully positioned further along the runway to give the impression that much more serious damage had been caused than was the truth and even they could not use the runway, which was not true.

Interim Summary

We have four British eyewitness accounts of the state of the main paved area of the runway, all of which support the view that there was no major damage to the paved area that had been left unfilled in. These have to be taken into account along with the evidence of Lieutenant Carlos Centeno. Conversely, we have no eyewitness accounts offering a contrary view.

FURTHER PHOTOGRAPHIC EVIDENCE

One of the photographs has been used by others to show that a 'Vulcan's bomb hit the runway' but this is not a 1000lb bomb crater, but rubble, as mentioned by Commander Gedge and Lieutenant Colonel Blundell, on the western end of the runway. Its juxtaposition with the control tower indicates its position as being to the north-west, whereas the one bomb that clipped the runway was to the north-east. Even if this is not rubble, then the only other credible explanation is that it is damage by a Sea Harrier and was easily repaired before Alberto Vianna landed his Hercules along the northern side of the runway.

In yet another AAF photograph of the whole runway, the bomb that clipped the paved portion can just be seen on the right in the distance, but no sign of anything towards the runway's centre, as it either did not happen or was placed there by the Argentines. There is no hint of a centreline crater. The dummy rubble is clear in the foreground on the right side of the paved area. A further photograph taken by the AAF before the end of hostilities shows no sign of any significant runway damage.

REPAIRS

The Royal Engineers began their survey on 17 June and in their Report of Proceedings there is mention of only one Vulcan crater on the runway.

Another excerpt is the Royal Engineers' chart of the runway damage as found on the 17 June, and corroborates the position of the one Vulcan bomb. The dummy craters are shown as such, but are depicted as surface scar'. General Menéndez's subterfuge had worked.

In yet another excerpt is the only photograph we have seen of a close-up, ground view of the one crater on the runway's edge. The main crater can be seen towards the left with rubble spread (we believe, from Argentine statements) by hand, towards the centreline.

The first British Hercules landed on the runway on 24 June, just seven days after the first engineer recce.

Final proof of the lack of serious damage to the runway is supplied by the AAF taken from a US satellite – KH-9 Mission 1217 on 12 June 1982.

SUMMARY

We have shown that the Black Buck raids played no part in the Argentine decision not to operate fast jets from Stanley runway and we have shown that the Black Buck raids 2 and 7 missed the target. Black Buck 1 hit the southern edge of the runway with one bomb, allowing flying operations, including the Aeromacchis AM-339 fast jet fighters, to continue along the full length of the northern section of the runway.

We have offered visual and written firsthand accounts, all of which – British, Falkland Islands, French, American and Argentine – state that no significant bomb damage could be discerned on the centreline nor on the northern half of the paved runway. We accept that there was superficial damage from Sea Harrier strikes. We show the original FAA photograph taken just a few hours after the Black Buck 1 raid which shows one bomb crater on the southern half of the paved section of the runway. We also show the FAA photograph taken a few hours after the Black Buck 2 raid, which shows no crater on the paved runway, but a white circle closer to the centreline.

We have General Menéndez's photograph of the nearest crater to the runway and his (probably vague) description of its position, and we have Vicecomodoro Vianna's description of landing his Hercules onto an intact runway, apart from well-repaired damage on the southern edge.

Conversely we have not seen one RAF eyewitness account, first-hand or written, that supports a bomb straddling the centreline of the runway but we do have one 'RAF photograph' showing a bomb crater straddling the very centre of the runway. Unfortunately, we have no clue to its origin, although it does appear to be a variation of the original and much clearer photograph taken on 1 May by the FAA.

Across the three Black Buck bombing raids, an estimated 1,000,700 gallons of fuel were used and sixty-three 1,000lb bombs were dropped, with just one hitting the southern half of the runway. We have shown that there was no repositioning of Argentine aircraft, as claimed by the RAF, following the first Black Buck raid.

CONCLUSIONS

The first and most evident conclusion is that the photograph sent to us by a RAF historian, (and attributed to the RAF) is not genuine. Of all the many other photographs and first-hand descriptions contained in this paper, not one refers to, or shows, a bomb crater on the runway's centreline. At best, the origin of this notated and fuzzy photograph (the original taken by the FAA and analysed by Admiral Woodward's staff) is suspect.

The second conclusion is that the Argentines were never going to operate fast jets out of Stanley airfield, but merely planned to use it as a refuelling and re-arming base by extending the runway using 231 aluminium planks preloaded into the Argentine merchant ship, ELMA *Córdoba*. That this extension was never possible, was nothing to do with the RAF and the Black Buck raids, but the direct result of the Royal Navy's surface and sub-surface operations that prevented all Argentine ships from sailing outside their own coastal waters.

The third conclusion is that the first crater on the southern half of the runway from Black Buck 1 was filled in before Black Buck 2, and replaced probably (as hinted by Commodoro Destri) by the faintish, pale circle close to, but not on, the runway's centreline. This was a rough circle of painted stones, part of General Menéndez's subterfuge and which Commodoro Héctor Luis Destri described as to:

...help the English break the track? So we decided to build two simulated impacts on the track so that the Vulcan would stop shaking us and the result was successful.

After the second Vulcan bombing, it was sought to make the enemy believe that he had achieved his objective. For this, two craters were simulated similar to the real one already repaired. We did an excellent job of trying to fool the English into believing that the runway was really disabled. We used stones, paint, etcetera.

Clearly this stratagem worked, although eventually Admiral Woodward saw through it.

Despite the obvious and highly laudable courage and determination of both the Vulcan and Victor tanker crews the inescapable assumption is that Black Buck 1 (and even less so Black Buck 1 and 7) did not meet the RAF's mission, as laid down in Operation Order 3/82 271440 Z APR 82, which was 'to impede Argentinian air operations from Stanley airfield'. All evidence tells us that the runway remained operational for C-130s, Pucara, Fokkers, as well as the Aeromacchis AM-339 fast jet fighters, from the first until the very last day of the campaign. The Pucara and Aeromacchis operated inter alia against HMS *Argonaut* on 21 May and the Pucara against British troops at Goose Green on 28/29 May.

No Argentine aircraft were moved north as the result of the Black Buck raids thus the threat to the Task Force was not diminished.

Our penultimate conclusion is that Flight Lieutenant Withers' statement, '*We had one bomb right on the runway and as a result the runway was never used for the rest of the war by the Argentineans*' is both misleading and historically incorrect.

Thus, we come to the inevitable decision that tactically, the four Black Buck bombing raids (1, 2, 3 and 7) were at best ineffectual, and at worst, expensive failures.

THE CONSEQUENCES

The consequences of the Stanley runway remaining open for Argentine flying operations throughout the campaign were profound.

In his book *One Hundred Days* (Fontana, 1992), Admiral Woodward says:

My own opinion was that frequent bombardment of that strip of tarmac from the sea would permanently discourage them from ever using it as a take-off or landing area for fast jets. I fully expected them to bodge it up with cement and rubble and packed earth sufficiently to run in the old Hercules freighters with supplies or even acting as ambulance planes to remove the wounded but I did not care too much about that. I cared about fast jet bombers striking at the British carriers and my general policy was to make life a misery for anyone planning to operate against us from Port (sic) Stanley. High speed aircraft need a very smooth and long surface to get off the ground or even to land and we intended to make sure that was an impossibility.

In this latter intention, both the admiral and the RAF failed, as the Aeromacchis AM-339s operated out of Stanley from the beginning to the end.

In other words the admiral 'did not much care' about resupply flights for the Argentine land forces, but only about the fast jets that might attack British ships. He would not have known of ELMA *Córdoba* and her load of planks, being prevented from sailing due to the Maritime Exclusion Zone followed by the sinking of ARA *General Belgrano*. Nevertheless, the British land forces most certainly did care about the almost continual resupply of food, fuel, ammunition and firewood, to the Argentine land forces.

Nor could the admiral have possibly known that in late May, three Exocet anti-ship missiles (the threat that he feared the most) had been flown into Stanley in an old Hercules, with four more arriving overnight on 5 June, one of these was to seriously damage HMS *Glamorgan*. With respect, if the admiral had cared a little more about preventing the Argentine Hercules flights, and had the Black Buck raids been the success the RAF continue to claim, not only would the British land forces have faced a more materiel-deprived enemy but HMS *Glamorgan* would have remained unscathed.

The Task Force faced the same number of enemy aircraft after the first Black Buck, as there had been before 1 May. The air threat was not diminished by the Black Buck raids.

SIGNATORIES

[Positions are those held in 1982, ranks are those achieved in due course.]

Dr Alejandro Amendolara, Argentine naval and military historian.

Santiago Rivas, Argentine aviation historian.

Mariano Sciaroni, Argentine military historian and lawyer.

Alejandro Pita, Argentine Navy midshipman at Rio Grande, son of *Capitán de Navio de Infanteria de Marina*, Miguel Pita.

Dr Anthony Wells: Head of Special Programs, UK Intelligence directorate, 1979–1983. Author of *A Tale of Two Navies* and *Between Five Eyes*.

Rear Admiral Jeremy Larken, Commanding Officer HMS *Fearless*.

Rear Admiral Jeremy Sanders, Staff Officer Operations on Rear Admiral Woodward's staff.

Major General Julian Thompson, Commander, 3 Commando Brigade, Royal Marines.

Major General Nick Vaux, Commanding Officer, 42 Commando, Royal Marines.

Major General Malcolm Hunt, Commanding Officer, 40 Commando, Royal Marines.

Commodore Michael Clapp, Commander Amphibious Task Group.

Captain Gordon Wilson, Royal Navy, School of Maritime Operations.

Captain Peter Hore, Royal Navy, Joint Logistics Officer, Ascension Island (J4).

Colonel Richard Preston, military adviser and SF coordinator to Rear-Admiral Woodward.

Colonel Ivar Hellberg, Royal Corps of Transport, Commanding Officer, Commando Logistic Regiment.

Commander Laon Hulme, First Lieutenant, HMS *Brilliant*.

Commander Tim Gedge, Commanding Officer 809 Naval Air Squadron.

Commander Graham Edmonds, Operations Officer, HMS *Broadsword*.

Commander David Baston, Commanding Officer 848 Naval Air Squadron.

Commander Nigel MacCartan-Ward, Commanding Officer 801 Naval Air Squadron.

Commander David Hobbs, DG Aircraft (Navy) Department, naval historian and author.

Lieutenant Colonel Peter Cameron, Commanding Officer 3 Commando Brigade, Air Squadron.

Lieutenant Colonel Roger Blundell, Fleet Royal Marines Officer, C-in-C's staff, Northwood.

Lieutenant Colonel Ewen Southby-Tailyour, OC Task Force Landing Craft Squadron.

Major Mike Norman, Officer Commanding Naval Party 8901 and J Company, 42 Commando.

Lieutenant Commander Lester May, Supply Officer HMS *Hydra*.

Michael Shuttleworth, retired Royal Marines officer and helicopter pilot.

Dr Andrew Rastall, Royal Engineers.

16 November 2020

Chapter 10

Operation Kettledrum, 1982

Paraphrased from *Exocet Falklands* by the author

The following is an extract from a published account of the 'Exocet war' within the overall 1982 British campaign to retake the Falkland Islands.

From the very first days of the campaign, concerns were expressed about the number of Exocet air-to-surface missiles Argentina possessed; furthermore there was uncertainty about whether or not those five aircraft and missiles that had been delivered in 1981 had been married, without French assistance, to form a potent threat to the approaching British Task Force.

This ambiguity was shattered on 4 May when one of two missiles launched, hit HMS *Sheffield*. On 25 May two missiles hit MV *Atlantic Conveyor*. The fifth and final air-launched missile missed its intended target, HMS *Invincible*, on 30 May. On the day HMS *Sheffield* had been struck, Rear Admiral Woodward [the Carrier Battle Group commander] asked that action be taken against the mainland naval air base at Rio Grande where the Super Étendard fighter bombers were based. The Special Air Service was tasked with two mainland operations against Rio Grande. One, Operation Plum Duff, was aborted after three days and the other, Operation Mikado, was cancelled. Subsequently, and for reasons yet unknown, the Royal Marines' Special Boat Squadron [it became the Special Boat Service in 1987] was tasked with a similar operation but against an altogether different target.

Elsewhere, a third implausible plan for a mainland operation had been maturing.

Lieutenant Commander Andrew Johnson, commanding officer of the diesel-electric submarine HMS *Onyx* brought his boat alongside HMS *Fearless* in San Carlos Waters as his log and additional supporting comments for 31 May 1982, show:

0530 Surfaced
0830 Dived on aircraft sighting
1200 Position 50° 35'S, 59° 30'W

2100 Rendezvous with HMS Avenger for lead in to San Carlos Water
0045 Berthed alongside HMS Fearless to collect SBS and associated equipment.

Dived at short notice when possible aircraft sighted. Bright light on steady bearing. In retrospect, consider it was a planet, but better safe than sorry! Spent day making slow transit to rendezvous, with brief periods of snorkelling [recharging the batteries at periscope depth through the use of a snorkel to provide fresh air for the diesel engines] *to keep battery high. Lead in to San Carlos went well, using periscope to follow, con and fix. Delayed while other movements took place, but arrived alongside HMS* Fearless [the amphibious flagship] *about midnight. Long chat with* [Captain] *Jeremy Larken, the Commanding Officer and a fellow submariner,* (and from whom he received, in Johnson's words, 'much useful, avuncular advice') *then briefly with the Commodore Amphibious Warfare before full briefing sessions with the SBS*

Having expended the last of their Exocet missiles unsuccessfully on 30 May – the day before *Onyx*'s arrival in San Carlos – the four Super Étendard fighter bomber aircraft had been flown back to their home base at Base Aeronaval Comandante Espora on 1 June, so Rio Grande was no longer a prime concern, but Espora could still have been. Although the Secret Intelligence Service were adamant that no replacement Exocets had reached Argentina, a tiny doubt remained, and as long as that tiny doubt remained, the Super Étendards were a target, wherever they were. Nevertheless it was towards Puerto Deseado, and not Espora, that HMS *Onyx* was about to be ordered to sail on 2 June.

With HMS *Onyx*'s berthing had also come a 'rather scruffy cardboard tube' that Andrew Johnson was at last able to hand to its addressee: the officer commanding the Special Boat Squadron, Major Jonathan Thomson. When the seals were broken, the SBS command team in the amphibious flagship 'simply could not believe the contents' for they were the outline orders for an attack against Puerto Deseado. This was an air base that had not featured in any 'direct action' plans by the British for two simple reasons: it was 400 nautical miles from Stanley, let alone Admiral Woodward's two aircraft carriers, and there had never been any indication that an attack – by Super Étendard, Mirage, Dagger or Skyhawk – had ever been launched from there.

Yet an SBS team was now required to embark in the submarine, sail north, observe and attack, if feasible, any relevant aircraft that they might detect, at an air base in a country with which the UK was not, in any legal sense, at war.

While there had been a brief, advance warning of the possibility of a mainland operation, nothing else was known until the submarine's arrival, especially not the destination, although it had been assumed to be Rio Grande and the Exocets.

The collective view among the SBS officers was uncompromising:

We think it was the timing that annoyed us most, because Operation Kettledrum, as it was called, had clearly been dreamt up some considerable time before but no one in England had thought to tell us in San Carlos. Had they done so we might have had a chance of doing some realistic planning and perhaps have been able to bring some up-to-date reality to the discussions. Instead we were reduced to having several DSSS conversations [Defence Secure Satellite Communications System, known rather more simply as the 'D triple S'] *with people at home who kept on telling us that 'the birds were expected to come in there'* (Puerto Deseado) *and other such inanities.*

SBS officers recall that these discussions were backed up by signals to which Jeremy Larken, as the Commanding Officer of *Fearless* and as the Flag Captain to the Commodore Amphibious Warfare, was properly privy. As a result he was able to offer practical advice, tempered with the observation that, in his experienced view as a submariner, the Royal Marines and HMS *Onyx* faced 'a bit of a problem'. Apart from Jonathan Thomson, Colonel Richard Preston, having earlier been the Special Forces adviser to Admiral Woodward, (in whom Thomson had confided his concerns) and Jeremy Larken the only other three officers 'in theatre' who knew anything at all about Operation Kettledrum, then and now, were Andrew Johnson of *Onyx*, Colin Howard, the SBS's Operations Officer, and (once at sea in the submarine) Lieutenant David Boyd, the Royal Marine who would command the operation.

The one officer who should have been consulted at the very beginning but was not, was Michael Clapp, Commodore Amphibious Warfare, responsible to the Land Force Commander [Major General Jeremy Moore] for SBS operations. He had certainly welcomed Lieutenant Commander Andrew Johnson to his amphibious domain and had discussed in outline, the use of the submarine operating with the SBS around the islands but no more than that, as far as Operation Kettledrum was concerned. Without Clapp's prior knowledge the submarine sent south to do his bidding was about to be removed before HMS *Onyx* had hardly arrived. As with the earlier loss of one of the commodore's 'junglie' helicopters [Royal Navy troop lift helicopters, as opposed to the 'pingers' who search for submarines by lowering a transponder below the surface] for Operation Plum Duff, the normal amphibious chain of command, long-established to, inter alia, safeguard and control invaluable assets, was once more being ignored by those far removed from San Carlos.

Captain Brian Woolvine, an SBS officer on Admiral Fieldhouse's staff, had handed the sealed cardboard tube to Johnson when the submarine had called at Ascension Island, on its way south in the middle of May. Apart from the orders, this scruffy cylinder also contained one map, one chart and a handful of satellite-derived images. Richard Preston, now back with General Jeremy Moore's Land Force Headquarters in *Fearless*, wrote in his diary:

> *Onyx arrives tomorrow night to start training with the SBS for a possible mission against the Argentine mainland air bases. This kind of strategic task should be mounted from the UK. We have no need to know about it; neither are we able to provide adequate briefing.*

Following the submarine's arrival, Preston's diary continues:

> *Jonathan is very worried at the way the operation is being set up. It is unbelievable that anyone should be expected to plan, let alone execute a mission of this complexity without comprehensive intelligence and topographical information. We* (Headquarters, Land Forces Falkland Islands) *signalled Fleet* [Headquarters in Northwood, England] *expressing grave misgivings over the operation. It is a Boys Own Paper scheme which is likely at best to create only political embarrassment and at worst could lead to our whole team being killed and I suspect it would achieve nothing.*

Preston also noted:

> *The only map Thomson has been given by Fleet Headquarters looks like a piece torn from an RAC road map. It has the outline of the coast and roads but little or no other information and certainly no indication of the target or any contours. I am horrified.*

Marginally more detail was to be found on the 1:35,000 scale, Argentine chart number 23071, titled Rada Puerto Deseado. This second edition was based on surveys by the Argentine Naval Hydrographic Service to 1969 and published by the US Defense Mapping Agency Hydrographic Center on 20 November, 1976.

Preston continues:

When the SBS officers sought my views I could not believe that anyone sane would have considered mounting a military operation on the basis of the information that they had been given, and said so. They appeared to agree and that, I assumed, put an end to the madness, especially as their Officer Commanding, Jonathan Thomson, also consulted Jeremy Larken.

Preston added later: *I have to say that I was surprised to learn subsequently that they had launched the operation.*

The senior SBS officers 'down south' were not happy either, with one major (who wishes to remain unnamed) stating unequivocally: *We were in a period where people in the UK were prepared to believe in the myths as much as the reality. However, we in the SBS were not prepared to believe in myths and said so. But once that discussion was over, we were ready to mount the operation against the Puerto Deseado air base despite thinking it politically unwise and probably militarily impossible. We felt we had a wider duty to say that myth and reality had more than parted company, but when overruled by Fleet Headquarters we had to get on and attempt to follow orders. If you don't do that, you get chaos.*

The same member of the SBS command team in theatre continued to elaborate their collective views: *Argentina was a country against which we were not, formally, at war. Having men killed or captured on the Argentine mainland would have been counter productive in the global media war in which the United Kingdom was then engaged.* And that opinion certainly influenced the SBS command in its discussions with Northwood and the eventual decision, made by Fleet Headquarters, to abort the operation.

No one in the SBS wanted to be associated with pointless failure, nor as is now known, with an operation that not only was based on outdated intelligence but one that was aimed at an Argentine base that had never been of any military significance. Further comments from the same source in Headquarters SBS have recently surfaced:

Now that we know that the airbase was of little tactical importance, it just makes the whole thing more serious, for it implies that the Special Forces planning staff in the UK had lost grip of reality. We in the SBS had had enough of living that sort of dream by then and were trying to concentrate on the much less glamorous, but realistic and essential, mission of supporting the landing force.

Following discussions between the South Atlantic and Northwood on the 'D triple S', described at the time as being a series of 'remonstrations from San Carlos' (caused in part by conflicting orders on the target that were also flowing from the Ministry of Defence) the SBS planners in HMS *Fearless*, having made their point, complied with their orders.

The precise details of those orders – the aim, or what is now termed 'the mission' – are lost, although the declared reason for this operation was that Puerto Deseado was believed to be a 'staging, refuelling and mounting base' with 'pilot accommodation' and the 'command needed to know how, precisely, it was being used, by whom and when'.

This rather vague 'mission statement' was based on an unfounded worry that the Super Étendard pilots might have been using Puerto Deseado as a diversionary air base for rest and security immediately following a mission. The basis of this rather spurious deduction – given that only two aircraft and two pilots were all that had been involved in each sortie – offered to the SBS during their planning, was that Puerto Deseado had 'large accommodation facilities'.

It has to be remembered, too, that these orders were written in the United Kingdom three weeks earlier and then delivered, 'by hand of officer' to HMS *Onyx* at Ascension Island before she continued her voyage on 16 May. At that stage of the campaign there had been three Exocets 'unaccounted for' but, in the meantime and while the submarine 'swam south' for two more weeks, all were to be expended. By the time of the submarine's arrival in San Carlos there were no missiles left, and that much was known in the Task Force, if yet to be appreciated at home.

According to the SBS Operations Officer at the time, a s with Plum Duff and Mikado, no one in the United Kingdom had done their sums, for the landing itself at Puerto Deseado would have been equally as fraught as any attack or reconnaissance. The river is very narrow, very fast flowing and the submarine would not have been able to get close enough because of a ledge. Indeed, the British Admiralty's *South America Pilot Volume II* talks of a complicated approach for surface vessels that also face tidal streams running up to 6 knots at 'springs', with just five minutes of slack water at each change of tide, and the landing was planned for two days before the 6 June's full moon.

Concerned that he was sending his men on a mission that was unlikely to succeed, the officer commanding the SBS himself decided to lead the attack. Although not trained as an SBS officer Thomson felt strongly that he could not send his men on a 'raid' that all regarded as 'stupid, with a near certainty of death or capture', without him being with them. On this occasion there would be no underwater work involved but a straightforward landing by rubber Gemini assault craft followed by an overland approach to, and possible raid upon, a well-defined target prior to a lengthy escape towards a neutral country: on the face of it the normal fare for a Royal Marines major.

However, that was not Thomson's job whose task was to advise the Land Forces Commander and the Commodore Amphibious Warfare on maritime Special Forces operations, while also providing de-confliction advice on such operations in relation to conventional plans.

Additionally, according to Preston who had been personally involved in the early stages after *Onyx*'s arrival, the operation also presented an interesting aspect of moral philosophy. When given a task that is clearly impossible and one that would, at best, end in failure and political embarrassment (with, inevitably, the commander held as the scapegoat as happened to Captain Andy 'L' who had led the aborted Operation Plum Duff) and at worst lead to the capture or death of all involved, do you have an obligation to lead the attack yourself? There is also the problem of a commander leading his men who have placed their trust in their leader yet who, personally, believes the task to be unachievable. 'In the end you just get on with it as part of your contract,' but it is still a dilemma.

To meet the pre-arranged timings contained in the orders there was no occasion to prepare plans prior to the submarine's departure, thus the main planning could only be conducted once HMS *Onyx* was on her way north. The controlling Special Operations Group in London (and thus, it has to be presumed, with the War Cabinet's agreement) had originally ordered that the operation should involve fourteen men but Thomson felt that this was twice as many as were needed for what was, after all, not an 'invasion' but a 'quick nip in and out', leaving the smallest of footprints. Quite apart from that, there simply was not enough room in the submarine while the allotted small team was already well-formed and self-contained.

Without yet knowing the reasons behind the failure, Thomson was also conscious that Operation Plum Duff had been aborted and that his own men did not have, as the SAS team had had, a nearby international border to make for: the nearest point of Chile lies over 250 miles to the west of Puerto Deseado. To limit any damage when things went wrong just six men would conduct the operation. Another reason for reducing the numbers was that this was expected to be, contrary to how the SBS prefer to operate, a one-way journey. Any chance of successfully conducting a lengthy 'escape and evasion' would be greater with the fewest men possible.

HMS *Onyx* sailed from San Carlos at 0700 GMT on 1 June for a day of pre-Operation Kettledrum trials with her embarked force of SBS led by Lieutenant David Boyd and Sergeant 'Wally' (William) Lewis, who with their four Royal Marines, had been waiting in *Fearless*. Also on board was the SBS's Operations Officer, Captain Colin Howard who could now view the 'Northwood mission' for the first time in detail. Once at sea Howard was able to produce a first draft of his operation order as he explains:

I then wrote the orders with Andrew Johnson and of course with David Boyd and his team conferring. We did not really have much technical information to go on but the chart and 'surrounding information knowledge' painted the picture! The assault team was not going to retrace its entry down the river either as that would have been near impossible without the river taking charge.

The fact that my boss, Jonathan Thomson, tasked me to go forward in the submarine meant that London would get an SBS operational order for their approval, written with the team that would conduct the landing, after we had all analysed the available information and balanced that with the team's capabilities. Boyd's team was 'good to go' and prepared to be ordered! However, for obvious good measure we required answers to a list of carefully thought out key points that needed clarification.

David Boyd was to write:

Much of what happened I had long since forgotten and some I was never aware of as a young, relatively inexperienced officer just getting on with a job. This was because Jonathan Thomson was quite determined to do everything possible to protect Operational Security to the point that none of my team, including me, were told of anything until HMS Onyx had departed San Carlos. We were to remain on board until the task commenced or, as it happened, was aborted and diverted elsewhere.

Boyd's most enduring memory of the operation was the paucity of up-to-date intelligence.

*The air photographs we were supplied, presumably through the United States,
pre-dated the Argentine invasion of the Falkland Islands, let alone the outbreak
of conflict. I also recall that we had little in the way of stand-off munitions to
deal with the target we were assigned; which meant we were back to the 'get
up close and personal' with a target in a potentially heavily defended air base.*

Although on a far smaller scale than the cancelled Operation Mikado [the landing
of two Hercules, heavy-lift aircraft with, between them, up to sixty SAS troopers
embarked, direct onto the Rio Grande runway] this mainland operation too, was
beginning to exhibit all the makings of a backroom-driven disaster.

HMS *Onyx*'s log adds some detail to this bizarre affair:

1 June
0700   Slipped to clear San Carlos before daylight.
2130   Surfaced for lead in by HMS Avenger.
2350   Alongside HMS Fearless for SBS dry drills and briefings.

*Day spent loitering off North Falkland Sound. Weather deteriorated through day,
so no chance of SBS drills. Change of plan resulted in return to San Carlos for
further briefings. Planning proceeding slowly but too many unanswered questions.*

The 'too many unanswered questions' were posed on this day in a three page
signal, sent by Howard and Johnson in *Onyx* via Thomson (still in the amphibious
flag ship) to Northwood for discussion by the Special Forces coordinator, and
then onwards to the London-based Special Operations Group. Nevertheless,
before receiving any answers the submarine slipped once again from alongside
Fearless and proceeded northwards for the operation.

2 June
*0245   Sailed for Operation KETTLEDRUM. Landings on Argentine
              mainland.*
1200   Position 50° 37'S, 59° 57'W
*2124   Action stations for wet drills. Rigged casing lines then dived to repair
              ballast pump defect.*

*Very quiet forenoon with snorts to keep battery up while crew recovered from
two nights at diving stations. Still much info required which may arrive by*

signal – hopefully. Briefing/planning in afternoon. This was for operations against one of the airfields – not sure which at this stage. Sea calm with long swell, bright moon and some mist – not good for secrecy, but convenient for rehearsals.

The questions that needed addressing centred around one of many concerns: was the operation to be in-and-out or one-way? Careful study of the chart suggested that for seabed profile and security reasons the Gemini [inflatable assault craft powered by a 40hp outboard engine or paddles], would need to be launched as far as 20 miles offshore where the water begins to shoal sharply from 230 feet to 100 feet. This would mean the use of noisy outboard motors that, if a one way operation, would be jettisoned over the side before the men began their final approach using just paddles against the possible six knot current. An added fear, following the experience in South Georgia when all outboard motors failed, was that they would behave likewise off Puerto Deseado – less than 500 nautical miles north of Cape Horn and in the autumn – leaving the crews stranded at sea and almost certainly in an offshore wind. If an in-and-out operation was to be planned the craft – with their motors – would need to be hidden on the river bank, probably to the west of Puerto Deseado town although an approach via the exposed Atlantic beach to the north-east of the airbase was a possibility but one that needed unseasonably calm weather. If a one-way journey was what the planners in the United Kingdom had in mind then the craft would need to be sunk without trace on the river bank and that is not an easy task.

An in-and-out operation, although preferred by the SBS, had its problems as elaborated by Howard in his lengthy signal. The river journey past the docks and built up areas would need to be conducted twice beneath a moon two days short of being full. On their return, the team would have to rendezvous with the submarine 20 nautical miles out at sea using standard SBS operating procedures through the use of a hand-cranked, underwater noise-making device called a 'trongle', towards which the submarine would 'home'. Yet this distance offshore was simply too far if, as was likely, the weather was bad.

A one-way operation, with Chile over 250 miles away, produced other worries. Howard needed to know if there was an established 'pipeline' of safe houses and sympathisers that his men could contact: he needed to know the status of his men vis-a-vis the Geneva Convention if they were captured, and a vital consideration, he needed to know what their precise action on the target was to be – reconnaissance or direct action.

Not one of these points, plus many more other operational concerns, had been aired in the original 'orders'. Additionally, because all Exocets had by then been launched, Howard and Johnson pointed out there were far more valuable tasks that the submarine should have been conducting around the shores of the Falkland Islands, than being despatched on such an indistinct mainland operation to the north.

Unlike the aborted Operation Plum Duff, but similar to the cancelled Operation Mikado, there was no half-plausible excuse for six, heavily armed SBS men attempting to enter Puerto Deseado air base. The diplomatic fall-out would have been impossible to laugh off while the military embarrassment would be acute, and all for no readily discernible reason.

To assist in the planning of this contentious operation the officer commanding the SBS flew by helicopter to join the submarine in north Falkland Sound shortly after she sailed. The major's transfer from HMS *Fearless* to HMS *Onyx* was described as 'hairy' by both Johnson and Thomson, not only because all such operations involving a conventional submarine under way in the dark and in typical Falklands weather are 'hairy', but because the helicopter pilot with his night vision goggles was furthermore, confused and blinded by the well-lit British hospital ship SS *Uganda*.

The next day brought further changes:

3 June
0600   *Action stations. Wet drills.*
1200   *Position 49 43S, 61 53W*
p.m.   *Operation KETTLEDRUM cancelled. Returning to Falklands.*
2250   *Action stations. Wet drills.*

Surfaced at 0600 for SBS drills. Launch completed by 0715. Static dive very slow. Gemini engine failed, [confirming our worst fears] otherwise no snags. Further drills in afternoon, then more planning. Operation KETTLEDRUM cancelled at about 1800, turning back to Falklands but still did full run through at 2300 to check out drills. Operations Officer SBS had embarked on 31st May and was still keen to utilise the submarine which seems sensible. Heading back to San Carlos for a decision.

While planning continued, in between action stations and wet drills when two Gemini were brought onto the submarine's casing, inflated, launched (the submarine submerged beneath the craft), recovered (the submarine surfaced beneath the craft), deflated and struck below (while the first lieutenant monitored every move with a stop watch), the 'direct action' team plus the Officer Commanding SBS and his operations officer, all in *Onyx*, waited.

Then, as the boat's log states, the signal to abort Operation Kettledrum came from the United Kingdom at about 1800 on that day. The signal, drafted by Preston on Moore's staff, the three-page signal from Howard combined with Thomson's personal remonstrations on the 'D triple S' – had all finally found their target in Northwood. Lieutenant Commander Johnson immediately ordered a reversal of his submarine's course.

While the ire of Northwood's staff may well have been risked during the earlier conversations over the 'D triple S', those in the South Atlantic had always known that Puerto Deseado was such an insignificant air base that it did not warrant a major military and diplomatic failure, and failure it would have been, as Santiago Rivas, a Buenos Aires military journalist, has since stated:

I don't know what was the intention of attacking that place. There was an Argentine battalion located in the town, but it wasn't a strategic target and had no importance to the operational theatre. The most valuable targets were always Trelew, Comodoro Rivadavia, San Julián, Rio Gallegos and Rio Grande.

As with the aborting of Operation Plum Duff – although at the time for more clear-cut reasons – the cancelling of Operation Kettledrum was too, the correct decision. Prompted from 'down south' it had also dawned on those in Northwood that for instance, the unknown status of Weddell Island (to where *Onyx* was originally planned to head after her arrival), was of far more importance to the amphibious and Special Forces planners in San Carlos when compared with what was almost certainly not happening in Puerto Deseado some 400 nautical miles away.

The Weddell operation had been planned long before Operation Kettledrum burst into HMS *Fearless*'s Special Forces operations room: indeed it was Boyd's team that were earmarked to conduct it. The island was an enigma to Clapp's amphibious staff, who wanted to know if the Argentines had managed to place a team there with a guidance system for their aircraft approaching the archipelago; if so, it needed to be taken out. Conversely, it would be helpful to have had a 'home team' inserted, able to offer last minute advice to San Carlos on how many aircraft were in-bound and heading in what direction.

Back on board the amphibious flagship, Thomson was now obliged to wrestle with the thought that he might have been wrong to suggest to Northwood, and through that headquarters upwards to the War Cabinet via the Special Operations Group, that the operation was 'as near to madness as it was possible to get'. He was conscious that officers and men in the armed forces are taught to receive orders and then carry them out: based on the assumption that those up the command chain see a wider picture. In this case the reverse was true which may explain why, on his return to the UK, no one was prepared to discuss Operation Kettledrum with him. And no one has since.

There may have been another reason: very few at Northwood had known about the operation while even fewer in the theatre chain of command were aware of it. This would certainly not have been the case had Thomson lacked the moral courage to try to prevent what would surely have become a diplomatic and military disaster, this time instigated by the naval rather than the army staff. In truth, and with hindsight, on the Task Force's return, all at Northwood were delighted that both military and common sense had prevailed, and all felt that there was no point in further discussions so long after the non–event.

Although the submarine was to conduct a number of Special Forces landings and extractions around the Falkland Islands, any chance that HMS *Onyx* would again be employed in an excursion to the mainland was destroyed on 5 June as her log explains:

0410   Slipped HMS Fearless. Proceeding south through Falkland Sound to attempt SBS insertion at Chatham Harbour.

1200   Position 52° 16'S, 60° 23'W.

1314   Struck rock pinnacle south of Cape Meredith. 5 and 6 tube bow doors and shutters damaged.

p.m. Weather unsuitable for landing at Chatham Harbour; moving on to carry out reconnaissance of Weddell Island. (This with Boyd's team still embarked.)

Dived at 0915 south of Falkland Sound, heading west at periscope depth initially, then down to 180 feet as water allows. Up to snort 1000 – 1230 then down to 180 feet again to sprint. Struck bottom off Cape Meredith at 150 feet – glancing blow only, luckily – 25 fathom patch among minimum sounding of 42 fathoms! All well except 6 tube shutter. Bow cap sprung so unable to drain tube or move bow cap. Hopefully will be able to investigate in San Carlos at some stage and repair/remove shutter. Slowed down considerably to sort out trim, damage etc. so not arriving off Weddell until midnight.

In an aside to himself, Andrew Johnson later added:

The SBS operations officer was sitting in the seat nearest the wardroom door when this happened – we were having lunch. He was trampled by the rest of the wardroom who literally ran over him to get into the control room. He arrived some minutes later wearing a lifejacket and enquiring politely if everything was all right!

With Howard's arrival in HMS Onyx's *control room came the inevitable request for him to don his diving gear and exit the submerged submarine to carry out an initial inspection. Howard's response was, perhaps, equally inevitable, as we could not 'hover' but still appeared to be motoring well at, at least, one knot, I gave a 'polite' negative answer!*

Johnson's summing up is alarming: *We were much less concerned about the grounding at the time…and were some weeks from discovering, once in dry dock in Portsmouth, that both bow tubes were damaged while the torpedo in one tube was cracked like an egg, with the safety range clock 'wound off' as the battery had partially energised!*

In 2013, Andy Johnson explained just how close his submarine had come to destruction, not only at the time of the 'grounding' but throughout the 8,000-mile journey mile journey home.

The cracked torpedo was a Mark 24 Tigerfish. It has a battery which is salt-water activated, so with the torpedo casing damaged, the battery developed part of its charge – enough to turn the motor and propeller slowly which 'winds off' an interlock for releasing the safety device designed to make sure the torpedo doesn't turn 180 degrees and attack it's launching submarine. As I understand it, this device was released. However, the torpedo wasn't armed in the true sense, as this only happens when it acquires a target.

Nevertheless, when we returned to Portsmouth, this situation was so rare that the experts in the armament depot had no idea how to dismantle the torpedo while it was still in the tube – and we couldn't move it forward or back. In the end, the dockyard staff cut away the area of the torpedo tube around the warhead, then an engineer from the dockyard, with myself and one of my 'fore-ends men' hacked the sonar head off the torpedo with drills and crowbars in the middle of the night. The area around the floating dock had to be evacuated and the cross-channel ferry terminal closed while we did so.

So I guess from that we can conclude that the torpedo was in quite a dangerous state. One expert assured us that it could certainly explode at any time – not that we knew that until we entered Portsmouth. Ignorance is bliss! I have the sonar head at home, presented to me by the Squadron Weapons Officer.

Chapter 11

Gestation of 539 Assault Squadron, Royal Marines, 1984

539 Assault Squadron, Royal Marines is named after a Royal Marines Landing Craft Flotilla that served with distinction during the D-Day landings onto Gold Beach on 6 June, 1944.

A paraphrase of the historical records states:

539 Assault Flotilla consisted of 16 Assault Landing Craft (LCAs) – their HQ Infantry Landing Ship (LSI) being SS Empire Halberd. *On D-Day, this vessel was part of Assault Group G2 (Gold Beach) whose HQ was HMS* Squid *at Southampton with the HQ Ship being HMS* Kingsmill. *Most of this group (HMS* Kingsmill, *4 LSIs, 2 Motor Launches (MLs) and an assortment of smaller craft, all escorted by HMS* Ursa *and HMS* Undaunted*) assembled at West Solent and departed 1935 hrs on 5th June, arriving at the lowering position, 7 nautical miles off the beach, at 0455 hrs on 6th June. Embarked in this assault group were the 69th Infantry Brigade consisting of 5th Battalion East Yorkshire Regiment and 6th and 7th Battalions of the Green Howards.*

It was during these operations that Corporal George Tandy of 539 Assault Flotilla was awarded the DSM for steering his LCA six miles to the beach with his feet on the rudders, after the control lines had been damaged while his craft was being lowered into the water. Despite his insistence, he was prevented from taking part in the second wave. After his death and in accordance with his wishes, his ashes were scattered from a landing craft south of Plymouth Breakwater by ranks of 539 Assault Squadron and survivors from the original 539 Assault Flotilla.

After the war the Royal Marines continued to deploy landing craft from specialist ships but the flotillas were changed to squadrons. These squadrons served in the Royal Naval Rhine Flotilla and subsequently in the Amphibious Warfare Squadron in the Mediterranean and Persian Gulf. The landing craft were then embarked in Assault Tank Landing Ships (LST(A)) such as HMSs

Anzio, *Messina* and *Striker*, eventually, when the Landing Platform Docks (LPDs) HMSs *Fearless* and *Intrepid* were commissioned, they were transferred to these ships as the LST(A)s paid off. Additionally, the Landing Platform Helicopters (LPHs) HMSs *Albion* and *Bulwark* (and latterly *Hermes*) were equipped with a squadron each of four LCAs.

During the 1970s and early 1980s when the Royal Marines' 3 Commando Brigade deployed to Norway for its annual winter training, it relied, as it did for operations and exercises elsewhere across the globe, on its own 'air force'. The Brigade Air Squadron (now known as 847 Naval Air Squadron) provided aerial reconnaissance, communications and artillery spotting. Very small parties of men could be also be inserted and extracted. At sea level the Raiding Squadron (a unit of Headquarters and Signals Squadron – now known as the Command Support Group) offered a small-scale, sea-lift capability using Rigid Raiding Craft (RRC) Mk I and Gemini inflatable raiding craft (IRC).

For lifting guns, ammunition, food and fuel or the movement of large numbers of men, two Naval Air Squadrons (845 and 846) could be deployed ashore from the 'duty' LPH or, more usually in Norway, they would self-deploy from their UK base at Yeovilton. Further afield an LPH was – and remains – vital, but as they were phased out an aircraft carrier (CVS) occasionally took on this temporary role. Now the UK has its first custom-built LPH, HMS *Ocean*, (sold to Brazil in 2018), but she is alone in this task and a CVS is still required when she is in refit. These air squadrons would come under brigade control and be tasked through the Commando Helicopter Operations Support Cell (CHOSC, or CHAOS as some named it) which was itself an organic unit of Brigade Headquarters.

For similar surface movements, the landing craft carried in each LPDs were four Landing Craft Utility (LCU) and four Landing Craft Vehicle and Personnel (LCVPs) while the LPHs carried four LCVPs to conduct the initial surface assault, and any follow-on operations. They never came under command of the brigade, remaining very much under the control of their parent ships. Thus, in simple terms, the Brigade Commander had his own air force – when needed – but never his own navy. Few naval commanding officers would sail from the Amphibious Objective Area without their ship's full fit of landing craft, for the very simple (and occasionally proved) reason, that should they be diverted for a real crisis elsewhere, they would look foolish without their own organic assets immediately to hand on board.

This was a severe restriction to the swift movement of commando forces (an integral part of their *raison d'être*) and especially among the fjords of north

Norway in winter, where often the roads around their edges would be blocked by snow, while helicopters could not fly because of blizzards. Cross-country movement, too, was slow, circuitous (some fjords almost bisect the country) and easily ambushed in the many choke points that mark operations in that part of the world. The Russians – the potential enemy – knew all this only too well.

However, in 1971 the Commanding Officer of 45 Commando approached the COs of HMSs *Albion* and *Fearless* to ask if he could take their landing craft under command for a task in the Harstad area that would last at least three days. Despite this being a radical move and one not without its risks, both captains were quick to recognise the military sense of the experiment. The plan included a covert night approach and pre-dawn attack against the 'opposing' NATO forces (in this case the Italian San Marco Battalion) from a direction they were least expecting and, anyway, assumed impossible.

The small flotilla of *Albion's* four LCVPs and two of *Fearless's* LCUs was placed under command of the LPD's Officer Commanding Royal Marines, and once the laden LCVPs had been lashed alongside the equally laden LCUs – between them they had embarked 500 men of the Commando. The two vessels hoisted lights indicating that they were fishing. Although hunted by the Norwegian Navy – which had been purposefully informed of this move – they were never discovered, probably because for much of the twelve hour round-journey, they were only feet from the sheer cliff faces – without lights – and the navy was looking for six craft. The Italians were severely routed and called 'foul' at the subsequent NATO wash-up!

Thus was formed the idea for the Commando Brigade's own 'navy' and while all agreed that it was a 'good idea' there were no spare craft and no spare men. Later, in 1979, a 'spare' LCU was purloined from the training pool and for a number of winters was shipped out to Norway. There it took part in trials in camouflage (static and mobile), covert navigation, drifting among ice flows (cut off by the LCU itself – the radar echo could be similar), nautical ambushes, carrying smaller raiding craft, acting as a mobile, hidden Brigade HQ or hospital ship close to the action, and even a signals relay station (rather than having one in an exposed position on the peak of some mountain).

When in 1982 the brigade deployed for the Falklands campaign, the Landing Craft Squadron did not yet exist, but thanks to the work in the Arctic, it was quickly formed in the waters of San Carlos. All the fleet's minor landing and raiding craft – whether ships' commanding officers liked it or not and (in practice, they did!) were involved, and based in a Forward Operating Base off a beach close to the initial Brigade Headquarters, only returning to their parent ships when they were in the vicinity for rest and fuel. This independent squadron (eventually named after 539 Flotilla that had operated with distinction off the Normandy beaches in June 1944) did so well during Operation Corporate that within two years, permission was granted by the Admiralty to formerly introduce it into the Royal Marines' Order of Battle. Thus, it reformed in 1984, with two LCUs Mk 9, four LCVPs Mk 4, eighteen RRC Mk 1 and eighteen IRC, plus its own Amphibious Beach Unit, transport, signals and engineering sub-units. Of almost more importance, it provided not only in-house expertise in the practicalities of the amphibious art but a tasking cell compatible with that for the helicopters. The brigade's flexibility was hugely enhanced while it was believed that there was no other comparable unit then in existence.

Since 1984, the Royal Marines' 539 Assault Squadron has seen service in every conflict and civilian evacuation undertaken by British forces with small Landing Craft Air Cushion (LCAC) and RRCs operating in the Congo, a good example of the use to which this remarkably flexible unit has been put. More recently, Operation Telic (Iraq) has been no exception. Indeed it has proved – if proof were needed – of the worth of a small independent 'navy' under command and control of a major military formation. One of the added advantages of the Squadron is its ability to take under command a large variety of other craft, in order that the brigade has only one headquarters with which to deal – thus whether they are British Army floating bridges, United States Navy heavy-lift hovercraft, Australian landing craft or US and UK EOD teams, there still remains just one line of command.

For Operation Telic, 539 Squadron was also augmented by a number of other UK units: 4 Assault Squadron Royal Marines (ASRM) from the now paid-off HMS *Fearless*; 9 ASRM from HMS *Ocean*; 10 Training Squadron from 1 Assault Group based at Poole, and 2 Raiding Squadron from the Royal Marines Reserve.

With the premature and difficult-to-understand demise of HMS *Fearless* and the consequent capability gap until HMSs *Albion* and *Bulwark* become operational, the Royal Navy was forced to rely on ships taken up from trade to lift the squadron to the Gulf. In practice this would have happened even if an LPD had been in service, as one can never have enough small craft for such an operation, and anyway, 539 Squadron does not have its own organic lift assets. In the early days there had been talk of the Royal Navy procuring a semi-submersible heavy-lift ship, but the plan was never advanced.

[The squadron is now named 539 Raiding Squadron.]

Chapter 12

Sea Soldiers

Written in 2010 for *Jane's Amphibious and Special Forces*

Sea peoples, sea soldiers, marines, naval infantry – slightly depending on the era under discussion and local sensitivities – trained to live and fight at sea as well as on land, have a history as long as mankind has sought to expand his frontiers. They were used – and are sometimes still used – to guarantee maritime trade, to protect communication routes, to seek space for an expanding population, to acquire land for food, rivers and lakes for potable and irrigation water, to control the source of fossil fuels, or simply in the pursuit of power and prestige.

Down the centuries these duel-trained men have, in various guises and with many titles, been used to conduct amphibious operations, to board and capture vessels, to man ship-borne heavy and light weapons or to establish, secure and defend footholds ashore for future land-based operations. The earliest account of these specialists comes from before 1000 BC when 'sea peoples' fought in ship-to-ship actions in attempts to conquer Egypt, while Greek 'marines' from 600 BC are depicted on an Etruscan vase. In 500 BC, Greek ships were recorded as having their ships' companies divided into seamen, marines and rowers, while at the Battle of Lädê in 497 BC (some say 494 BC), more than one hundred Greek ships had on board forty armed men specially chosen and embarked for the occasion, thus implying that these were not regular ships' company.

Greek ships of this era carrying *Epibatai* (marines in modern parlance) also embarked *Eretai* – slaves, who manned the oars – and the *Nautai* (general hands) who carried out all other duties concerned with the handling of the ship. Large bodies of these *Epibatai* could also be embarked in transports; remaining in preparation for a landing anywhere that the fleet might need assistance in its shore-side operations.

The first recorded amphibious operations were the Persian landings at Marathon in 490 BC followed by the exploits of Alexander the Great (who died in 323 BC), which included amphibious operations against Egypt and along many other eastern Mediterranean coasts.

The Romans employed amphibious tactics to help build their empire, first in the Mediterranean and then in England from 55 BC. Roman tiles bearing the initials TR, CL, and BR, have been found in both Lympne, near Hythe in Kent, and across the channel. It has been generally accepted that the last of these letters are an abbreviation for the 'Tribune of British Troops' trained for sea warfare. The headquarters of the Roman Channel Fleet was at Boulogne where the *Classiarii* – soldiers trained for service at sea – performed the same functions as the Greek *Epibatai*. They wore a sea-green uniform that matched the colour of their shields, a designed colour scheme that might be considered the earliest military camouflage. The Romans also maintained a small force of *Lembarii* who served on board small war-vessels known as *lembus*, a word that translates as a small sailing vessels with a sharp prow.

As part of their order of battle the Greeks and the Romans trained and equipped men for both service at sea and ashore. In the case of the Romans in south east England, northern France and along the Mediterranean coast, these men would have been, as was the custom, recruited or pressed from among the local population. There was certainly at least one marine cohort of between 500 and 1,000 men in Britain between 96 AD and 117 AD. Prior to returning to defend their imperial city against the 'hordes of Gothic warriors that threatened', the Romans placed one of their corps of marines under the Count of the Saxon Shore's direct command, to face would-be invaders from the north and east: Vikings, described by a Roman poet at the time as 'Foes, fierce beyond other foes and as cunning as they are fierce: the sea is their school of war and the storm their friend; they are sea wolves that live on the pillage of the world'.

Once the occupying force finally departed, Britain was left with neither marines nor a navy to employ or transport them. It can be argued that the corps of *Butescarles* that served in Alfred the Great's navy were the natural successors to the *Classiarii* but with this brief exception, alone the sea soldier – at least in northern waters – would be extinct, or nearly so, for some centuries.

The amphibious fleets of the Greek and Roman eras were a much closer match to those that exist today when compared to those of the British Middle Ages. Throughout this last era, merchant ships would be pressed into service to augment the very few king's ships – effectively also in trade – when they would be retrofitted (in modern terminology) with fore and aft castles from which they could be fought. Some would also carry men-at arms for specific operations. Edward III made provision for a marine force, and when in 1417, Sir Thomas

Carew fitted a squadron of eleven ships for service, the largest embarked a force of 75 men-at-arms plus 148 archers.

The Elizabethan era was not without its sea soldiers either. Drake's expeditions all included soldiers trained for service at sea and ashore, while, with many such deployments, it was not always clear who was in command. Previously, ships were merely used to transport troops to wherever their commander needed to go, but with the advent of more efficient sailing vessels it was often unclear who was – or should be – in command.

The specialist role of the 'sea soldier' was given a more modern impetus when Spain formed her *Infantería de Marina* in 1537. Portugal followed with her *Corpo de Fuzileiros* in 1585, Great Britain (Motto: *Per Mare Per Terram* – By Sea By Land) with her Marines in 1664 ('Royal' in 1802), and the Dutch *Korps Mariniers* (*Qua Patet Orbis* – As Far As The World Extends) the next year. 1775 saw the formation of the United States Marine Corps (*Semper Fidelis* – Always Faithful), and then Brazil joined the club in 1808 with its *Corpo de Fuzileiros Navais* (*Adsumus* – Here We Are).

Today many maritime nations possess a marine force of some sort, although with very few exceptions – notably the Americans, United Kingdom and France – most do not serve permanently at sea. With modern, fully automated, heavy weapons currently operated by a 'weapons electrical' specialist rather than a 'gunner', marines around the globe have lost this traditional role. Nor do many marine corps have any amphibious assault capability, but merely replace sailors for security duties and the defence of naval areas: the word 'marine' can imply anything from the most highly trained amphibious shock troops to local guards.

Conversely, there remain nations with an amphibious capability and aspiration yet no specialist amphibious troops, Australia being a good example, although its Special Air Service Regiment does have an amphibious troop within each squadron. There are two reasons why this is so often the case: one self-evident and one misguided and erroneous. The first is that good marine training is lengthy and costly, and the second is that regular army units – envious of the money and time spent on a marine corps' training – argue that there is a bogus mystique attached to such elite soldiers. The *non-cognoscenti*, or simply, the unwilling to learn – often argue that this mystique purposefully generates an air of false complications in order to ensure that the naval infantry remain in business as specialists. An example will be found during a successful amphibious landing conducted by a tiny British army force from HMS *Fearless* off the southern Oman coast in October 1966. On completion, the army brigade commander voiced the opinion that he could see nothing complicated with amphibious warfare, and suggested that the army could take over the role. What he and others in similar situations failed to appreciate, was that the Oman operation – Operation Fate – was an unopposed, single ship, single unit (embarked only the day prior to the landings), landing unopposed in daylight.

A more representative amphibious operation might involve a brigade, supporting arms from all three services, naval and marine surface, sub-surface, air and electronic warfare, Special Forces advance force operations, naval gunfire support, intelligence acquisition and complicated diplomatic involvement up until the last moment, plus the rest. The British Army's 5 Brigade in the Falklands conflict believed, as had the land commander of Operation Fate, that it was a simple business of transport by 'ferry' and then advancing along a coast made even more simple by resupply across an open (the sea) flank. How very wrong they were proved to be, a fact summed up by a British admiral at the time thus: 'Amphibious operations are at the scholarship level of military operations'. By this he meant everyone involved from all three services had to be trained to the highest level, but specifically, he was implying that 'sea soldiers' needed to be at that scholarship level, specially trained and able to wholly integrate – and remain permanently integrated – into the force.

It is worth repeating Winston Churchill in 1942 before the Tobruk landings in North Africa: 'An amphibious operation has to fit together like a jewelled bracelet'. That dictum still applies and continues to reinforce the argument that such operations cannot be undertaken by an ad hoc collection of troops, ships and aircraft brought together at the last moment to fulfil a sudden need.

For amphibious troops – marines – and their embedded specialists, amphibious training will involve long periods onboard ships and in (to basic infantry soldiers) an alien environment, while non-amphibious commanders will be equally frustrated by the nuances of naval warfare and the restrictions imposed on their actions, up to and after the initial landings. Naval infantry understand this, and working alongside their naval colleagues, are able to fit in, tolerate and even take part in naval warfare operations under the water, on its surface and above it. They are part of the whole: it's a state of mind as much as anything.

While some marine forces are trained merely to protect naval installations, others operate small craft in coastal or riverine operations, land from ships by sea or air for a specific task such as capturing a beach or port – an entry point – to enable later landings by heavy forces. Nevertheless, a few elite marine corps have gone further and embraced harsh training to Special Forces standards. The British Royal Marines joined a few army units of volunteers in the commando role during the Second World War – as traditional a role for marines as any, as a mere glimpse of their actions over the preceding centuries will show.

Raiding from the sea, often across seemingly impassable coastlines or up vertical cliffs – anywhere but the place from which an enemy might expect an attack – has been the business of marines down the centuries, together with manning both ships' heavy guns and light weapons. It was not surprising, therefore, that at the Second World War's end, the British army's commandos reverted to a standard infantry role, while the Royal Marines continued as commandos – a most natural extension and expansion of their role as sea soldiers.

A few other marine forces followed the example, and if not always called 'commandos' or something with a similar meaning, they at least carried out the same tasks. French, Indian and Indonesian marines all have the additional command skills that allow them not only to fight by land and sea, but to conduct very complicated, arduous operations under the toughest conditions the globe has to offer – and not necessarily confined to the littoral battle space. Additionally, many marine corps go one step further and find their country's maritime Special Forces from within their ranks.

An added bonus in a very few marine corps – the Dutch and the British are prime examples – is that the navy's raiding and landing craft (including hovercraft in the case of the British) are also manned by commando-trained marines. As with naval pilots in support of naval operations and army pilots supporting land operations, the coxswains and crews of assault craft understand the amphibious battle. Far better that such operations are supported by amphibious boats crews, as is the case with specialist naval and army aircrew overhead.

Chapter 13

Commando Forces

Written in 2012 for *Jane's Amphibious and Special Forces*

Although fifty-eight countries are listed (at the last count) as possessing 'commando' or 'para-commando' forces in some form or another, the word 'commando' nowadays means different things to different nations. In very few cases is the word allied with amphibious operations, and more often than not since 1945, with elite, rather than Special Forces. Likewise the title 'commando' is not always synonymous (as it should be) with advanced specialist training and supreme fitness.

For the purposes of this overview I am dealing only with the word 'commando'. There are other elite units of similarly trained personnel such as Rangers, *Jeager*, *Spetznaz*, Pathfinders and so on. Additionally, and quite simply, a number (but certainly not all) of the various marine corps and naval infantry units around the world might also be grouped under the same elite heading. Some of these might also be 'commandos' in all but name.

Notably of course, some marine units are indistinguishable from commando forces. France, India and the United Kingdom possessing prime examples, but even here the marines are marines first, with their commando attributes being an additional specialisation. In other words, in most cases marines or naval infantry are trained to fight from the sea in amphibious operations, whereas commando training (whether within a marine corps, naval infantry or an army battalion) takes the man to a significantly higher level of expertise and fitness, yet may not necessarily include any amphibious capability. It can be argued therefore that marines and naval infantry may be elite forces but they are not 'Special Forces'. Nevertheless those who have received commando training are at a level above the standard infantryman and are certainly approaching the status of a special force.

During the Second World War, commandos or their equivalent from whatever country, were regarded as 'Special Forces' but now with the advent of Special Forces dedicated to asymmetric warfare, counter-insurgency and strategic reconnaissance, the commandos (and, with them, airborne forces) are numbered among the elite rather than the 'special'. So who deploys today's commando units and for what are they used?

The *Oxford English Dictionary* would appear to be rather xenophobic in its description describing commandos as 'a unit of British amphibious shock troops'. It goes on to explain that the commandos were British troops of Combined Operations Command during the Second World War. They were trained originally (in 1940) as shock troops for the repelling of the threatened German invasion of England, later for the carrying out of raids on the continent and elsewhere. Further on, the dictionary regards them as having been a unit in the Boer War, of the Boer army composed of the militia of an electoral district.

Wikipedia, on the other hand, describes a commando as a soldier or operative of the elite light infantry or 'special operations' forces, often specialising in amphibious landings, parachuting or abseiling. Regardless of the above, in most (but certainly not all) countries, today's commandos are distinctive in that they specialise in assaults on unconventional, high-value targets whether in amphibious, airborne or ground assaults. The reason why I say 'certainly not all' is that there seems little doubt that to possess commando forces is a measure of kudos, but not necessarily a measure of ability. Any navy, army or air force can name one of its sub-units 'commando' purely for 'shop window' reasons. However, for the purposes of this overview, it is assumed that all commandos are indeed trained to what most consider to be many levels above the basic infantry standards in capabilities and fitness.

The word commando (and thus, in broad terms, the *modus operandi* of modern commando forces) originates in the Afrikaans language where it is spelt *kommando*, and roughly translates to a mobile (originally by horse) infantry regiment. Additionally, Wikipedia states that the Boer commandos were able to use superior marksmanship, field craft, camouflage and mobility to expel an occupying British force that was poorly trained in marksmanship, wearing red uniforms and unmounted.

There is no question that the ethos and spirit of modern commando forces were formed by the Boers between 1899 and 1902 in South Africa. Apart from a unit of artillery, the Boers had no standing force, but relied instead on raising bands of men in different districts. They received no pay nor uniform, and additionally, were required to provide their own horses. Their tactics from the very beginning were swift and deadly using the 'get in fast – get out fast' principle, and when they 'got out' they melted into the bush, long before their British opponents could take retaliatory action.

Britain failed to learn the lessons at the time, although two decades later T.E. Lawrence (Lawrence of Arabia) was to use many of the same tactics while supporting the Arab revolt against the Turks in the Middle East during the First World War. It was to be some years later before amphibious operations were to be married to these commando tactics. Although individual, small-scale amphibious operations had by and large helped to forge many empires during the eighteenth and early nineteenth centuries when it came to the Dardanelles operation in 1915, it is clear that no lessons had been learnt and indeed those that might have been learnt had been long forgotten.

Small scale amphibious raids continued to take a back seat until 23 April 1918 and the blocking of Zeebrugge by the British Royal Navy and Royal Marines. Although now it is easy to see this as a classic commando-style, amphibious operation, its importance as such was not to be realised until 1940. Nevertheless, in 1924 a recommendation was made that a 3,000 strong Royal Marine brigade should be established for the sole purpose of conducting amphibious operations: in other words raids on an enemy coast similar to that conducted at Zeebrugge, while also including the capture and defence of bases for naval use. It was not for yet another twenty years that this concept saw the light of day, when during the Second World War, many nations began developing their own commando-style forces for similar such tasks.

Earlier, during the First World War the Italians had deployed specially trained 'trench raiding teams' against Austria and Hungary where they fought mainly in the Alps. Known as *arditi* (which can be roughly translated as 'daring' or 'brave') they too, would appear to have embodied the commando ethos or spirit: in other words supremely trained, shock troops used for swift 'in-and-out' actions, such as demolition tasks in enemy territory and lightening raids with a limited aim.

While the uses to which these elite troops were put (the word 'commando' was not used until the British did so in 1940), the procedures and tactics were broadly based on those of the original Boers. Thus we see in the First World War, German raiding troops called *Sturmtruppen* deployed on what one might call 'special duties' into no man's land and the enemy's trenches. Following their successes, Germany formed the Brandenburger Regiment, although this was officially named as the 800th Special Purpose Training and Construction Company.

During the Second World War, Benito Mussolini was rescued from captivity in the Gran Sasso raid in 1943 by Otto Skorzeny. Skorzeny was an Austrian-born *SS-Standartenführer* in the Waffen-SS and involved in a number of operations, including the removal from power of Hungarian Regent, Miklós Horthy.

Skorzeny also conducted special operations personally ordered by Hitler while commanding a number of SS commando units. It is believed that one of these units may have conducted a commando raid on a radar station on the Isle of Wight in 1941, similar to a number of such raids conducted by the British against comparable German targets on the northern French coast.

Also during the Second World War, the Japanese *Teishin Shudan* (raiding group) with their *giretsu* (heroic) detachments, conducted airborne assaults on Allied airfields across a number of the Pacific Islands, including the Philippines and Okinawa. The Japanese navy also contained 'commandos' such as the *S-toku* – special submarine attack units – that infiltrated enemy submarine bases. These were part of the Japanese special naval landing forces.

Italian frogmen of the *Decima Flottiglia* were hugely successful in sinking or damaging a significant number of British ships in the Mediterranean, indeed they led the way in such work. Their preferred method of attack was either with explosive motorboats or early examples of what became known as 'human torpedoes' known then to the Italians as *maiali* (pigs). Nowadays these naval Special Forces are known as the *Commando Raggruppamento Subacqui ed Incurisori* (or simply the *Incurisori*), and are famed for remaining in the forefront of underwater operations.

Also during the Second World War, France supplied a number of minor units within the British commando organisation, most notably during the attack on Walcheren in November 1944. To this day, the French navy still operates Commandos Marine units, one of which, Commando Hubert, is designated a Special Forces unit formed, by and large, for underwater combat much in the manner as the British Special Boat Service and the United States' SEALs.

Although New Zealand has no commando troops in the twenty-first century, in 1942 the country established the Southern Independent Commando in Fiji, in order to combat expected Japanese forces. When it became clear that no such attack was imminent, this independent commando undertook reconnaissance tasks in support of United States' forces at Guadalcanal and New Georgia. It was disbanded in May 1944.

Australia, too, formed army commando units that first saw action in 1942 against the Japanese. These Royal Australian Navy commandos operated in the Borneo campaign until the end of the war when all were disbanded. Now one battalion of the 4th Royal Australian Regiment is commando trained.

Greece formed commando units that fought alongside the British Special Air Service in Libya and with the British army's Special Boat Service in the Aegean. As with so many other similar units they too were disbanded in 1945.

Perhaps less well known, is that in 1941 the United States Marine Corps formed battalion-sized commando units although they were named Marine Raiders despite their initial name of Marine Commandos. This latter title met with considerable opposition, with one general stating that the term 'marine' is sufficient to indicate a man ready for duty at any time, and the injection of a special name such as 'commando' would be undesirable and superfluous – perhaps omitting to understand that commando skills (if indeed that is what they were trained in) are considerably in excess of those required by the 'ordinary' marine. They fought with distinction throughout the Pacific theatre until 1944, when the four Marine Raider battalions reverted to regular United States Marine Corps units.

Brazil's modern commandos are also marines and enjoy the title 'amphibious commandos' of the Brazilian Marine Corps, while in Chile, all three services (navy, army and air force) have commando units that wear a distinctive black beret, as opposed to the more normal (but certainly not universal) commando-green beret.

In India, the 'para-commandos' form an integral and vital part of that country's Special Forces, trained almost exclusively to operate behind enemy lines, while the Indian Air Force operates the Garud Commando Force composed of quick response teams to counter attacks on airbases. This unit is also trained in search and rescue as well as forward air control. The Black Cat commandos, more formally known as the National Security Guards, are trained in counter-insurgency and hostage rescue operations.

Indonesia's *Kesatuan Komando Tentara Territorium* was formed in 1952, with the original shortened name of *Kopassus*. There is no doubt that this organisation embodies all that is meant by the word 'commando': direct action and unconventional operations, raiding, counter-insurgency and reconnaissance. The standard of fitness of its members is superb.

The Democratic Republic of Congo is one of a number of countries where the title 'commando' is honoured in the breach rather than in the field. The various para-commando battalions were and are little more than standard infantry units, some of which were formed by mercenaries with little cohesive commando or even conventional, training.

Canada's commando forces are interesting, for in practice they are airborne battalions. The Canadian Special Operations Regiment is also commando-trained although its counterpart, the Canadian Joint Task Force, is technically a unit specialising in counter-insurgency operations, rather than what might be called conventional commando operations. In this and other instances, it might justify the title Special Forces rather than elite forces.

Portugal's commandos were formed in 1962 in northern Angola during the Portuguese Colonial War to conduct irregular operations. Other commando units were soon spawned although they took names such as *Caçadores Especiais* (Special Hunters) of the army, the *Caçadores Paraquedistas* (Parachute Hunters) of the air force, and *Fuzileiros Especiais* (Special Marines) of the navy. They still exist to this day but with slightly different titles.

Pakistan's Special Forces Group is an independent commando division within the army, although their role is more focused on counter-terrorism than traditional commando operations.

An interesting variation on the use of the word 'commando' was produced by the North Vietnamese in the Vietnam War, who were notoriously effective during the Tet Offensive against United States forces in 1968. Originally these commando units were designated as sappers that operated in support of the infantry by often spearheading the attacks themselves, supplying assault and fire support elements.

Israel has the renowned naval commando unit *Shayetet 13*, whose operations mirror those of the British Special Boat Service and the United States' SEALS.

Although formed in 1664, it was not until 1942 that Britain's Royal Marines took on the mantle of commando troops; this was two years after the army had formed the first commando units that set a near worldwide trend. At the end of the Second World War, the British Army relinquished its commando aspirations allowing the Royal Marines to be the only British force to continue in the commando role, while adding to that, retaining their centuries-old tradition of amphibious warfare. The army's Special Forces mantle was then taken up, initially, by the Special Air Service (there are now a number of additional special service units that support the SAS), while the Royal Navy (through the Royal Marines) continues with the Special Boat Service.

To return to the present, the word 'commando' worldwide, stems from the British use of these elite forces during the Second World War, and it is from that beginning that the lineage of all modern commandos can be traced. Yet it is still a truism that one man's commando may be another man's marginally higher-trained infantryman! Nowadays, commandos are no longer considered – Special Forces – as they had been during the Second World War, but with the advent of smaller specialist units they certainly remain elite, along with all airborne forces.

Thus, bearing in mind that the word commando can mean many things, the following countries are known to have forces especially described as 'commando' or 'para-commando' within their ranks. Very few of these are also amphibious, while a fair number are not, in effect, 'commando trained' to the supreme level of physical fitness as is understood in, for instance, the United Kingdom, France and India.

Countries known to have commando forces:

Albania, Algeria, Argentina, Australia, Austria, Belgium, Benin, Brazil, Bulgaria, Cameroon, Chile, Colombia, Cuba, Democratic Republic of Congo, Djibouti, Egypt, El Salvador, Eritrea, Finland, France, Gabon, Georgia, Germany, Greece, Guinea, India, Indonesia, Iran, Iraq, Israel, Italy, Kuwait, Lebanon, Libya, Mali, Mauritania, Morocco, Netherlands, Nicaragua, Nigeria, Norway, Pakistan, Peru, Poland, Qatar, Russian Federation, Saudi Arabia, Senegal, Singapore, South Africa, Sri Lanka, Thailand, Togo, Turkey, United Kingdom, Venezuelan, Yemen, Zimbabwe.

Chapter 14

Airborne Forces

Written in 2015 for *Jane's Amphibious and Special Forces*

(Balloons) appear…to be a discovery of great importance, and what may possibly give a new turn to human affairs. Convincing sovereigns of the folly of wars may perhaps be one effect of it; since it will be impracticable for the most potent of them to guard his dominions.

Five thousand balloons, capable of raising two men each, could not cost more than have ships of the line; and where is the prince who can afford so to cover his country with troops for its defence, as that ten thousand men descending from the clouds might not in many places do an infinite deal of mischief, before a force could be brought together to repel them?

It is a pity that any national jealousy should, as you imagine it may, have prevented the English from prosecuting the experiment, since they are such ingenious mechanicians, that in their hands it might have made a more rapid progress towards perfection, and all the utility it is capable of affording.

Benjamin Franklin, 16 January 1784

Jane's Amphibious and Special Forces contains information on 157 countries, of which, at the latest count, 107 claim to have viable airborne forces. This figure may well be higher, for some countries are listed as simply possessing a 'special force', 'commando' or 'airborne' unit of undetermined size, trained along the lines of for example, the US Navy's SEALs or Rangers, the United Kingdom's SBS, Royal Marines, Parachute Regiment, SAS or, even Germany's GSG-9 police unit. These ambiguous descriptions do not necessarily confirm a nation's ability to conduct a parachute assault – correctly, an airborne assault – capable of achieving any significant task. Nor do these entries indicate at what readiness these paratroopers are, nor how current they are with their training. Nor is there much point in having airborne troops, if in practice, the transport aircraft are not available or perhaps not even in existence.

In the absence of any real clues, other than an entry – or lack of it – in *Jane's World Air Forces*, listing the numbers and types of aircraft available, the trick is to make an intelligent guess. The aim being to gauge, without help from 'in country' defence attachés who can be remarkably reticent regarding which description most accurately describes a nation's capability. It is not unknown of course, for defence ministries to make exaggerated claims when discussing the possession (or hiding the non-possession) of elite or Special Forces.

Finally, with a number of such entries, there is little or no indication whether 'airborne' actually means a parachuting capability into, or close to, a combat zone. This is because there can be confusion with a second category of airborne troops – those who enter directly into a battle space by glider (now probably an extinct process) or by helicopter or tilt-wing aircraft and who can then be supported and manoeuvred around the battle space by these same aeroplanes. These air assault operations should not be confused with paratroopers' airborne assault operations.

A third category is that of the Tactical Air Landing Operation (TALO), when a laden, troop-lift aircraft lands on an unprepared strip: a strip that may, or may not, have been staked out by Special Forces, themselves parachuting in earlier using either the High Altitude/Low Opening (HALO) or the High Altitude/ High Opening (HAHO) procedures. There may be little difference in the wording but there is considerable difference in the actions.

Either way, airborne assault troops will be largely unsupported in the initial stages of deployment or combat. That self-reliance, plus the simple fact that it requires a special mentality and courage to jump from an aeroplane in the dark, into battle with upwards of seventy pounds (32kg) strapped to your leg has to be a vital asset in any country's armoury. Parachute training – regardless of whether or not it will ever be needed – requires a physical and mental fitness and that, transferred to the ground battle, is an invaluable asset and one that no nation should discard without very careful consideration. Lose the parachute training – even if you lose the need to parachute into battle – and you run the risk of losing that special fighting quality that makes the 'red devil' a feared adversary.

Fourthly, there are air mobile operations for which men are trained to move great distances by air to a secure landing site in fixed-wing aircraft. On arrival they are ready to deploy forwards with their first line, and perhaps even much of their second line, equipment that will have accompanied them. For these operations, host nation support is a must.

Among the world's infantry there is a further distinction between those trained to parachute en masse direct into battle to fight as infantry, artillery and (less often) as an armoured force – cavalry – and those trained to parachute covertly or even clandestinely in very small numbers – almost always not directly into battle – prior to executing Special Forces tasks.

With so many options of approaching a battle, is the parachute as vital as it was once considered to have been?

With the ability to land within, or behind, an enemy's front line – or even on it, as was the case at Arnhem, and, to a certain extent in Normandy – has to be, on paper, a battle-changing operation in terms of the shock and disruption such troops are designed to cause. Yet they were not always regarded as important during the Second World War and had their considerable doubters. One was Royal Air Force Marshall, Sir John Slessor, who in his 1954 *Strategy for the West*, wrote:

It would probably astonish the reader were I able to…state the cost in manpower and material of the airborne forces of the late war, complete with all the aircraft and manpower devoted to training and carrying them…compared with the impact on the enemy. They would certainly find no place in the early stages of another great war. They are too vulnerable.

Slessor was a fanatical believer in the power of aerial bombardment, rather than the infantry, to win wars. He was certainly keen to exploit every tiny example of vulnerability to suit his argument, although he failed to appreciate that 'in the early stages' of that 'great war' German paratroopers were all but invincible and had considerable impact on their enemies. His prophecy was at fault too, for during the two next 'great wars' – Korea (UN) and Indochina (France) – parachutists from, respectively, the US's 187th Airborne Regimental Combat Team and the French and Vietnamese armies, plus the Foreign Legion, were used most effectively, though perhaps not in the earliest stages. The same is true for both Indo–Pakistani wars, in Indonesia in the early 1960s, and in Rhodesia in the mid to late 1970s. The list continues. In Vietnam, a large number of operational parachute drops were conducted but very seldom were these more than a handful of men engaged on 'special tasks'. The battlefield helicopter was coming of age, fast.

Had he not been such a believer in the bombers' ability to win wars, all but single-handedly, Slessor, worried about vulnerability, might have gone on to agree with an unknown author:

Air assault troops flown by helicopters to a point near or in a combat zone, with long-range support from ships offshore, ground-based artillery and 'fast air' operating from a carrier, are much more important and far less vulnerable than those dropped by parachute.

Following the first ever opposed helicopter assault from the sea, at Suez in November 1956, by the UK's 45 Commando, Royal Marines, the United States in Vietnam became far more dependent on this form of airborne assault. Although still vulnerable and with perhaps less range than true parachute-capable units, this method of arriving by air direct into combat was and remains a far more manageable and effective method. But helicopters were, and remain, expensive and limited in payload.

Had Slessor lived during the 2001-2021 Afghanistan War – and others in the latter years of the 20th century and the first decade of the next – he might have come to appreciate that modern warfare, far removed from the unsustainable theories of Blitzkrieg and the carpet bombing of civilians, is a finely tuned matrix that includes, *inter alia*, infantry supported by fast air and, yes, bombers – but bombers practicing precision attacks within minutes, if not within seconds (very few seconds if the aircraft is already on-call) of tasking. Now, with terrain-following radar and the latest navigational systems I would hope that Slessor would eventually have come to appreciate that there still remains a role, if not for mass parachute drops, then most certainly for small, specialist teams whose influence on the outcome of a battle is belied by their small size. He would too, I trust, have come to appreciate the helicopter as an invaluable asset that has very largely, negated most of his arguments concerning the vulnerability of airborne or air assault forces.

So, where would his argument be now, with heavy lift helicopters and the Osprey tilt-wing aircraft suggesting that a mass airborne assault by parachute is an out dated and certainly an expensive option? Probably back where we started, for Slessor's views are coming true at last, yet they were not true during the period of which he wrote, nor for some years afterwards. Nor were they ever true for the insertion of Special Forces as the briefest of looks at the successful parachuting of dozens of British and Allied Special Operations Executive agents, US Office of Strategic Services' men and women, and Free French forces into occupied Europe between 1939 and 1945 will prove. Nevertheless it would be a naïve defence ministry that abandoned contingency plans that did not involve the option of at least a battalion-strength drop of airborne forces.

Slessor should too have appreciated that it was his (or rather, Marshal of the Royal Air Force, Lord 'Bomber' Harris's) views and decisions that were often at fault, and that it was some (admittedly a few, but enough to catch the headlines) of his aircrew, that helped to give airborne forces a poor record. Being dropped in the wrong place and at the wrong time – and thus in 'vulnerable' circumstances – was not the fault of the soldiers, but of Slessor's airmen. Towards the latter stages of the Second World War some transport aircraft pilots were concerned less with accurate navigation and more with an avoidance of flak to ensure their personal safe return. On a number of documented occasions, passengers (parachutists) were forced to produce pistols to make their point. In his book *Overlord: D-Day and the Battle for Normandy 1944,* the military historian Sir Max Hastings describes some of these instances, while recording that many paratroopers on D-Day itself, were released with 'near-criminal carelessness'.

Nevertheless, in general, any country with the ability – declared to exist for political reasons even if it does not actually do so in practice – to insert anything above a company strength unit into theatre by parachute, must still be considered to possess a useful and viable capability. This in spite of the fact that, in the case of the United Kingdom, the last mass operational parachute drop (other than small teams of Special Forces) was as far back as November 1956 at Suez. Israeli forces have only ever conducted two drops in their existence and both were at Suez, yet both countries continue to maintain airborne brigades. While the USA's airborne forces have often been stood-to for operational drops over the last 30 or so years, they have seldom been used in their primary role. The last two significant occasions of mass drops being during Operation Urgent Fury when more than 500 men parachuted into Grenada in 1983 to capture its airport, and in 1989 during Operation Just Cause to seize Torrijos International Airport and other objectives in Panama.

It is a moot point whether or not airborne troops are Special Forces or 'elite forces'. By and large, what they are not are amphibious forces. They may well be part of an amphibious operation, such as at Suez (French, Israeli and United Kingdom) in 1956 during Operation Musketeer, but except in very small numbers, they do not parachute into the water in anything above, perhaps, section strength, and then very much with a Special Forces mission in mind. Certainly during the Second World War, mass parachute descents were often used in conjunction with amphibious landings – usually to take an airfield to prevent enemy disruption of an assault landing – as at Sicily in July 1943 during Operation Husky and as a pincer movement as at Nadzab, where parachute drops were conducted in concert with amphibious landings at Lae in New Guinea in September 1943.

Military parachuting can be said to have begun its evolution during the First World War, when artillery spotters found it necessary to escape from their balloons. Prior to that, parachuting was more of a civilian spectator 'extravaganza', along with ballooning itself while only a few, Benjamin Franklin being one, were beginning to hypothesize on the military advantages to be gained by airborne – even balloon-borne – soldiers as shock troops. Although mooted by all the belligerents during the First World War, hostilities ended before any plans – particularly American plans – could be executed. Between the wars the Italians – using the same inventiveness that allowed them to lead the way with underwater warfare in the earlier stages of the Second World War – carried out the first operational drop in November 1927. Russia soon followed in the 1930s with the training of entire units, a military evolution that was quickly taken up by Japan, France and Poland. Germany's first mass operational drops – of many conducted during the Second World War – were made against targets in Norway and during the invasion of Holland in May 1940, when vulnerability would certainly not have been an accurate accusation.

Shortly after the outbreak of that war, both Winston Churchill and President Roosevelt called for the formation of an 'elite corps of troops'. Apart from Special Forces' operations (the expression was not yet in vogue) beginning in February 1941, the UK's first mass drop was in November 1942, when the 3 Parachute Battalion seized Bone airfield in Algeria. Many other such battalion-sized operations followed across the globe; for example in February 1942, 460 Japanese paratroopers seized oil refineries in Sumatra. And so the airborne expertise, across most nations, began its expansion.

Throughout the post-war years the range of missions undertaken became almost limitless. Beyond the seldom-conducted basics of seizing vital ground in advance of a larger scale assault, many one-off operations were conducted to, for example, to rescue a single downed airman (USA, Alaska 1954), to re-enforce a cut-off garrison (Laos, 1955), to seize a pass (Israel, Mitla, 1956), collect intelligence (Tibet 1959), investigate a bomb threat (UK, *Queen Elizabeth 2* (QE2) in mid-Atlantic), destroy a railway and three bridges (Rhodesia 1979), capture an airstrip (South Africa, 1981), deliver Special Forces via a water jump (UK, South Atlantic 1982), plant a radio beacon prior to an attack (USA, Grenada 1983), recover a pilot's body (France, Chad 1984), enforce a curfew (South Africa, Owambo 1984), destroy an oil pipeline (Iran, 1986), assist survivors of a crashed C-130 (Canada, 1991) and so on and so on. But in all these and dozens of other cases, only small numbers were involved.

Thus airborne operations would appear to be diminishing in favour of air assault operations. If airborne operations were considered by some to have been vulnerable between 1939 and 1945, then they have become considerably more so in the 21st century, with the falling numbers of such operations proving the case. During the eleven years since 2000, just four countries conducted a mere ten airborne assaults of mass drops, whereas during the previous thirty years, from 1970 to 2000, twenty-three countries carried out an estimated 160 operations – a high proportion of which were drops of a company strength or larger. Admittedly this period includes extensive operations in Vietnam and Rhodesia, with among many others, operations conducted by France in Zaire, Turkey in Cyprus, Indonesia in East Timor, and the UK in the South Atlantic. These figures indicate a lessening in mass drops and thus, in many respects, indicate that the need for such a capability is reducing quickly in favour of helicopter-borne air assaults.

Despite modern designs and 'smart' weaponry, allied to sophisticated counter-measures such 'vertical envelopment' – to use a military colloquialism – of mass parachute drops remains fraught with difficulty, even without the rear certainty of disruption by an enemy. Thus the slow demise of the airborne-art continues and it is easy to see why. For sake of argument let us assume that all mass drop aircraft are a variation of a Hercules C-130, for with over 70 countries operating them, they must be the most ubiquitous of modern parachute-capable aircraft. Of course there are many other types, but the operating parameters remain much the same and within these parameters come some of the same difficulties that so influenced Slessor when he called these airborne operations vulnerable.

Although accuracy of navigation is now far less of a problem, it can still be an immense worry to pilots and navigators, especially if cloud is suddenly encountered over the dropping zone (DZ). The approaches to a DZ might be helped by a pre-positioned beacon, but essentially, the final drop itself has to be conducted by eyesight alone.

Thus the weather will always play its part for an unexpected last-minute change in wind direction – but especially in strength – which can cause an operation to be aborted even with the aircraft on 'finals' – and that after many painstaking, low-level hours of approach. Wind limits for military parachutists are precise and low, with a maximum night-time wind speed of 9 knots and about 13 knots by day. Another factor not often considered, is the prevalence of air sickness among even the most hardened of troops. Three hours in, the cargo bay of a Hercules flying at 250 feet to avoid detection, in windy conditions, plays havoc even with the strongest of stomachs. One hardened, experienced parachute jump instructor is quoted as saying 'The moment that green light flashes on you'll be glad to jump out of the aircraft even if you have forgotten your parachute!' Perhaps this is not the best state in which to begin a hard fight.

The numbers of aircraft required for even a small mass drop (not such an oxymoron as it might first appear!) is high, with this adding to the overall and continuing maintenance bill for a little-used exercise. As an example, a brigade of say 1,500 men involves six waves of six C-130s, thirty-six aircraft in all. The men drop in waves, followed by two or three waves dropping heavy loads – vehicles, light armour and stores. For all but the mightiest of military powers, that is a large number of aircraft to be kept in readiness for what is becoming a little-needed operation of modern warfare.

Each wave of aircraft flies a 2,000 foot trail offset to port and starboard. With about a mile between waves, the whole formation is some 18 to 20 miles long. The aircraft fly most of the journey at low level – about 250 feet – before popping up at the last moment to 650 feet, making them vulnerable to radar and visual detection, and then reducing speed to 115 knots, thus rendering each aircraft vulnerable not just to missiles but to a man with a rifle.

The idea that such an armada could fly around Europe during the Cold War, or across any other theatre, without being detected, was considered laughable by the aircrews who believed that such a mass drop should only have been planned against a Third World country. The vulnerability of such formations, 'large, lumbering beasts with a very limited ability to carry out evasive manoeuvres against ground fire particularly SAMs', was never lost on either the aircrew or their passengers.

Eventually, and in line with many other nations, the United Kingdom recently reduced its parachuting lift from a brigade requiring thirty-six aircraft, to a battalion needing just fifteen. This is a figure that remains common among all proponents of the art, but one that is still too large to fly with guaranteed impunity against a sophisticated enemy defending his own air and ground space. Additionally, mass drops of below battalion strength will provide their own problems of vulnerability once the men are on the ground – and alone. Even in this milieu there has to be strength in numbers.

Additionally there are considerable weight restrictions when carrying paratroopers, as the weight of the parachutes alone reduces the cargo carrying capability of each aircraft by as much as a third, while the time to prepare a heavy-lift aircraft for such operations is about four times as long as for a normal sortie. Multiply that by thirty-six, or even just fifteen, and the problem becomes immense. Such operations cannot be planned at a stroke.

Then there are the further considerations of air superiority and escorts by fighters with a mere fraction of the radius of action of their charges.

Assuming the retention of a small mass drop capability, it is essential that terrain-following radar is fitted in each aircraft, in addition to the most up-to-date navigational systems and night vision aids. A 'blind drop' facility is also essential, as is a fighter escort. Lacking all these and more, involving large amounts of money, formations of even fifteen aircraft are unlikely to succeed. Without prolonging the discussion on the alternative approach to battle, this is precisely where modern helicopters and tilt-wing aircraft take over low altitude, nap of the earth flying, men delivered accurately and in a concentrated space, with near instant availability. Yet these advantages do have to be balanced against the shorter range of such a rotary wing force, while the numbers of men likely to be involved are fewer. Helicopters are always in short supply. They are also expensive to purchase and maintain for a far smaller payload than a C-130.

Where parachuting is still effective and where it is increasing in use (and where it apparently remains affordable, at least in the UK) is within the Special Forces world. HALO (High Altitude, Low Opening, or HAHO (High Altitude, High Opening) operations are the most effective for the insertion of strike teams. HAHO exercises and trials have shown that thirty to 40 nautical miles of transit are possible, while under the canopy, thus allowing the aircraft to stand off from the target with a consequent enhancement of security and safety for both aircrew and troops.

Sensibly, contingency plans exist within most parachute-capable nations, for say, the mass evacuation of expatriates from a country in turmoil, and that requirement often lies (usually hidden) behind decisions among the middle-ranking nations to maintain the art of at least a small mass drop. In a simple, hypothetical case, a Special Forces team would drop to secure a DZ into which a battalion would parachute, to establish not only a base for say, the collection and processing of civilians, but also to prepare a strip landing site from which all can eventually be evacuated.

Yet paradoxically, it is these Tactical Air Landing Operations, (TALO) that offer yet another reason to side line mass parachute drops. Using current flying techniques coupled with modern aircraft and air-to-air refuelling, pilots can now use flat beaches, desert scrub or farm land lanes as strip landing sites a long way from the home base. They need less than 2,000 feet to land and even less for take-off. Using these landing zones (LZs), one single aircraft is able to deliver more troops into a tighter area than the same aircraft could have delivered by parachute.

This is because the aircraft's payload will not have been severely reduced by the weight of say, sixty-four main parachutes plus sixty-four reserve parachutes. TALO operations are now much practiced, especially at night. This is not new, for such night landings were commonplace across Europe during the Second World War, but instead of the payload being one or two agents, and the distance from the home base being measured in a few hundred miles, now the payload may be as high as ninety-two passengers and the distance measured in thousands of miles.

The helicopter – plus sturdy, heavy-lift aircraft – and not the parachute, now rules on the battlefield, but that does not mean the latter has had its day. It is just that the parachute has become more selective over who it takes into combat.

Both Franklin and Slessor were nearly right, but Franklin was by far the more prescient.

Chapter 15

Development of British Medium-Lift Hovercraft

Written in 2001 for *Jane's Amphibious and Special Forces*

The need has long been felt for a medium-lift hovercraft to operate stealthily in covert or clandestine operations, in addition to conventional amphibious warfare, while retaining a high degree of survivability for long periods under arduous conditions. Until now medium and heavy-lift hovercraft have been unable to meet these specifications, yet in theory they should be ideal for this work. Currently they tend to be used for communications along waterways, tourism and military ship-to-shore operations with the amphibious fleets of those few nations that possess such a capability.

But now, with modern construction methods offering enhanced capabilities this adds the previously missing stealth and survivability to the hovercraft's arsenal.

Introduction

The British Royal Navy and the Royal Marines trialled light hovercraft when they were in their infancy with those trials, including security operations in Hong Kong and general patrolling duties among the Falkland Islands. It was quickly found that although the principles of hovercrafting had clear potential, the then construction materials and propulsion systems prevented their use in anything other than comparatively unsophisticated and overt logistic supply duties. They were eventually withdrawn as being too costly, too noisy, too delicate and with an inappropriate range and payload for their size.

However, during the 1982 Falklands conflict, the newly formed Brigade Assault Squadron having proved its worth, was formally commissioned by the Ministry of Defence in 1984, yet it still lacked speed and stealth for all but the transport of small packets of lightly armed men in fast raiding craft which could be hidden, among the rocks or, at a penalty of reaction times, at the back of a beach. Shortly afterwards a small hovercraft became available and trials were conducted: the principles of hovercraft operations were established.

By the mid 1990s, and with the ordering of the new LPHs, LPDs and logistic support ships to modernise the British amphibious fleet, it was clear that Medium-Lift Hovercraft (MLHC) would be needed to meet a number of specific operating parameters, mostly in support of amphibious and covert operations. Experience showed, that in addition to such subjects as speed, power and payload, hull construction had to be as maintenance-free as possible yet strong enough to operate for long periods isolated from formal base areas. Any repairs would have to be effected in situ, quickly, in silence and without lights.

The requirement was identified therefore, for a robust craft capable of carrying serious weapons fit and an embarked assault team of useful size and composition plus a vehicle or, perhaps, canoes and fast raiding craft, over a good range and at speed. The craft had to be large enough to be self-contained for supplies and repair (including the possibility of debris or battle damage) over long periods, yet small enough to hide, clandestinely, in what is called the 'pounce mode', in support of a government's counter-insurgency, anti-smuggling, anti-terrorist, anti-piracy or drug enforcement policies. The same craft would need to be adapted for conventional amphibious assault or disaster relief, which duties could include a command post for a military commander or civilian government official respectively, and the possible use for example, as a mobile hospital or air-sea rescue craft.

The operating parameters that had to be met by these medium-sized, medium-lift hovercraft included the ability to operate over sand, mud, flat rocks, snow, smooth and broken ice. The expected temperature range would be between -25°C and +50°C and the craft had to be capable of operating in heavy dust storms and the highest humidity. It had to be constructed to all USA, British and the International Maritime Organisation's codes of safety. It had to have a hull life of at least twenty years. It had to lift at least ten tons of disposable load, be able to maintain a laden speed of 40 knots, have a bow ramp capable of operating a light vehicle or tracked over-snow vehicle or canoes and light raiding craft. It should be able to fit, side by side, with another in the stern dock of the Royal Navy's LPDs and logistic support ships, and it had to be light enough to be craned onto a flight or cargo deck for quick deployment by sea to a distant operating area. The radar signature had to be minimal and note was to be taken of the requirement to lie dormant without heat emission for long periods in ambush or surveillance roles.

The customer needed to choose from a variety of superstructures and control positions depending on the uses to which he would put his craft, be it amphibious assault, logistic supply, weapons platform, air-sea rescue, pollution control, disaster relief, seismographic work, drug enforcement, passenger transport, internal security, anti-terrorist or anti-piracy duties and so on.

Requirements such as strength, acceptance of battle damage, low cost, low noise, minimal maintenance in the field, small crew, negligible radar cross-section, high thrust-to-weight ratio, 2.5-metre-wide bow ramp for light vehicles, sea-keeping ability and speed and endurance were designed in at the beginning. None of these aspects were to be 'added back' to meet military specifications.

The design had to be kept as simple as possible to ensure that battle damage could be repaired, and regular maintenance could be carried out by the two- or three-man crew on the beach or among for instance, the mangroves of the Far East. To this end the engine compartment had to be 'walk-in' for ease of access at sea.

Suggesting that this latest generation of hovercraft (or any hovercraft for that matter) is the panacea for the world's amphibious or counter-insurgency problems is clearly foolish, but the use of such a craft with its enhanced operating parameters working for, and in conjunction with government forces, has to be a leap forward providing it is reliable and easily maintained. Fibre-reinforced hulls with off-the-shelf fittings and world-wide-available truck engines, with spares back-up to match, tend to be just that.

To assess some of the uses to which this craft could be put, we conducted comprehensive trials in the Far East with a smaller version and, on request, studied the operational requirements of a number of countries in all hemispheres who face serious problems of border security, arms smuggling, terrorist insurrection and piracy.

In addition to the enhanced speed, payload, endurance, manoeuvrability and low radar echo of the MLHC, we have found that it is ideal for operating in what I term the 'pounce mode'. We would set the scene of an anti-piracy operation along the littoral of the Malacca Straits, where it was necessary to lie in ambush, waiting for the enemy to emerge from among the waterways, when as so often, their craft arc channelled by mud flats, debris, fishing nets and shoals. We would pre-position our camouflaged hovercraft high and dry among the mangroves, with all machinery and active sensors turned off. If the enemy had had radar it was unlikely that he would have detected us. If he had had thermal imaging equipment, likewise. Nor would he have seen us using passive night goggles and thus he would feel perfectly safe from government intervention. On his approach though, we would pounce from our hide, taking less than thirty seconds to reach full cushion-speed from a cold start, and head-off a very surprised 'pirate' from a totally unexpected position. As an example of our hovercraft's effectiveness it was always an impressive demonstration and there were plenty of others in a similar vein.

Because of its size the third-generation MLHC can stay hidden thus for days on end, while supporting its crew, an embarked assault team and weapons operators. Craft for craft, the weapons fit has a greater range and power than an adversary operating in close or shoal waters. To achieve an effective escape speed, an enemy craft would have to twist and turn through the channels, thus making it difficult for him to bring his weapons to bear accurately. Additionally, the type of craft capable of such evasive manoeuvres would be small and unable to carry the same weight of firepower. This third-generation hovercraft is a steady platform under such circumstances (and in open water) for it travels in a straighter line and avoids banking – which is minimal anyway. The normal range of infantry anti-tank, anti-aircraft (anti-ship) missile systems (Milan, Javelin, Stinger, Blowpipe for example) can be carried and deployed with ease.

In more conventional warfare, pressure, magnetic and contact sea mines will cause little concern, yet if one was to be command-detonated, experiments have shown that unless the operator understands hovercraft, the shock-waves reach the surface after the craft has passed, and even if not, the cushion is known to absorb much of the blast.

It goes without elaboration that with its near comparable well-deck area, the hovercraft offers facilities comparable to those of the current Landing Craft Utility. As with these ancient but much respected landing craft, the comparably sized hovercraft can be used in conventional warfare as an ideal mobile, 'just-about-anything-you-like-conveyance', command post, forward dressing station, communications centre or relay station, transport and mother ship for covert or clandestine operations operating canoes or other small insertion craft, troop transport in the assault or over longer distances and inevitably, the handling of Main Supply Route (MSR) work.

The great advantage that this hovercraft has over anything else in the field is its true amphibious nature and the ability to hide much more effectively, and certainly where least expected. It is not though perfect and cannot carry a MBT.

In order to help our design teams meet the various perceived uses of the third-generation hovercraft, we studied the defence and security requirements for most Gulf States, India, Sri Lanka and a number of Far East governments. Empirical observations in jungle areas were added to our knowledge of hovercraft operations in the Arctic, the desert and the West Indies, to the point where there is now no doubt that the third-generation medium-lift hovercraft offers an important advance in world wide amphibious concepts, procedures and mobility, whether in conventional warfare, counter-insurgency, disaster relief or simply troop transport.

Conclusion

Forget all about loud noise, high running and crewing costs, complicated maintenance, high radar definition, corrosion-prone aluminium long down-times and high power for low payloads, this new generation finally lays the ghost of all the anti-hovercraft arguments. Military medium-lift hovercraft are at last able to operate in amphibious, covert and even clandestine operations using high speed, high payload, long endurance in time and distance, stealth and excellent survivability for the highest chances of success. They are also excellent for military aid to the civil community in times of natural disaster.

Chapter 16

Maritime Terrorism

Written in 2015 for *Jane's Amphibious and Special Forces*

In overall terms, the world's primary piracy hotspots can be listed as: the north, west and east coasts of South America; the west coast of mid-Africa; the southern Red Sea; short stretches of Mediterranean coastlines such as Corsica; the Gulf of Aden and the Somalia coast; the northern Gulf; the west coast of India and the coast of Bangladesh; the northern Sri Lankan coasts and much of Southeast Asia. In other words, wherever there tends to be widespread poverty, although the two are not necessarily linked.

It is perhaps a paradox that in September 2008, Malaysia despatched three naval ships with embarked commandos for service in the Gulf of Aden, off the Somalia coast. One of the ships was the Newport-class LST *Sri Inderapura* with an undisclosed number of Special Forces personnel from the three services. Rumours that they were intent on a rescue mission were dispelled, for apparently they were in the region purely to escort five Malaysia International Shipping Corporation (MISC) vessels through these much-troubled waters. Nevertheless, it was well-known that two other Malaysian-flagged MISC vessels had, earlier in August, been seized by Somali pirates and were still being held hostage for an undisclosed ransom.

The paradox being, that until recently, Malaysia and her neighbours faced the world's most severe piracy problems in the Straits of Malacca. With piracy on the decrease in that area, although still prevalent, it is comforting to acknowledge that Malaysia now feels able to spread and share her experiences.

To go back in time, briefly. It was declared in 1999 that out of a world wide total of sixty-six attempted or successful piracy attacks during the first three months of that year, thirty-eight of these had taken place in the Straits of Malacca. The area was then described in a leading British newspaper as a 'sea speckled with deserted islets that offer ideal safe havens for pirates'. The three interested countries, Indonesia, Malaysia and Singapore, with tacit support from Japan, whose interest in the safety of its commercial interests was vital – established joint patrols. Over the years these have increased in both efficiency and efficacy, despite the fact that this area was, and remains, ideal piracy territory thanks to the coastline of thick vegetation and mangrove swamps, but piracy has been reduced dramatically. Conversely, as will be discussed, the coast of Somalia is far from ideal as a haven for pirates, yet piracy is rife and increasing.

These two choke points may see the majority of the world's oil pass through them, but other commodities of every description also pass, enroute, in both directions between the Far East and Europe. A prime and uncomfortable example will be found in the capture of the Ukrainian freighter MV *Faina* bound for Kenya with a cargo of Russian tanks, whose final destination was southern Sudan. A list of ships targeted or captured in the Gulf of Aden would be lengthy, but the pirates are not put off by size as they attempted to capture a Japanese 264,000 DWT VLCC (Very Large Crude Carrier), while Italian forces prevented the seizure of a 32,300 DWT bulk carrier. Every type of ship that passes through the area is vulnerable and that list includes private yachts. In this regard the French have scored more than one notable success with the recapture of the yacht *Carré d'As IV* being a prime example. It might be instructive to pause a moment and consider how the French managed this text-book coup.

The 53ft (16m) yacht was being delivered by a husband and his wife from France to Tahiti when it was boarded by pirates off the Puntland coast on 2 September 2008. For two weeks the crew suffered on board along with seven pirates, while a ransom of £800,000 was demanded from an insurance company. On hearing that the vessel was to be taken to Eyl, the French authorities acted. The La Fayette-class, 3,750-ton frigate *Courbet* shadowed the vessel from just over the horizon until weather conditions were suitable. here were delays due to strong winds and heavy seas before its helicopter was able to be launched, believed to have been an SA 565 Panther, with a *combatant nageur* team from *Commando Hubert* embarked. The *combatant nageur* team entered the water, with one report suggesting they parachuted while the helicopter kept its distance, then swam (using a modern version of the DC55 breathing apparatus with its minimum bubbles plus night vision goggles) to board the vessel via short ropes and grappling hooks. The pirates were caught by surprise, overwhelmed and captured, although one of the seven was killed in the process. Not believing that the Somali authorities would convict and jail them the maritime terrorists were taken to France to stand trial. This was not the first time that the French had acted positively and with unqualified success. An attack off the same coast in early April against another French yacht, the *Ponant,* led Paris to place its forces based in Djibouti on alert. A frigate was despatched to track the yacht, while a reconnaissance aircraft flew over the hijacked vessel to gather further information. By 11 April, Paris announced that the thirty hostages including twenty-two French nationals had been freed and the vessel released.

This rise in maritime terrorist attacks off the Horn of Africa led, on 2 June 2008, to the UN Security Council adopting Resolution 1816, which 'condemned all acts of piracy and armed robbery against vessels off the coast of Somalia' and gave authority 'for states operating with the transitional government to enter Somalia waters for the following six months to repress piracy and armed robbery at sea'. It must be argued though, that it is not at sea where the problem should be tackled, although it is a good start.

Piracy off Somalia has been a scourge for many years but only in recent months – and particularly after the capture of the supertanker *Sirius Star* – has the public learned how widespread this form of terrorism is. And it is maritime terrorism of a particularly pernicious kind, for these are not pirates in the mould of Sir Francis Drake or Sir Henry Morgan, whose lives have been – with a tiny modicum of vindication – immortalised and glamorised in films and books. Many traditional pirates of legend were actually in the employ of their sovereign, for one nation's pirate was another's provider of wealth. But that is to go off on another tack, despite some who argue, with justification, that the occasional, modern Far East state has not been averse to the same practices in order to gain riches.

Modern-day pirates though are terrorists, and even those that operate out of Somalia, while trying to hide behind the 'poor little me' attitude of the by-product of a failed state, are themselves nothing less than terrorists. There are naturally, one or two fundamental differences: conventional terrorists, by-and-large, kill and destroy to intimidate a government or community, while their maritime counterparts need to preserve their quarry in order to intimidate commerce through ransom or rather, criminal coercion. At the same time, they also intimidate governments through embarrassment as there would appear to be little that can be done short of direct action and that has its problems as will be seen. Not all pirates are so careful to preserve life, as examples in the West Indies, South America and, particularly, in the Straits of Malacca have shown. In the latter case, crews have been killed in order that the captured ship can begin a new life under a new identity, often managed by the state itself.

Unlike other areas, Somalia hijackings are normally resolved peacefully through negotiations for ransom, but that does not lessen the seriousness of the crime, nor should it remove from that simple crime, the stigma of terrorism by another means. The stakes are high. In 2008 alone it is estimated that $30m (£17m) – has been paid in ransoms, although the Kenyan government gives a higher estimate at around $150m. What is the money used for and by whom? In other words, what is the driving force behind the desire for access to such readily available funds?

Before that question is answered, it has to be said that thankfully, some countries do not favour paying ransom money, as the French have demonstrably shown. For its part, the United Kingdom's Foreign and Commonwealth Office has reinforced the British view on the payment of ransoms by stating: 'It is very important that the international community stands firm against the scourge of hostage taking whether it be on boats, or in an aeroplane or elsewhere.' British governments, of all persuasions, have a strong record on this line dating from well before the Iranian Embassy siege in 1980. The United States, China and France are also loathe to pay. Private companies will often take a different, more commercial and perhaps more pragmatic view, but one that does not help the long term prognosis.

Denmark has a chequered history in this business. In August 2008, HDMS *Absalon* (operating as a member of the international Combined Task Force 150 off Somalia) captured ten pirates in two small ships off the coast of Somalia. To begin with, the Danish Ministry of Foreign Affairs decided the pirates should be tried in Denmark, as they would face the death penalty in nearby states. However, after much debating the pirates were freed, after the authorities had expressed their concern that it would be difficult to deport them back to Somalia once they had served their sentences. The pirates were allowed to keep their vessels but not their weapons, which as with most, had come from Yemen. On the other hand and on another occasion, one vessel was sunk by HDMS *Absalon* and seven pirates landed in Yemen. The country faced another dilemma with the capture of the Danish flagged merchantman *Svitser Korsakov*, but whether or not ransom money was paid has not been revealed. Of note, between 2008 and 2015 HDMS *Absalon* was by far the most successful warship operating within Combined Task Force 150 and is credited with capturing 88 out of a total of 150 pirates detained by the task force.

Spain was also presented with a similar challenge late in April 2008 and sent a frigate to rescue the crew of the fishing vessel *Playa de Bakio*. The twenty-six crew and vessel were released on 26 April following negotiations and possibly the payment of ransom money.

Somalia, though, is not alone at the top of this unfortunate league table, for Nigeria also ranks alongside the Straits of Malacca as one of the world's most feared areas for piracy. These attacks are aimed almost solely at oil company workers who are often released unharmed after 'commercial' money has changed hands. According to an International Maritime Bureau (IMB) quarterly report on piracy, released in April 2008, Nigeria suffered the greatest number of attacks in the first three months of 2008, with the Gulf of Aden and India the second worst-hit spots, the Straits of Malacca having slipped down the table. At the same time, vessel hijackings and crew abductions were reported to have moved from the east coast of Somalia to the north and northeast coast of Puntland, and thus well into the Gulf of Aden, which was always an area prone to such acts.

In theory, the coast of Somalia is less easy for a piratical network to operate along when compared with say, the Straits of Malacca, for it is a largely uniform coastline facing a vast open ocean. Yet this is where countries of all persuasions are being forced to concentrate their major efforts. Although the coastline of 1,632 nautical miles very roughly compares with that of the USA's eastern seaboard (an argument that is often but erroneously used to explain the difficulties) unlike that seaboard, it contains very few safe havens and harbours. It is also known, from modern surveillance systems, precisely from where the pirates operate, and yet this scourge is still increasing almost daily. But this sea area of international interest, within which one-third of all global piracy incidents are now taking place, is more than one million square miles in area and thus difficult to police.

Without wishing to concentrate solely on Somalia, it has to be asked why is this area suddenly so dangerous. The answer isn't simply that of stealing money to help members of a failed state, for there are reports that much of the ransom money that is paid goes towards the country's Islamist insurgents, with whom the pirates are now reported to be in a loose form of co-operation. Thus there tends to be a two-way trafficking system, with the pirates shipping captured arms and ransom money to insurgents, who in return, are offering pirates suitable modern equipment for the betterment of their nefarious work. One unfortunate spin off is the lack of World Food Programme aid now reaching Mogadishu. That in turn exacerbates the poverty in Somalia, a poverty that is certainly not alleviated by the riches obtained by a comparative few who live in the lawless, self-declared, autonomous state of Puntland embracing as it does, both sides of the Horn of Africa.

With the civilised world ranged against them – for few countries do not benefit from trade that passes along this coastline – how is it therefore, that these Somali pirates are able to operate in small craft, often far out at sea from well-known and identified bases? Before taking a glance at the practicalities, it is well to remember that the legal status of a pirate is not totally understood. If they were treated as terrorists, as they should be, the matter would indeed be crystal clear, but for instance, Article 100 of the Law of the Sea Convention requires that a warship first sends an officer-led party to suspected pirates' ships to verify suspicions. The warship cannot just open fire, even on the strongest of evidence except in self-defence. Neither do other pointers help clear the air. The European Parliament towards the end of 2008, adopted with a huge majority, a proposal to downgrade piracy from an 'act of war' to a simple 'criminal act'. If this is eventually ratified then a naval vessel may not attack at all, but will need to arrest the suspects and hand them over to an international court, where no doubt, they will plead human rights and sympathy by citing the destitute squalor of living conditions in Puntland in particular and Somalia in general. The fact that no pirates' money reaches the poor of these benighted countries is an understatement.

Nor is there any internationally-agreed legal system for treating pirates once captured, for each receiving country deals with them as best they think fit at the time. Some have been tried in Kenya, others have been tried in France, while the British Navy and others, have killed 'in self-defence'.

Now, leaving aside the politics, why is it often difficult to tell who is a pirate until he is actually on board your ship? One trick employed by these criminals is to appear to be a stranded dhow far offshore – sometimes as far as 390 nautical miles – even to the point of sending out false Mayday calls, then when a passing merchant ship stops to help, it is boarded.

Nor is this aspect helped by the hundreds of local, genuine fishing vessels working the area and once described by a journalist embarked in a warship as 'the whole of the Yemen fishing fleet in similar vessels to those used by the pirates and often taken over by the pirates as cover'. Identification is not easy until the pirates declare their hand by committing their unlawful acts, and then it is too late as they have already seized their prey. The security forces (*pace* France's remarkable *Commando Hubert*) are then powerless to intervene without endangering hostages' lives. These piratical acts are not conducted by just a handful of ill-trained men in a brace of speed boats operating from a hijacked mother ship. The MV *Faina* was attacked by a well-led, well-trained gang of sixty-two men – three times the number of her crew. The vessel is still in custody, as are many others.

What are the methods by which this problem may be combated at sea? While some advocate the use of on-board, private, armed security personnel, the International Maritime Bureau (IMB) believes that 'the legalities of the situation do not allow for an armed private security presence'. Yet some continue to believe that it is time merchant vessels became more proactive and engaged in their own self-defence, which brings us back to the use of private security firms. Views remain divided, for there is no doubt that while the pirate is not intent on killing, he will be forced to do so, if he has to fight to secure his prey. Security guards have been the catalyst for casualties before 2008 and yet it has to be assumed that the maritime terrorists off the Horn of Africa want to destroy neither the ship, its cargo nor its crew: ransom money cannot be demanded for a burnt-out derelict, a hulk on the sea bed, a destroyed cargo or a dead crewman.

So what other acceptable alternatives are there, short of direct-action operations such as attacking the pirates in their bases or sinking every suspect seen at sea – with no questions asked in advance, to the detriment of the genuinely innocent?

Firstly and perhaps most obviously, is the forming of convoys with naval protection, but this can be a convoluted affair, with ships and shipping arriving at inconvenient intervals and with each ship having its own commercially important timetable for transiting the Red Sea and thus the Suez Canal, overturned. Nevertheless, this is probably the safest form of preventative action and is already underway.

Additionally and collectively, whether in convoy or not, there are a number of other actions individual ships can take. Various ploys are being used or being experimented with, through which unwanted boardings in any one of the hotspots around the g lobe can be reduced. Old-fashioned methods such as barbed wire handrails, electrified guardrails and high-pressure hoses are already in vogue. The Chinese merchantman *Zhenhua 4* fought off pirates with water cannon and Molotov cocktails, although the timely intervention of a Malaysian naval ship probably helped to save the day. A sustained speed above 20 knots and a freeboard above twenty feet are also useful deterrents.

Technology too, is coming to the rescue, with such weapon as the Long Range Audio Device (LRAD) and the Magnetic Acoustic Device (MAD). These are classified as non-lethal, but even so, they are most disorientating for an approaching vessel, and have been used successfully on at least one occasion. An 8,500-ton chemical tanker was targeted by three small, fast boats. When they were within a mile the alarm was activated and the maritime terrorists forced away.

More formally there is Task Force 150. Under overall US command, this flotilla consists of ships from twenty navies, with at any given time, fifteen warships in the area off Somalia, supported by aerial reconnaissance. Extra US ships can be made available if necessary as can be, apparently, Russian warships. China has announced too that it will send naval ships to the area by the end of December

2008 – two destroyers and one supply ship – for as many as five Chinese ships pass through the area every day. Seven Chinese ships were seized in 2008.

Even Iran has sent a warship to the Gulf of Aden to protect its merchant shipping, with officials stating that their ships would be prepared to use force against the pirates if necessary. The spokesman went on to say that the Gulf was an international area and that Iran's armed forces would 'carry out any decision made by their superiors'. In October 2008 though, Iran paid a ransom to free the crew of a captured merchant ship and in November, an Iranian-operated cargo ship carrying 36,000 tonnes of wheat was seized. Maybe Iranian views on ransom-paying have now been reversed.

Meanwhile, an Indian naval frigate destroyed a Somali pirate mother ship which was accompanied by two speed boats. As these did not then have enough fuel to reach a safe haven, their fate remains unknown. It must be hoped that more commanders will consider equally robust responses as being the correct means to suit the proper end.

While this is all progress, Somalia's internationally recognised transitional government has invited foreign navies to do whatever is necessary to stop the pirates, even agreeing to them being attacked ashore if necessary. Helpfully the UN Security Council confirmed this as an option. World leaders, in December 2008, while calling for greater action to deal with the problem, approved a UN resolution that allowed foreign troops to meet Somalia's invitation by pursuing pirates on land. As nearly all of the pirates come from Puntland and live in a single town, Boosaaso, and harbour their captives in three ports – Eyl, Hobyo and Haradhere – this ground interdiction is, in theory, made easy, but this would be expensive in amphibious and airborne resources, when most western forces are committed to Afghanistan, Iraq and the Gulf. It is though, the only permanent solution.

US Naval Forces Command has now established a Maritime Security Patrol Area in the Gulf of Aden, conducting sea and air patrols by Combined Task Force 150 in a bid to contain attacks. Additionally, in early December 2008, a fleet of six European warships operating under the codename Atalanta began escorting World Food Programme ships into Somalia's ports under robust rules of engagement. These are accompanied by Somalia's run-down coastguard of just three patrol vessels, all operating under a relevant set of ROE. The only aspect lacking in all these maritime operations, are suitable numbers of patrol aircraft, for the pirates are known to dislike this form of surveillance above all others, as they have no methods of dealing with it. Extra Maritime Patrol Aircraft (MPA), in addition to those already in theatre, would provide a more complete maritime picture to help establish where the pirates operate from and their general modus operandi when at sea.

Yet in the absence of a durable, workable, legal solution, maritime terror attacks off Somalia will continue. Even if such a law did exist and was workable at sea, or if the international community was willing to take the war to the enemy in his homelands (as asked for by Somalia and given tacit approval by the UN), it would still be hampered by poverty, lawlessness and support from Islamist extremists. Yet again, despite all this, the over-riding desire to help the innocent civilians of this part of Africa is powerful, but is that desire powerful enough to by-pass so many antiquated perceptions of piracy. Modern pirates are far from being old-fashioned and should be treated for what they are, maritime terrorists, and not as the European Parliament would have them treated, as simple criminals. They should be hunted down ruthlessly by land, by sea and without compassion until eradicated once and for all. They are so rooted in their way of life that it is doubtful that the return of a stable, all-embracing, Somalia government would now make much difference.

Finally, interestingly and in support of much of the above, Dmitry Rogozin – Russia's ambassador to the UN has stated that in the view of Russian experts, it is not a sea operation that is needed but an amphibious operation to eradicate the pirate bases – a view that was long held for the Straits of Malacca – and that any such operation should be co-ordinated with Russia.

Quite so. 'Any port in a storm' should be the cry, and this one would prove to be the best choice for the longest-term solution.

Chapter 17

Riverine Operations

Written in 2014 for Jane's Amphibious and Special Forces

Since man first expanded his military horizons, narrow waterways, and lakes and rivers have been the ideal conduits for incursion into another's territory, accordingly they were probably the first areas that needed specialist equipment to attack and defend.

Rivers separate nation states and bisect single nations. Rivers, by their nature, tend to lead deep inland and for a myriad of reasons, usually pass through centres of population, commerce, trade and military installations. Rivers often, literally, carry the lifeblood of a nation, but are equally as often, the most vulnerable of a nation's Achilles heels. If a transgressor can control a river he can control much of the hinterland either side. For both defender and attacker, a river is a supreme tool and yet a soft underbelly.

Rivers and canals can squeeze traffic into narrow defiles – good for the defender, bad for the attacker, yet they can also offer surprise as well as lengthy warnings of approach. They can reduce the worry of navigation, and yet almost without warning, can throw up unseen – unseeable and unpredictable – navigational hazards. River banks can offer ideal hiding and camouflage conditions for both defender and attacker, while some offer little more than billiard table conditions and visibility for miles. Some are tidal, some are a one-way flow, some are benign in summer, and yet under winter conditions, turn in a near instant, into unusable torrents of debris-strewn, dangerous water. Flotsam can be a serious hindrance to fast travel, while there will always be some bystander only too eager to report the passage of friend or foe. Except in the largest estuaries, a populated river bank is seldom far away.

Whether a help or a hindrance, whether attacker or defender, riverine operations are here to stay, as more and more of those intent on asymmetric warfare come to appreciate the pluses and minuses (mostly pluses) to those intent on criminality along the world's rivers. For it is along rivers and in shoal, coastal waters, that many of today's disaffected are now operating.

In the recent past, riverine warfare played a major role in many operations, although the equipment had so often to be borrowed from other theatres, and then more often than not, altered to suit, not always successfully. Riverine craft are not limited to the small and the fast, hence for instance, Romania's two classes of river monitors, and nor is riverine conflict a modern form of warfare.

General James Wolfe fought a river-supported operation at Quebec in the mid-eighteenth century when he used flat-bottomed barges (known as flatboats) to cross the St. Lawrence seaway on 13 September 1759, in order to take the Plains of Abraham during the Seven Years War with France. The USN's riverine experiences also date back to the latter half of the same century. During the Second World War small craft were used to infiltrate river systems in search of targets, with the British raid on German shipping 90 miles up the Gironde estuary in December 1942, using canvas canoes a prime example. More recently – and from the British point of view – confrontation in Borneo during the early 1960s required intensive riverine operations, yet the only craft available were small Assault Landing Craft/Landing Craft Vehicle and Personnel (LCA/LCVP) and army aluminium assault craft. On the face of it these craft were small and unsuitable, but with their shoal draft and ability not only to lift heavy weapons, but offer a steady platform when manoeuvring, they were remarkably successful. The same craft – plus many commandeered, local vessels – had been used by allied forces against the Japanese in Burma. In New Guinea, Australian infantry adopted local dug-out canoes for their riverine patrols. During the Vietnam War, US forces adopted and adapted craft for riverine operations along the Mekong River system, but then when that conflict drew to a close, they quietly abandoned the art.

Rivers can be well populated with pleasure craft, fishing vessels, ferries and commercial shipping, that in many cases, will offer ideal cover for those prepared to use indigenous craft for both defence and nefarious purposes. Rivers can also, over quite short lengths, offer a wide range of protection/camouflage and operating conditions: mangrove swamps, reed beds, sand banks, swamps, rapids, shoals, placid pools, narrow defiles, deep gorges and wide, sluggish, many-branched deltas all have their advantages and disadvantages. They can also be the habitat of poisonous snakes and dangerous reptiles, considerations ignored at an operator's peril, as those who work in such areas will testify. The hinterland from which an enemy may attack or a defender may defend vary too, from the dense, jungle banks of South America to the muddy, flood-prone deltas of the Indian sub-continent and the myriad *chaungs* of the Malaysian Peninsula. The list is almost endless.

By and large most littoral states will have a river system, although there are obvious exceptions. The Mediterranean coasts of Africa and those of the Red Sea and Gulf are prime examples. Some landlocked states, far from the sea, have extensive river systems which need serious patrolling. Rivers in Paraguay and Bolivia are good examples, as are the many countries through which the Danube flows in Eastern Europe. The Mekong river's upper reaches are in China, before it flows through Cambodia, and are also far from the sea, yet ones that require substantial vessels to guarantee the security of those who depend on it for their livelihood.

That having been said, almost any craft can be co-opted into use for the myriad of tasks that riverine warfare requires, tasks that can be encapsulated as: area control and denial, interdiction of lines of communication, fire support, insertion and extraction of conventional ground forces, ambushes, anti-smuggling patrols, and maritime counter-insurgency.

Inevitably, craft specifically designed for riverine work must meet a mix and match matrix, depending on the likely adversaries, the depth of water, ranges of weapons and speed required, troops/payload likely to be carried and/or inserted or extracted. Whether the operation is overt, covert or clandestine, the size and capability of enemy and his own craft, fast and light versus slow and heavily armoured. Below surface propulsion and steering gear is prone to debris damage. Is stealth a priority or are noise and radar signature inconsequential? It helps too, if the craft can safely take the ground either to hide, resupply, or simply lie-up for rest or disembark and embark troops quickly and tactically.

The following is a brief summary of some of the countries around the world who are capable of operating in a riverine environment. Of course any nation with access to comparatively shoal draft vessels suitable for local conditions, can conduct riverine operations, but as with much in the military world, operations are more successful when the correct equipment is deployed. Though having the correct equipment does not guarantee success in any field. Some nations with no rivers of their own may feel the need to be able to operate in such conditions elsewhere.

The following list is not intended to be a full inventory of countries and their equipment, nor an update on current operational activity. Many of the craft listed will not have been acquired specifically for riverine warfare, but will in extremis be useful. It may also be the case that crew training lets the craft down. It must also be borne in mind that almost any craft can be employed in riverine/brown-water warfare, but perhaps, not as efficiently as those designed for the purpose and crewed by those trained for the job in hand.

To the uninitiated riverine operations may seem a mere extension of brown-water/coastal warfare but this over simplification is not borne out in reality.

Argentina has 11,000km (7,860 nautical miles) of usable rivers which need patrolling, especially as she has a lengthy border with Uruguay along the Uruguay river. The country operates just four Guardian craft armed with a 12.7mm machine gun, and four 7.62mm machine guns, although four LCMs and fifteen assorted patrol and fast-attack craft could be brought into play.

Australia has no craft designed for riverine warfare, nor any earmarked for such operations, although the four 6.5-ton LCVPs could be used in the archipelago to the north.

Bangladesh certainly has a need for riverine experts and amphibious equipment, for combating natural disasters such as floods, as well as preventing insurgents using the extensive river system. Yet the country possesses only a limited number of slow but capable landing craft and army personnel. Medium-lift hovercraft and relevantly trained forces would be more suitable, but finances do not allow for such luxuries.

Bolivia, with 20,000km (10,787 nautical miles) of inland waterways, has a small force to secure these conduits. Most operations are aimed at drug runners and dislodging illegal Brazilian immigrants, but with the size of riverine assets available, and despite the known efficiency of the Special Forces, plus help from the USA, they are hardly viable for the distances concerned. Progress in this aspect of operations remains an uphill struggle.

Brazil has a vast network of rivers (in excess of 42,973km, 23,220 nautical miles), centred mainly on the Amazon basin in the north and west, the Paraná basin in the south, and the São Francisco basin in the east. A number of vast coastal lagoons also need patrolling. Five army jungle brigades and a Marine Corps riverine operations battalion form the basis for all fluvial operations.

With Peru, Paraguay and Bolivia all being accessible via rivers flowing through Brazil, or along common borders, the need for extensive riverine expertise is obvious. Many of the larger landing craft can and do operate in the rivers, but that has not prevented the country from developing specialist craft. One such vessel is the river hospital ship, *Doutor Montenegro*, that complements the two in the Amazon Flotilla, while other specialist vessels are the river transport ships used for logistics and troops. The Amazon Flotilla operates three Roraima-class patrol ships, and the elderly (commissioned in 1938) river monitor *Parnaiba*, which is fitted with a helicopter deck. Two shoal draft river patrol ships are also within this squadron. The 1st Jungle Battalion, based on the Amazon in the Manaus region, trialled the Combat Boat 90 in 2004, so successfully that it was used during a live operation later in the year.

Bulgaria has 470km (253 nautical miles) of the River Danube running along the northern border with Romania – a waterway that can carry in excess of 2.5 million tonnes and 26,000 passengers a year. To police this river, the Bulgarian Navy has three Boston Whalers and an unknown number of RIBs. So clearly, no significant threat is anticipated.

Cambodia lies between Vietnam and Laos, all of whom are connected by the mighty Mekong river (500km, 270 nautical miles). The Mekong, with the Tonle Sap river and lake, divide the country into thirds. 2,000-ton vessels can use the Mekong, yet the only suggestion of riverine forces is the existence of about 170 motorised and manual canoes.

Canada has no riverine threat and is not equipped to conduct such operations elsewhere. A number of coastguard-operated hovercraft can assist in flood relief.

Chile's rivers are by and large, unnavigable and the country has no aspirations for riverine operations elsewhere.

China has a vast riverine network of which at least 110,000km (59,330 nautical miles) are navigable by ocean going vessels – including the largest amphibious ships. Internally – apart from smugglers – there is probably little need for specialists in riverine warfare, although the large number of hovercraft might suggest otherwise. A growing number of small, water-jet propelled inshore patrol craft – especially of the Swedish Combat Boat 90-type, may be significant for riverine and shoal water operations.

Colombia has a large river network of which 14,300km (7,713 nautical miles) are navigable. the past the rivers were vital for the transport of people across 40 per cent of the country, but now they are used more often by drug smugglers. This domination is being challenged by the navy with US help, and the procurement of fifty LPR-40 river patrol craft (propelled by water-jet) to add to the large number of dedicated riverine craft (reported to be over eighty) already in existence. Of added interest are at least eleven river support ships with one fitted as a hospital. Colombia takes its riverine operations very seriously and has a compelling need to do so.

The Democratic Republic of Congo is dominated by the vast 4,650km (2,508 nautical miles) Congo river system that provides easy access to the hinterland. The river is navigable up to 148km (80 nautical miles) from the sea by ocean-going vessels. Above Stanley Falls at Kisangani, the Congo river becomes the Lualaba and is navigable for a further 965km (520 nautical miles) – from Bubundi to Kindu and from Kongolo to Bukama. However, although there is surely a need for riverine vessels, there are no reports of what is used by the army's River Command based at Kinshasha.

Croatia has a navigable river network of in excess of 785km (423 nautical miles), with the country deploying at least four heavily armed river patrol craft.

Ecuador's 1,500km (809 nautical miles) of navigable rivers are mainly in the remote Amazon basin (bordering Peru in the east) and offering the only access to the hinterland. There is a growing need for riverine forces to keep these vital waterways open and clear of drug smugglers. Ten specialist jungle infantry battalions can call upon a number of fast, light-draught, heavily-armed riverine vessels such as the Swiftships-class. Nevertheless, considering the distances that need to be covered, there is clearly a need for many more.

Egypt owns much of the navigable Nile, and in total, about 3,500km (1,888 nautical miles) of inland waterways, and yet is not reported to possess any form of riverine force nor associated equipment and vessels. This suggests that all is quiet at home and with no aspirations further afield.

El Salvador operates six Piranha and nine Protector river patrol vessels on her few navigable rivers, but of interest, the navy also operates eight minimal-draught, 'air' patrol boats (propelled by aircraft propellers) on the swamps and lakes.

Estonia's navy operates one Griffon 2000TDX Mk II hovercraft (16 troops or two tons) along her 500km (270 nautical miles) of navigable waterways.

Finland has 187,888 lakes in addition to 6,675km (3,600 nautical miles) of waterways. Without external threats, she concentrates on her coastline where she operates hovercraft and fast raiding craft.

France, as with most European maritime nations, has no homeland riverine threat, but her amphibious force is capable of such operations worldwide. These are limited as it is not believed that she possesses any dedicated riverine vessels.

Germany possesses a limited amphibious capability and certainly no riverine forces, nor equipment for home or worldwide use.

Greece has no navigable rivers – although the country is worried about the river routes (often deep defiles used by personnel) into the hinterland – and so no riverine forces. Abroad, the navy relies on a conventional amphibious fleet (including four heavy-lift hovercraft) for conventional amphibious operations, and looks no further than the coastline. The navy's Special Forces, high-speed insertion craft and well-armed Special Forces diving support craft could be used for riverine operations. The coastguard though, does operate three Combat Boat 90s and a number of fast insertion/interception craft.

Guatemala has 260km (140 nautical miles) of waterways that increases by about 730km (394 nautical miles) in the rainy season. These are patrolled by marine and navy battalions using shoal-draught, Machete-class troop carriers and a variety of small, out-board propelled river patrol vessels. The quarry are guerrillas of the *Unidad Revolucionaria Nacional Guatemalteca*.

Hungary's 1,622km (875 nautical miles) of rivers require a riverine presence. This is supplied by the Danube River Flotilla and its maritime wing, operating three 72-ton Nestin-class minesweepers and 45 AN-2 Mine Warfare/River Patrol Craft. Many of the country's armoured vehicles are amphibious and more than capable of crossing the local rivers.

India has a wide range of riverine requirements, both on the mainland and within her offshore island groups. India's waterway network extends for 14,500km (7,820 nautical miles) but she has no riverine vessels, other than a variety of Griffon hovercraft. She has no need for more, while her conventional amphibious capability is also considered to be all that is needed among the islands.

Indonesia certainly has a need for specialist riverine troops and craft – if only to try and contain the piracy scourge that often emanates from inland. Kalimantan, Sumatra and Papua have long riverine networks, while Java and Madura have smaller systems, all of which add up to about 21,579km (11,639 nautical miles). Apart from conventional amphibious forces, there are no specialist riverine troops nor equipment that have been reported.

Iraq's rivers include the dominating Euphrates (2,815km - 1,518 nautical miles) and the Tigris (1,899km - 1,024 nautical miles) together with their confluence at the Shatt al-Arab. There are also numerous and substantial lakes. The Iraqi Riverine Patrol Service operates small aluminium outboard propelled craft, under the original guidance of the UK's Royal Marines. In due course, this force will need expanding, while procuring more suitable craft as foreign forces scale back their operations. The Iraqi Coastal Defence Force, although primarily responsible for general maritime counter-insurgency tasks, will need to look closely at approaches to the river system as well as the offshore oil platforms.

Italy has no need for riverine craft to patrol her 2,400 km (1,295 nautical miles) of waterways, nor does she deem it necessary to augment her substantial amphibious forces with such craft and expertise.

Japan has no need for riverine craft to patrol her 1,770km (955 nautical miles) of waterways nor does she consider it necessary to augment her growing amphibious forces with such craft and expertise, although the six heavy-lift LCACs might be useful.

North Korea may not possess a riverine capability as such, but her forces are well trained to infiltrate South Korea's coasts and rivers using a variety of insertion craft – both high and slow speed.

South Korea has 2,406km (1,600 nautical miles) of navigable rivers, some of which are exploited by North Korea, yet there are no reports of special riverine craft: however the numerous light-lift hovercraft are certainly useful. There are reports of plans to build up to 20 further small hovercraft for Special Forces. It is feasible that these could be used offensively abroad up rivers rather than defensively at home.

Malaysia, in company with her neighbours, has an urgent need for riverine and brown water specialists and vessels, in order to counter the many and serious piracy problems of the region – a number of which operate out of the thousands of shoal-water creeks and *chaungs* of the peninsula. In addition to her coastline – including the Straits of Malacca – Malaysia needs to secure over 7,000km (3,775 nautical miles) of inland waterways. While she has no craft specifically designed for such work, the smaller, amphibious vessels – including, among others, the 130 Damen Assault Craft and the seventeen Combat Boat 90 – are extremely useful.

Mexico has nearly 2,900km (1,564 nautical miles) of navigable rivers and coastal waterways on both coasts. No specialist troops or equipment exists other than the Mexican Marine Corps who can call on a number of Combat Boat 90 variants and water-jet propelled Pirana rigid raiding craft.

Myanmar has a vast river network that transports at least 5 million tonnes of freight and 45 million passengers each year. It is vital for the country that these lines of communication are kept safe. The primary task of the Myanmar navy is to patrol the country's coasts and rivers in support of the army's counter-insurgency operations. Yet apart from nine 37-ton river patrol craft and four 98-ton river transport vessels that can be armed with 20mm guns and the navy's meagre range of LCUs – largely unsuitable for river work – there would appear to be little or no specialist riverine equipment and expertise.

The Netherlands has 4,800km (2,589 nautical miles) of safe waterways most of which are in constant use. Apart from conventional amphibious vessels, no specialist riverine craft are considered necessary at home or abroad.

Nigeria's riverine and brown water areas – mostly the Niger and Benin/Benue delta – require considerable expertise in preventing attacks on the near-shore oil platforms, but the country possesses neither specialist vessels nor expertise. The Nigerian army patrols the delta in armed assault craft, and while a number of fast patrol craft have been procured in recent years, these by and large, are not suitable for rivers. The Marine Police, which operates on Lake Chad and other inland waters, plus the Port Security Police, operate their own craft.

Norway has no need for riverine craft either at home or abroad, although the Coastal Ranger water-jet propelled Combat Boat 90 would be highly suitable should the need arise.

Pakistan's rivers are used only for small-scale local traffic, nevertheless the army does deploy its troops in inflatable craft, Klepper canoes, four light hovercraft and a number of fast insertion craft that are also available for river and near-coast operations.

Paraguay's 3.331km (1,800 nautical miles) of rivers are used for smuggling and human trafficking. The Marine Corps is mostly deployed on the upper Paraguay river between Bahia Negra and Olimpo and at Saltos del Guaira, Ciudad del Este and Encarnacion, on the Parana river. With no dedicated amphibious forces, the Marine Corps is deployed and supported by the navy's riverine forces. A small number of river patrol craft are available as are three LCVPs.

Peru's large fluvial system includes 8,600km (4,639 nautical miles) of Amazon tributaries and 208km (112 nautical miles) of Lake Titicaca. To help control and police these waterways the Marine Corps has two jungle-trained battalions which it can call upon and an array of specialist riverine craft for deployment and support.

Included amongst these vessels are two 365-ton Mara and two 250-ton Loreto river gun boats. Two river vessels (one fitted as a hospital), act as transport along the rivers while a venerable (built in 1872) hospital craft is also stationed on Lake Titicaca. Additionally, the marines and the army have the use of sixteen five-ton lake and river patrol craft.

The Philippines's shoal water interests tend to focus on the Spratly Islands, while the Philippine Marine Corps operates fast, heavily armed rigid inflatable craft for coastal defence. The limited river system is shallow and only suited to craft drawing less than 1.5m (4.9 feet).

Poland has a rich network of rivers totalling about 3,997km (2,156 nautical miles), but with no reported serious threats to the nine million tons of trade carried on them, just two light-lift hovercraft are considered ample.

Portugal's river systems allow access to the interior for displacement vessels, but with no obvious threat either here or abroad the country possesses no riverine expertise.

Romania's river network includes the vital Danube, where commercial shipping and especially passenger and car ferries, are regularly targeted by insurgents.

To counter this threat the Romanian Navy operates a maritime flotilla, the River (or Danube) Flotilla and the Naval Infantry Battalion. The Danube Flotilla is organised into a river brigade with a further (maritime) brigade further downstream. For riverine support, the navy operates an extensive range of vessels and craft, including about twenty river patrol craft (which include three Boston whalers and a light-lift hovercraft), five 410-ton Brutar, and three 575-ton Kogailniceanu river monitors.

Russia's riverine specialisations tend to centre around the smaller amphibious vessels, landing craft and hovercraft, ranging from the 550-ton Pomornik down to small, five-seaters. Apart from the very few smaller landing craft, no other vessels suitable for riverine deployment either at home or abroad are reported.

Serbian riverine forces patrol the river Danube with a river detachment (now part of the army) which operates twenty-one assorted river patrol craft and minesweepers. One 29-ton river patrol boat is deployed, capable of landing troops using its own embarked rubber assault craft.

Singapore has many small waterways, most little more than large brooks that tend to be blocked by low bridges. Despite needing riverine forces for homeland defence, the country possesses a number of useful assets should they be needed abroad, including no less than 450 five-metre assault craft, each of which can carry twelve troops and are designed to fit beneath the local bridges. A few hovercraft are available but these tend to be experimental.

South Africa's Operational Boat Squadron, with its six Lima assault craft, each capable of carrying twenty-four troops at a top speed of 38 knots, is certainly capable of operating in most rivers at home or abroad, although whether such specialist training is undertaken is unknown.

Spain has no need for riverine forces to operate at home, but within her extensive, modern amphibious fleet, there are certainly craft capable of such operations. For instance seventeen inflatable raiding craft, each of which can carry twelve marines, have been procured.

Sri Lanka certainly needed a sophisticated riverine capability to counter the threat from the Liberation Tigers of Tamil Eelam (LTTE), also known as the Tamil Tigers, fighting for an independent Tamil state in Sri Lanka, yet no specialist craft were listed, while the one medium-lift hovercraft was mainly used for logistic supply.

Sweden has no need for riverine forces despite a substantial river and lake network. Nor is the country prepared to operate such forces overseas. However, an impressive range of shoal water, assault craft – based mainly on the Combat Boat 90 hull – is available for shoal-water operations as are a growing number of medium-lift hovercraft.

Taiwan's major interests lie in home defence and with few navigable rivers on the islands there is little need for a riverine expertise: nevertheless over 100 assorted LCVPs and armed assault craft are in commission.

Thailand has over 4,000km (2,147 nautical miles) of major waterways and many more minor rivers capable of accepting small craft. To patrol these vital conduits (in addition to other tasks) the navy's Riverine and Seal Squadrons operate: three light-lift hovercraft and 13 PBR Mk II River patrol craft powered by water jets. Three SEAL assault craft fitted with stern ramps are also in commission, as are ninety assault boats. Conventional amphibious vessels and minor landing craft can support riverine operations especially abroad.

Turkey's river system is only suitable for small-scale incursions. Two fast intervention/insertion craft are in commission should they be needed abroad.

Ukraine has three important river systems, of which the Dneiper (Dnipro) and its tributaries with a long string of inter-connecting lakes is by far the most important as a conduit to the country's interior. Nevertheless, there are no specialist riverine forces reported, the navy's two Pomornik heavy-lift hovercraft being impractical for such work.

The United Arab Emirates has no river system but plenty of craft suitable for such work, should the need arise elsewhere. In addition to long-range SDVs, at least sixty-six high-speed RIBs are in service although none with water-jet propulsion – the preferred system in rivers. Three Boghammer craft and an unknown number of fast intercept craft could be used, but these are better suited to coastal areas, where their high speeds are more useful for the distances involved.

The United Kingdom has no need for home land, specialist riverine craft, and expertise although such craft have been deployed on various occasions during anti-drug running operations on, for instance, the Thames. The country's approximate 3,200km (1,726 nautical miles) of canals are considered safe from waterborne threats, but should this situation change the expertise does exist. The UK does though, need riverine craft and specialists as part of her amphibious forces for her global commitments. 539 Assault Squadron, Royal Marines – under command of the 3 Commando Brigade – is the specialist unit operating four light-lift hovercraft and (as far as riverine operations are concerned, the wrongly-named but very heavily-armed Offshore Raiding Craft) plus a variety of rigid, rigid inflatable and inflatable craft. Klepper canoes are still used by the country's maritime Special Forces, as are the more modern, High Speed Insertion/Intercept-class of delivery vessels. All riverine forces and equipment can be transported either by air, by conventional surface combatant or by amphibious shipping. Some can be delivered by parachute and by submarine.

The United States possesses a vast riverine and canal network. For instance the Mississippi/Missouri/Ohio/Red River systems of about 24,059km (13,000 nautical miles), almost bisect the country from north to south. As a useful conduit for terrorists into the heartland this cannot be ignored. The US also has riverine responsibilities in a number of global theatres and compliant countries; these are most usually involved in assisting anti-drug running operations.

The US Navy's first riverine squadron since the Vietnam War was formed in 2007. The Riverine Squadron One (RIVRON1), under the command of the Navy Expeditionary Combat Command operates ten former USMC Small Unit Craft (SURC). Other craft are being considered. The Northrop Grumman/ Aluminium Chambered Boats consortium is experimenting with a ramped, 12.4 metre (40ft 10") shallow draught craft (0.6 metre, 26 inch) capable of negotiating Class V rapids and powered by water jets.

The USMC operates thirty-two Riverine Assault Craft and 72 nine-ton, water-jet propelled RIBs, while the US Special Operations Command operates 116 1.2 ton Light Patrol Boats, formerly known as Counter Drug Patrol Boats.

Uruguay shares a lengthy border of lakes and river (the Uruguay) with Argentina, with neither country considering riverine forces to be a priority, although the Uruguay Marine Corps does practice riverine training from the Paysandu naval base on the Uruguay river.

Uzbekistan's two major rivers – the Syr Darya and the Amu Darya (Oxus), are patrolled by two armoured gun boats, particularly on the latter river which runs along the border with Afghanistan.

Venezuela's largest navigable river system is the Orinoco with its tributaries the Apure and Aracua. The total length of its inland waterways is 7,000km (3,776 nautical miles), a substantial part of which forms the Venezuelan/Colombian border. To patrol these delicate areas, the Marine Infantry has two major amphibious commands, one of which is the River Command. This is formed from, among other units, the River Brigade which operates a number of useful riverine craft, including seven 15-ton river patrol craft, twelve Boston Whalers and ten Rio Orinoco-class. The coastguard operates seven 5-ton, 50 knot Polaris High Speed Interdiction-class vessels.

Vietnam encompasses the deltas of the Red River in the north, and the Mekong in the south. Both areas tend to be rich with pirates. To counter this threat a number of classes of conventional minor landing craft are in commission, which would hardly seem either adequate or appropriate.

Chapter 18

Beach and River Reconnaissance

Written in 2013 for *Jane's Amphibious and Special Forces*

'Time spent in reconnaissance is seldom wasted.' This most well-known military advice is more than pertinent when it comes to planning a landing from seaward. The Romans in 55 BC knew that. One thousand years before, the Egyptian 'sea people' knew that. And the Persians landing at Marathon in 490 BC knew that to put men, horses, food and equipment ashore across a beach, whether defended or not, required a prior reconnaissance. The British at Gallipoli, and the Allies elsewhere in the First World War knew that. Hitler's men in 1940 knew that and so did the Allies in the Mediterranean, the English Channel, the Indian Ocean and the Far East, as did the Japanese and Americans across the Pacific during the Second World War. The French and British knew that at Suez in 1956, and the British again in the Far East in the 1950s and 1960s, as did the Israelis, Turks and Egyptians during their post-WWII campaigns. So the list continues for amphibious nations up to the first and second Gulf Wars, via such operations as Somalia, Grenada, the Falkland Islands, Sierra Leone and even Libya.

Unlike almost any other phase of warfare, there are three distinct opponents involved in amphibious landings: the human enemy, the weather and the topography (above and below the waterline). Take a standard battalion attack on land as a simple but useful example. The enemy lie atop a well-fortified hill and must be dislodged, in order to allow friendly forces to maintain their forward momentum.

Unmanned aerial vehicles conduct real-time intelligence sorties, foot patrols scout at night to seek out the enemy's alertness and their mine fields and the general lie of the land. Approaches can be studied from afar through binoculars. Signal and satellite intelligence is fed into the command post. The latest ordnance survey maps are studied, while the extremes of the weather are largely ignored, unless for instance, thick fog is forecast. The phase of the moon is a side-line, although its luminosity versus cloud cover will be noted. Assuming the attack will be successful, all-round defences of the new position are pre-planned, as are the precautions to be taken against counter attack, while the vital logistic resupply following the battle is assessed and routes approved.

Now we must project that same scene to one where the enemy holds ground, close to or even on a shore – a shore that friendly forces are keen to occupy in preparation for further operations inland. The force commanders have decided that to take that ground and to advance in accordance with the wider plan (this is a very simple scenario) a beach head must be established, from which those future operations may be conducted. In this case it does not matter if the beach itself is the objective (as at the Al Faw peninsula in the second Gulf War) or merely a stepping stone. What does matter is that that beach will need to be the subject of an intensive beach reconnaissance operation, a phase of war all of its own. In the first Gulf War for instance, no such beach head was required to be taken, for Kuwait offered host nation support (although an amphibious assault was conducted against the Iraqi-occupied island of Maradim) but this changed with the second Gulf War and the opposed landings direct into Iraq.

During the Cold War, beaches on both flanks – north Norway and the north-eastern Mediterranean – needed to be reconnoitred, should landings have had to have been conducted by American-led NATO forces. These recces were conducted in slow time over the years, while a comprehensive library of beach information was built up. But again, with host nation support (what is known in some NATO circles as the 'red carpet treatment' from, as examples, Norway, Turkey and Greece), these surveys were obtained under peaceful conditions. Nevertheless, the information required remained the same as that needed to be acquired under combat conditions.

So what information is needed, how is it gained, who will use it, and what, therefore, are the significant differences (and difficulties) between a beach or river reconnaissance, and any other?

Firstly, the main aim is to prepare the way for a landing from seaward of men, vehicles and logistics, preferably unopposed. A beach or river bank might be chosen as the most suitable place from the tactical (and, sometimes, strategic) point of view, bearing in mind the eventual objective and the forces and assets (size and type of landing craft for instance) at the commander's disposal. The landing area could be a port, but this would almost certainly imply an opposed landing against stiff opposition, whereas a beach or river bank, although imposing considerable extra complications, will widen the choice for the attacker, while keeping any defender guessing, and hopefully, diluting his defences. Ideally the beach will not be overlooked by flanking headlands or high ground and the route to it will not be past inhabited islands, or any islands. It will be reasonably clear of complicated shoals and yet be in an area that has some protection from the elements, as well as from enemy surface and sub-surface activity. All in all, a tall order.

If the landing area is overlooked by surrounding headlands or offshore islands, then these may need to be secured by advance force operations, using helicopters, small teams of Special Forces, or more simply, naval gunfire. Of course these operations, unless conducted at the last moment, perhaps simultaneously, may well cause the loss of the all-important element of surprise.

A beach may be excellent in all aspects but a fundamental requirement is can the landing force move inland from the high-water mark? Clearly not, if the back of the beach ends in a cliff face or everglades-style swamps or impenetrable jungle. Of course, if the force to be landed is small, and of a Special Forces nature, then maybe these are the precise obstacles that they will be looking for, in the hope that the defending force will consider them to be just that – impassable. Nowadays, all that might be needed is a quick glance at Google Earth, bearing in mind that it can be dated.

Nevertheless, no commander will give the 'yes' or 'no' without having had eyes on the ground. For instance, prior to the Allied landings on Normandy in June 1944, an invaluable source of information was pre-war picture postcards and holiday snaps culled from across the United Kingdom. Much the same applied prior to the British landings in the Falkland Islands in 1982. Even so, the commanders were not satisfied without a physical reconnaissance, although the areas of interest to be surveyed may well have been reduced or confirmed by such ordinary information.

Other factors will need to be assessed and checked out by maritime Special Forces. The gradient of the beach – from the high-water mark to seawards will need to be tabulated. This can change, not only over the years but sometimes over just one tide. In very simple terms, the steeper the gradient – within reason – the drier the landing. The gradient may alter across the width of the beach, so that at low water, a dry landing may be possible, whereas at high water, a long, deep water gap may face the landing force. The opposite can also be true and thus this will affect the time of the landing.

Another consideration is that the water gap (by definition, the exposed area devoid of any form of cover from the bows of the beached landing craft, to comparative safety at the back of a beach), is considered one of the most dangerous places in warfare. If the beach is defended, then this is the fiercest of killing zones. It may be mined and will certainly be covered by small arms, artillery and mortar fire. All these latter factors will need to be reconnoitred, and at the appropriate time, dealt with. The shorter the water gap, the greater the chances of gaining that vital first foothold at the back of the beach. Only a physical reconnaissance by specialists trained in the art of beach reconnaissance can assess that.

There are really only two ways to gauge the gradient and underwater obstacles (plus any man-made obstacles to navigation for landing craft) such as shallow sand bars and, their opposite, deep runnels. The usual way for this to be conducted clandestinely, is by maritime Special Forces using a simple lead line and distance marker, or more often these days, using an automatic beach profile apparatus that is run along the sea bed, by a diver landed perhaps from a submarine. This produces an electronic graph (that can be transposed to a paper print-out back at base), recording distance and depth, and thus gradient. If this is to be assessed accurately, it will need to be measured at high water, with the surveyor remaining underwater for the whole operation. In extremis it has been known for a simple holiday maker to wade out while making an intelligent assessment of both gradient and the nature of the sea bed.

Another assessment that needs to be made at this stage is the 'trafficability' of the beach surface. Will it stand up to wheeled or tracked vehicles, without them becoming bogged, or will beach trackway need to be laid, from the estimated beaching point (underwater and well to seaward of the estimated tide-line) to where perhaps, a more stable surface can be expected? Trackway takes time (and heavy machinery) to deploy, and can only be laid after the assaulting troops have secured the area. Thus for instance, armour and artillery support (if the latter is not lifted ashore by heavy-lift helicopters), may well take some time before they are available. A more modern consideration may be found with the use of hovercraft, but these can be halted by deep shingle, as the supporting air cushion becomes absorbed. Apart from the US Navy's LCACs (Landing Craft Air Cushion) and the Russian Navy's Pomornik, Aist, and Lebed-class hovercraft, none can carry such heavy equipment. (Other navies have procured some LCACs and Pomorniks.)

While a simple chart recce can be conducted to assess the basic topographical and hydrographic features of a proposed beach, from which an assessment may be made on the likelihood of surf (its height, length and periodicity), a follow-up reconnaissance will be essential. Likewise, with tidal conditions and onshore currents, including any transverse currents especially along river banks. The phase of the moon and the attendant tidal times and states (neaps or springs), will need to be studied very carefully and at an early stage of planning, for they can seriously affect the timings of an amphibious assault. If tide tables are not available then timings can only be ascertained by observation.

What will not be gleaned from a chart in any worthwhile detail is the state of the seaweed or kelp – a possible serious hazard to the propellers of small craft. Likewise, the presence of krill, jellyfish or plankton has been known to clog the cooling water filters of even large warships. Advance warning of the likelihood of these nuisances will need to be given. Rivers have their own dangers that need to be tabulated. Tree trunks for instance, fishing nets, even abandoned motor cars littering the river bed, can bring to a halt the most finely planned landing.

A beach suitable for an assault (as opposed to a swift in-and-out raid) may not be suitable for follow-up operations. If any such operations are planned, then the beach must also be able to accept a 'beach support area' – for food, ammunition and general stores (in other words a logistics conduit through which material from afloat is assessed, sorted and despatched to the correct end-user). The beach support area should include 'drowned vehicle' parking and maintenance areas, water and fuel distribution points; a substantial parking area for passing vehicles, coupled to a strict, one-way track system, plus room for the differing headquarters as they come ashore to regroup, while preparing for their next phase. Keeping all this together will be a complicated communications network that speaks seaward, using naval radio circuits, as well as inland using the military tactical and logistical circuits.

Beaches can be, and have often been, used as decoys. The careful planting by Special Forces of say, a swimmer's swim fin, or an abandoned canoe, can instil doubt and confusion in the minds of the defenders. Care may be needed (depending on the level of deception required) to ensure that the discarded item would have found its way naturally, to its position.

Beacons to guide the approaching first wave of landing craft through unmarked offshore rocks and shoals may need to be placed during an advance-force operation, although this too, could compromise surprise.

Another consideration that will need to be aired is the approach to the 'amphibious operating area' and its subsequent defence. Factors that will need to be dovetailed and balanced, come under the following headings: cyber, air, surface and sub-surface. Cyber defence and offense, as the amphibious task force approaches the coast, will be familiar to any land commander, but to other considerations may be less so. It is an axiom that no amphibious landing should take place without the landing force having air superiority. Considering that the approaching force will need to rely on sea-based air power, while the defender may be able to call on a far larger air force operating from across the hinterland, air parity may be all that can be achieved.

A self-contained amphibious fleet can advance (or retire) well over 300 nautical miles in a day, and so can hide over the horizon with its intentions, and certainly its destination, unclear to a defender, unless surprise is compromised by the pre-landing beach reconnaissance. This speed of manoeuvre is an enviable advantage denied to land commanders, while the main disadvantages of an amphibious landing – its overall complications involved in planning plus an almost convoluted chain of command (and the necessary chop of command between naval and military leaders as the operation progresses ashore) – will be less envied.

While air superiority is a must, so is the equivalent at surface and sub-surface level, thus the list of supporting ships for an amphibious operation can be very large indeed. Of course it all depends on the scale of an operation that can vary from two men in a canoe, to a division in an amphibious battle fleet. Most amphibious countries can conduct the former, but only the United States can conduct the latter, while many of the more sophisticated navies should be able on paper, to land a brigade.

Either way, that fleet will need protecting and escorting. And then there are the all-important minesweepers who, it can be argued, are part of any advance force reconnaissance.

Finally there is the weather. Almost unlike any other phase of warfare, the weather plays a pivotal role in amphibious operations. No matter what recent recordings will show, nothing can take the place of eyes on the ground in advance, to gauge the actual conditions, before assessing them against the forecast conditions. Unlike land operations (with the exception perhaps of disruptively large falls of snow or flooding) the past weather at sea is more crucial than the past weather on land. By and large only a covert reconnaissance can make a true assessment. For instance, strong winds may have died but they will have left a swell that can affect beaches for days – indeed for weeks if the weather hundreds or so miles away, continues to remain 'dirty'. Heavy surf from a persistent swell can last long after a flat calm has set in. This can alter, quite considerably, a well-established beach profile. Weed and debris can be washed downriver from rains that perhaps are falling hundreds of miles away. This detritus – large enough to foul propellers and rudders – will be totally unpredicted and indeed, totally unpredictable. Only eyes on the ground will be able to warn the amphibious planners of such a wide range of natural phenomena. No wonder then, that amphibious operations have been described as being at the scholarship level of military operations.

Chapter 19

Swimmer Delivery Vehicles – A Résumé

First published in *Jane's Navy International*, 2008

It is perhaps not generally realised, that swimmer delivery vehicles (SDVs) have been in existence for almost exactly 100 years. It is also not always understood that SDVs themselves need to be delivered, and that they need not necessarily be submersibles. For example, canoes have often been carried by submarines, surface ships, flying boats and so on, before transporting limpet-armed frogmen on their final, underwater approach towards a target.

Proposals for a 'human torpedo' – indeed for a midget submarine – were first mooted in 1909 by a retired British naval commander. By the following year an early type of oxygen rebreather for the 'frogmen' was about to enter service, although its primary purpose was to aid escape from sunken submarines.

During the First World War, the Italian navy developed a vessel to carry an explosive charge by modifying a torpedo, using compressed air as the propulsion system. This offered 4 knots over ten miles, depending on sea conditions. At the end of October, 1918, one of these human chariots set out from Venice, embarked on board a torpedo boat, and headed for the port of Pula, now in Croatia. Strong currents and harbours defences jeopardised the journey, but the two-man crew of Major Rossetti and Sub Lieutenant Paolucci succeeded in attacking the Austro-Hungarian dreadnought *Viribus Unitis*, which sank the following morning. That same year the Italian navy extended one of its submarines by ten feet, to house ten swimmers, in an attempt to actually capture Pula itself.

During the interwar years a number of ideas proliferated, in by and large, those navies that operated conventional submarines were suggested and as often as not, discarded, but one that refused to die was the midget submarine itself. Although not designed specially as an SDV (it would drop heavy side-carried charges beneath targets), it was able to launch and recover swimmers.

In 1935, the Italians planned to retake Malta, using the same methods as those employed against the Austrians, but their thoughts were also turning to displacement – explosive motor boats which succeeded in attacking British ships in Souda Bay, Crete, in 1941 and were successful again with similar targets at Gibraltar, but failed against ships in Malta's Grand Harbour. However, an underwater attack was successful on 19 December 1941, when three two–man human torpedoes placed delayed action charges on the hulls of battleships HMS *Queen Elizabeth* and HMS *Valiant*, the destroyer HMS *Jervis* and the tanker *Sagona*, in the supposedly-safe harbour of Alexandria. The leader of this attack by the *maiali* was Lieutenant Captain de la Penne, who had been transported to the operational area by the submarine *Scire*. This daring and most successful operation caused British Prime Minister Winston Churchill to agitate: 'Please report what is being done to emulate the exploits of the Italians in Alexandria harbour and similar methods of this kind. One would have thought that we should have been in the lead'. The Italian navy had made an earlier attempt against Alexandria, but this was foiled when the submarine *Iride*, with frogmen and limpets (but no *maiali*) embarked, was bombed by a Royal Marines pilot.

Meanwhile, another Royal Marines officer had submitted to the Admiralty, in May 1941, a paper proposing the use of underwater canoes for carrying a single frogman, or in today's parlance, a single combat swimmer, but it was not until after this latest Italian attack and Churchill's demands, that Lieutenant Colonel Hasler's submission was unearthed, prior to him having been invited to develop similar British methods. The British army were carrying out a number of attacks using canoes, launched and recovered, by either motor gun/torpedo boats or surfaced submarines, but these were mainly for reconnaissance purposes, attacking land targets, or ships using limpets placed directly from the canoe – in other words not frogmen. It was this method that was employed by Hasler during his celebrated raid against blockade runners moored at Bordeaux in December 1942, when frogmen were not used. Following his escape, Hasler – amongst other devices – built in 1943, 'the Sleeping Beauty'- a true SDV, although described at the time as 'the most dangerous vessel in which he ever went to sea'.

The continuing development of wartime SDVs deserves – and has received – many books on the subject, but there we must leave the Second World War and move to the Cold War and the numerous minor campaigns that accompanied it. Between 1945 and the early 1990s, covert methods of obtaining information, of landing and recovering agents and of attacking legitimate targets, were practised by many nations in a continuing game of cat and mouse. Men and women were often inserted for whatever reason by parachute and more normal land-based covert or clandestine methods, but all the while, underwater methods were forging ahead, although the principle remained much the same as those from an earlier age. Insertion by submarine, whilst not fool proof, and demanding specialist training, was always a two-way passage – one thing that a parachute insertion is not. It is almost invariably more expensive, but far the most secure method.

For instance, the French navy in the early 1960s, operated the submarine FS *L'Astree* which boasted a 'locking-in' and 'locking-out' chamber – called the SAS – which was permanently secured above the casing and forward of the fin, but with an air lock into the submarine.

For many years, miniature or midget submarines (as they were known during the Second World War) were not used by NATO nations, who preferred to launch agents from conventional submarines, or if not, through the use of what became known as a 'swimmer delivery vehicle' or to the US, as a 'Seal delivery vehicle'.

Some nations used a submarine's torpedo tubes for the transfer of divers, but this was always considered a hazardous operation, although still in use by the German navy.

In the modern world, the need to deploy frogmen – combat swimmers – remains much as it always has been, namely for beach or littoral reconnaissance, for direct action against a specific target, and for the insertion and extraction of agents. All these, unlike the use of parachute or clandestine aircraft landings (shades of the SOE in the Second World War) are two-way journeys. Other uses of modern SDVs includes the US Navy's search for mines during the first Gulf War or the Swedish need to test their own defences against Russian infiltration or direct attack. Helicopters too have often been used to land and collect swimmers and inflatable craft. Aircraft are used to parachute, but not collect – one-way operations – although of course, a rendezvous with a surfaced vessel or submarine can be used for extraction.

Another consideration is 'wet or dry'. A 'wet' SDV has a far smaller profile than, for instance a mini submarine, which has a far greater range but a larger profile. Some modern German SDVs have been so small and portable that they were carried to a suitable launching point by a Land Rover equivalent, and recovered in a similar fashion.

Helicopters have been used to launch swimmers and indeed small SDVs, but these are not considered the best form of transport, although the range is helpful. Attempts have been made to parachute SDVs – again in one-way operations – but on one occasion there was a malfunction and the SDV was destroyed when it landed in a field.

Many ships – including merchant ships and fishing vessels – can be used to transport the SDV itself, or under certain circumstances, when the distances are small, have launched frogmen direct into the water from underwater 'doors'.

Four Upholder-class submarines (diesel electric propulsion but nuclear style teardrop shaped hulls) were in UK service between 1990 and 1994 and operated with the SBS's combat swimmers, who exited and entered via a five-man chamber in the glass-fibre fin.

Meanwhile many nations have some form of swimmer delivery vehicles, so it might be useful to take a look at who has what and, in some cases, make an educated guess as to why. Many more countries than those listed below, operate combat swimmers but deliver them over very short distances from conventional surface ships.

Argentina operates two, two-man CE2F chariots astride which the crew sit, and there are even reports of ten, four-man submarines. The Argentinian navy's two Santa Cruz-class SSKs can also deliver combat swimmers when surfaced, as well as conventional commandos using inflatable craft.

Brazil operates five conventional submarines, from which it might be assumed some entry/re-entry training may well have been conducted by the navy's Combat Divers Group – GROUMEC – who train with both the US SEALs and the French navy's *nageurs de combat* course.

Although Canada bought four of the Royal Navy's Upholder-class diesel electric submarines, it is not believed that the five man lock-in/lock out chamber was retained for the country's clearance divers, who also have a maritime counter-terrorism role.

Chile operates some French Havas Mk 8, two-man SDVs but these are not transportable by the four conventional submarines in service and thus have a very limited operating radius unless transported by conventional surface vessels.

For its size the Colombian navy has a potent underwater delivery capability for it operates not only an unknown number of two-man chariots but also two 70-ton midget submarines, each cable of also carrying eight combat swimmers to an operational area but, if distances are greater, two SDVs. The surface range of the submarines is 1,200 miles (60 miles when dived) which brings its neighbours on the South American continent and those in near-by central America well within reach.

Croatia has always been of interest for it builds its own SDVs and particularly the free-flooding R-2 Mala-class which, although it does not strictly deliver swimmers, is manned by swimmers who can deliver 250kg of limpets to a target area. With a range of 23 miles at cruising speed (distances differ depending on the source), this would well cover neighbouring countries to the south.

The R-1 is a more conventional form of chariot, with a range of just 4 miles but is easily transported on a landing craft or any seemingly innocent civilian vessel, as well as off a beach having been carried in a lorry.

Croatia also builds and operates the Una-class midget submarine with a payload of six combat swimmers (there is a lock-in/lock-out chamber) and up to four R-1 SDVs over a 200 nautical miles range at 4 knots. There are, though, reports that this boat is no longer in service.

Cuba's combat divers are delivered and recovered by Zodiac and a collection of fishing vessel, yachts and motor boats.

Denmark's Frogman Corps (*Frømandskorpsets*) combat swimmers are also delivered and recovered by a motley collection of assorted craft while the Klepper canoe is still used as a surface SDV.

Egypt operates a number of CF2 FX but has to deploy them using four Seafox type surface SDVs each with a range of 200 nautical miles at 20 knots. As these craft displace 11.3 tons when fully laden it might be expected that for a distant target either in the eastern Mediterranean or along the Red Sea littoral these can probably be lifted by larger surface ships.

El Salvador's naval combat swimmers have no SDVs or submarines although the two high-speed insertion craft in service may well be used for night-time delivery and extraction.

France's *Commando Hubert* supplies the country's combat swimmers (*combatant nageurs*) who use a 220-ton diving tender which can transport two SDVs. Of necessity the range is limited.

During the Cold War, West Germany possessed an unknown number of two-man SDVs which are known to have been transported by road to beaches in the east for surveillance operations. The navy now operates one Orca-class dry SDV designed to carry out a number of tasks such as visual and sensor reconnaissance, intelligence gathering and anti-mine operations. When delivering up to five combat swimmers over a 150 nautical mile range, these exit via a locking-in/out compartment with access to both the top and bottom of the SDV.

Otherwise Germany's combat swimmers from the Combat Diver Group – *Kampfshwimmerkompanie* – are inserted into the operating area via the torpedo tubes of conventional submarines or by canoe. A delivery method frowned upon by some navies.

The combat swimmers of the Greek navy, the *Batrahantropoi* (frogmen) – is the navy's special warfare unit and is also called the Underwater Demolition Command, (DYK). They deploy via the torpedo tubes of the nine submarines, and an unknown number of Cosmos CE2F/x100T two-man chariots, although these men can also be carried (presumably under cover of darkness) in Zodiac 470 inflatable boats and the high-speed insertion craft. No doubt helicopters are also used across the Aegean Sea and among the islands to the east.

The Indian navy's eleven CE2F/X100 are operated by combat swimmers of the Marine Commando Force who are also trained to parachute into the sea.

Indonesia has two units of combat swimmers: the navy's detachment *Jala Mengkara* and a SEAL-type unit known as the *Kesatuan Gurita*, but there is no indication how they are transported to an operational zone, other than, perhaps, by helicopter or surface ship. The two Cakra-class, Type 209 submarines are not thought to be swimmer-capable but have been known to launch inflatable craft while on the surface.

Iran possesses a plethora of locally built SDVs, coastal submarines, submersibles and semi-submersibles that can carry torpedoes and/or swimmers as well as mines – limpet and laid. It might, perhaps, be awkward to suggest why these are all necessary but recent events involving Iraq and the islands at the entrance to the Gulf might offer a pointer.

The two Nahang-class coastal submarines are designed for shallow water operations and as mother ships to SDVs, three of which are operational. The 8-metre Al Sabehat 15 SDV – of which there are believed to be two – can each carry a two-man crew and three combat swimmers and are well suited to coastal reconnaissance, Special Forces insertion and mining (it can carry fourteen limpet mines). A second class of SDV has been spotted, but apart from a photograph there are no further details.

Two classes of semi-submersibles are believed to be operational – or nearly so – with both offering a high speed surface approach followed by a slow, stealthy, underwater terminal approach to the target. Two 30-ton (estimated) 68.9ft, Kajami-class were delivered to Iran from North Korea in December 2002. The 50-knot, surface approach precedes a three-metre depth, submerged passage towards the target using a snort mast – which in the relatively calm waters of the Gulf could compromise stealth. Although they each carry two light torpedoes it is thought that they can also deliver and collect combat swimmers although they may have to surface very briefly to do so.

Three Gahjae-class, seven ton, 49.2ft, semi-submersibles are in service. These 50-knot (estimated) North Korean craft – also delivered in 2002 – use a snort mast for the terminal approach to the target under the same operating conditions as the Kajami-class.

It is quite possible that the Iranians use their small hovercraft as surface SDVs: in theory, the six larger, 70-knot, Wellington-class could certainly handle the smaller SDV and with a range of 620 nautical miles at 66 knots, every Gulf country is within range of a fast insertion and extraction.

Israel's three Dolphin-class, Type 800 submarines each have a wet and dry container for use by their Underwater Company of combat swimmers and with a submerged range of 420 nautical miles all potential targets are accessible. No conventional SDVs are reported but much of what happens in this line and in that country is hidden.

Underwater warfare has long been an Italian speciality with their Special Forces continuing to pave the way. The Italian company COSMOS manufactures both SDVs – of the human chariot type – and Shallow Water Attack Submarine (SWAT) – the X 201 – that carry up to twelve combat swimmers. The X 201 supersedes the MG-120/ER-class and with a 200 ton submerged displacement is small and not easily detected. It also has the ability to crawl along the seabed.

The Cosmos chariot CE2F/X100 is a development of Italy's wartime *maiali* with which it retains a near- similar silhouette and is in service with a number of navies worldwide. The 'chariot' is a sturdy, two-man, wet submersible designed to navigate undetected in hostile waters. Because of their endurance they are normally transported to within their operating range by a parent ship such as a patrol submarine, helicopter or innocent-seeming fishing vessel. It carries two combat divers to their target, be it harbour, oil rig, or even coastal installation.

Jordan's small but effective Underwater Swimming Unit is believed to use surface vessels – four 17ft and four 14ft GRP boats – for insertion and recovery, presumably at night.

Montenegro's 82nd Combat Divers Unit (if it still exist following the break-up of the Federal Republic of Yugoslavia) deploys six swimmers at a time from the three Una-class midget submarines – with their submerged exit and re-entry chamber – which themselves can deploy four SDVs of the R-1 type. The two R-2 Mala-class SDVs have a range of 23 miles at 3.7 knots and thus in range of Montenegro's neighbours and particularly Croatia to the north.

North Korea probably possesses the largest number of midget submarines and SDVs. Twenty-three (plus ten in reserve) midget submarines of the 110-ton

Yugo and P-class are declared operational and have been used against South Korean targets. These are ideal submarines for the SDV role, able to swim combat divers in and out, with the conning tower (fin) acting as the wet/dry chamber. Because their submerged range is only 50 miles at 4 knots they are often carried to operational areas in one of eight dedicated ocean-going cargo (mother) ships.

The thirty-two 277-ton Sang O-class submarines can carry six combat swimmers each with them able to enter and leave the boat at periscope depth. With their 2,700 mile range at 7 knots these boats are used extensively for infiltration operations.

Coupled with the submarines employed as SDVs there are also about fifty two-man submersibles of Italian design but smaller – at 4.9 metres – than the more usual chariot. Additionally North Korea operates at least two classes of High Speed Interceptor Craft (HSIC), all of which are designed to carry combat swimmers. These infiltration craft are often transported to their operating area by a mother craft of between 50 and 100 tons posing as a fishing vessel. The HSIC (acting as a surface SDV) is usually launched about 25 to 50 miles off a coast and when within 100 to 200 metres of the shore swimming escorts for the inserting agent guide him to the beach. The reverse is true for collecting an agent with all traces removed. The 5-ton Cluster Osprey-class HSIC is believed to be submersible as is the newer 10-ton HSIC. It is thought that these have a top speed of 50 knots and are able to submerge to three metres using a snort mast with a top speed of between 4 and 6 knots. They carry four crew, two escorts and two infiltrators.

Finally, North Korea possesses up to 136 Kongbang-class of hovercraft that are certainly capable of inserting and collecting combat swimmers and could well work in concert with the midget submarines.

South Korea is not so well endowed as its northern neighbour with swimmer delivery vessels, submerged or surface, although the list is still impressive with eleven KSS-1 Dolgorae and nine Dolphin-class midget submarines all capable of delivering eight naval combat swimmers. There are no reports of smaller, more conventional SDVs.

There are unconfirmed reports that Lebanon operates six Yugoslav Mala-class SDVs.

Malaysia possesses an unknown number of SDVs – probably of the chariot type – for use by the Special Sea Unit of the *Pasukan Khas Laut* (PASKAL).

The Netherlands is in the forefront of underwater operations in close alliance with the UK's Special Boat Service (SBS). The 2,800-ton Walrus-class SSKs are each capable of inserting and collecting combat swimmers of the 7NL SBS. No conventional SDVs are reported but personnel do operate with their UK counterparts.

Norway operates six Ula-class SSKs which, while submerged, are capable of delivering and collecting combat swimmers of the *Marinjager* through the torpedo tubes – a method frowned upon by some other Special Forces; two men were lost in the 1980s using this method.

The Royal Navy of Oman operates some French-built Havas Mk 8 two-man SDVs.

Pakistan is another major player in the underwater-delivery business, with its three midget submarines each capable of carrying eight combat swimmers, and an unknown number of Italian CE2F/X100T chariots, all of which can be ranged against India or Iran without a larger level of SDV.

Poland's *Sekcje Dzialan Specjalnych* – SDS MW – a small, maritime special operations unit operates at sea, in coastal areas, rivers and lakes. The Baltic is generally too shallow for the Sokõl and Kilo-classes to deliver combat swimmers. Elsewhere, without SDVs, swimmers will be delivered by land transport.

Portugal, despite possessing sophisticated maritime Special Forces in the form of the *Destacamento de Acções Especaism* (DAE) there is no known method for subsurface delivery.

The Russian Federation operates an unknown number of locally-built Sirena-UM manned torpedoes (chariots) and an unknown number of Yugoslav-built R–2 Mala. Reports suggest that the former can be launched through a submarine's 533mm torpedo tube. Russian forces almost certainly are able to use helicopters to launch and possibly recover the Sirena SDVs. Other SDV delivery systems may well include the Pomornik and Aist-class hovercraft (ACVs). Maritime special forces likely to be involved in such operations are the three Spetsnaz – *Spetsialnogo naznacheniya* – Special Force brigades each of 1,300 personnel which includes one Swimmer and one Midget Submarine Battalion. The SDVs can be transported globally in any number of suitable – usually amphibious – ships.

Saudi Arabia now has naval commandos but no dedicated method of deploying them sub-surface. Nevertheless, distances likely to be involved are short and so they can be inserted and recovered, by for instance, the thirty-nine Special Forces craft of the Simmoneau type.

Although Singapore possesses two Naval Diving Units there are no SDVS reported and it is not believed that the submarines in service can deploy combat swimmers. The most likely surface SDVs are the six Fast Intercept-class with their 55 knot-plus speed, that are known to operate with the Diving Units. Such a delivery and collection was the normal method used by, for instance, the UK's SBS for many years – and still is under certain circumstances.

The Spanish navy's Special Combat Divers Unit (*Unidad Especial de Buceadores de Combate*) are not transported by conventional SDVs although at least one of the four Galerna-class submarines is capable of being fitted with a dry deck shelter. Currently, there are no further details and so it is assumed that combat divers are inserted and extracted by helicopter close to the operational area or by, quite possibly, by the VCA-36 hovercraft.

Sweden's maritime Special Forces have been in the forefront of such operations since the earliest days of the Cold War when the possibility of Russian incursions across the Baltic were a real and demonstrated threat. While Sweden had no plans to attack, DSVs and similar underwater vehicles were procured to test their own defences. Now their equipment is more offensive in nature and includes one midget submarine for use as an ASW target and a number of one and two man versions of the R-2 SDV operated by the Amphibious Corps The two Söndermanland-class SSKs have a lock-in/lock-out chamber at the base of the fins. It is also reported that the three Gotland-class SSKs operate with combat divers but no chambers are mentioned. Other methods of delivering combat swimmers will include the various classes of Combat Boat 90, the Gruppbat raiding craft and Griffon medium-lift hovercraft.

Thailand's naval SEAL teams are believed to operate the UK-manufactured SSK 96 Subskimmer, which approaches the target area at 20 knots and on the surface, before converting to submersible mode.

It is not known how Turkey's underwater, attack swimmers approach their target, but it is not by conventional SDV and thus more likely to be in the 50-knot-plus fast insertion craft.

The United Arab Emirates have in recent years, expanded and modernised their underwater capability to be one of the more sophisticated. Their potential targets are close and not entirely un-surprising as various islands are disputed with Iran who occupies a number of them. The Dubai Commando Squadron includes a diving team while the Special Operations Group of combat swimmers are equipped with at least ten locally designed and manufactured class 4 and class 5 long-range submersible carriers.

These are sophisticated vessels with on board computers, sonars with a range of 150m (492ft), GPS and other navigational aids. Both classes carry a crew of two divers, can cruise at 8 knots to a range of 60 nautical miles and operate down to 50m (164ft). Class 5 craft are the larger of the two with a payload of one ton.

Following the Italian successes in the Second World War, the United Kingdom moved to the forefront of specialist diving and associated underwater operations. Although there was a lull during the early days of the Cold War various one-man and two-man SDVs were designed and procured in the 1960s and 1970s. These were mainly of the human tug/chariot variety until the procurement in the late 1990s of three American Mk VIII Mod 1 SDVs after extensive trials in the Norwegian Arctic in the mid-1980s. These battery-powered vessels have a range of about 67km (35 nautical miles) and can carry six fully equipped combat swimmers in its fully flooded compartments.

When the Swiftsure-class of SSN was in commission a dry deck shelter was fitted to HMS *Spartan* under the name Project Chalfont. This was discontinued amid fears that the Astute-class when in service in 2008 would not be similarly fitted but the decision has been made to rekindle the project. Meanwhile one of the more enduring methods of inserting and recovering combat swimmers remains extant and which had been perfected during covert operations in the Second World War. Under cover of darkness the submarine surfaces, rubber craft are brought onto the casing, swiftly inflated and, with a team of combat swimmers embarked, the submarine submerges allowing the craft to float off. Time on the surface can be as little as three minutes.

Swimmers are also parachuted with or without their uninflated craft or they can be launched and recovered by submarine. The Chinook is able to launch and recover craft direct from the sea's surface. A number of other methods are used. The Royal Marines' SBS swimmers are well-practised in locking in and out of submerged submarines.

The 2,300 personnel in United States SEAL teams operate with 14 Mk VIII Mod 1 SDVs which can be carried in a dry deck shelter (DDS) fitted to some of the Ohio, Seawolf and Los Angeles-classes. The Ohio-class in particular can deliver sixty-six combat swimmers via specially adapted torpedo tubes.

The DDS was developed to fit on submarines for the carriage of SDVs and for the locking in and out of swimmers. The submarines are equipped with special fittings with modifications to their air systems, permitting the passage of swimmers between the hull and the DDS while submerged, and then to exit the DDS in the SDV. The air-transportable DDS can be installed on distant submarines in about twelve hours. SEALs also deploy by surface craft and parachute.

The newest design is for an Advanced Swimmer Delivery System (ASDS), which is a dry submersible, powered by electricity capable of deploying from a mother submarine such as the Virginia-class. 60ft x 10ft (18m x 3m), with a crew of two and space for eight SEALs. The range of an ASDS is 125 nautical miles at 8 knots, using a 55hp motor and four thrusters. This craft can also be carried by C-5 and C-17 aircraft.

The Vietnamese navy operates two Yugo-class midget submarines procured from North Korea, almost solely for combat swimmer operations. The six divers lock in and out through a chamber contained within the fin.

To conclude this brief résumé of which countries can deliver and recover its combat swimmers, it is clear that SDVs are considered a necessity, and although not cheap compared with surface or airborne methods, it is the more secure way to land and recover agents. Combat swimmers and their SDVs are also most suitable for ship attack and beach or harbour reconnaissance, as these operations can be conducted totally submerged. Despite modern detection systems, the sub-surface arena still has many advantages to offer and possibly, apart from cost, rather fewer disadvantages. If targets are close a simple submersible 'canoe' will often do the trick, and thus we are back to those basic ideas formulated over fifty years ago and that have stood the test of time.

Chapter 20

Situation Reports from the Former Republic of Yugoslavia, 1993–1994

SITREP TO HQ, Royal Marines, Whitehall

By 15 December 1993, while serving with the European Community Monitoring Mission (ECMM) in the Former Republic of Yugoslavia, I felt I had experienced enough to write twelve pages of A4 paper to my first cousin, Robert Tailyour, then a brigadier on the staff of the Commandant General Royal Marines:

Nothing in 32 years in the Royal Marines can prepare one for this place.

I am in a town called Knin, the so-called capital of the so-called Republic of Serbian Krajina or RSK. When Yugoslavia began breaking up, Croatia was formed but this land also contained a much older state of Krajina, which illegally, but understandably, then declared independence.

In the RSK, the ECMM is seen as a spying organisation in the pay of the Germans, largely because Germany supported Croat independence and also because we are all believed to be German! Nor are we liked, because the EU does not insist in supporting the arms embargo, not just against Croatia but all the others as well. Many Croat arms and much equipment is German in origin and, more worryingly, many Croat soldiers also wear Nazi emblems on their uniforms.

But neither is the ECMM respected in Croatia, because we did nothing to prevent the formation of the RSK within what the Croats regard as Croat territory. The fact that the Krajina has existed for 500 years as a race of people is ignored by the Croats.

From my brief involvement so far, the ECMM seems to be doing an excellent and invaluable job. For a start, it was the first international agency to be involved and all the monitors come from Europe, therefore there is no USA involvement and this pleases all sides as far as I can make out. We monitor the political scene at all levels and report back each day, eventually, to Brussels. In theory!

In addition, we monitor military movements in order to help the brokering of local ceasefires. We can cross borders and unlike UNPROFOR are actually seen to be absolutely neutral for we are involved on both sides of the border.

Although the RSK has declared independence from Croatia, it does not yet want to be part of a larger Serbia, Croatia does not like this because the RSK owns the water supply (therefore, the electricity) and has cut the north–south railway line. Croatia on the other hand, has the ports and outlets to international trade. The stupid thing is that both countries need each other for trade. Neither can exist in isolation. One of our other jobs is to repatriate the dead and prisoners of war across the border.

Political awareness is limited. Serbs with money, experience and an understanding of international politics have left for foreign countries, leaving the RSK with few educated people. This does not help in our daily talks.

I am writing this in the middle of a thunderstorm by candlelight in a half-built motel on the outskirts of Knin.

All international bodies are treated with suspicion and are blamed for the situation:

The ECMM for being spies.

The UNPROFOR for having no teeth.

The International Committee of the Red Cross for being too selective in its work.

The United Nations High Commission for Refugees for being too selective in its distribution of aid.

None of this is true of course, but tell that to a Croat or a Serb. Apart from the British monitors, most of the rest are civilians or serving military personnel and are here for a year. Consequently, not many of them have their heart in the job so the attitude is far too often 'it is impossible'. I'm used to saying let's give it a try but one French marine officer and one Belgian warrant officer in my team will find every excuse not to go on a patrol. They will be glad when I move away to the coast next week.

Our daily work starts about 0600 with a briefing. Then we are on the road visiting local hamlets with those very few Croats who still live in them, making sure they have not been massacred by the RSK. We carry French tin hats and flak jackets as every day there are cross-border shellings on to civilian villages. For instance, 1000 artillery rounds were fired into Croatia the day before yesterday, then 70 rounds came back during a three pronged attack into the RSK in our area. This includes the RSK shelling of a school deep in Croatia to show just how far they can reach.

There is far too much hatred on all sides, each country proclaiming itself to be whiter than white but they are all as black as black as far as I am concerned. I have personally seen ethnic cleansing on both sides and hear of horrifying atrocities. We are vulnerable and unarmed. Yesterday two of our Land Rovers were shot at, each by about 15 high velocity rounds. Each night there is shooting around our hotel, but usually just drunken, immature soldiers.

Next week I will move to the coast where the ECMM has a number of teams. In Split I will be working with a Belgian monitor. One of our jobs will be to negotiate a new border crossing point in the south of the RSK, so that aid and food for ECMM and UNPROFOR can get into the RSK more easily. I don't hold out much for our chances or the route. Both being mined on all sides … Other tasks will be to help the EU decide where money for the regeneration will best be spent.

My other job, I have been told by the SIS (nothing to do with the ECMM or the FCO) is to keep an eye on the Algerian and Iranian influence in the port of Split. They (along with the US and Germany who are helping Croatia) are believed to be breaking the embargo by supplying logistic support to the Muslims in Bosnia. I shall also be monitoring the political and economic positions in the ports and on the islands.

I have conducted a covert beach reconnaissance on the edge of a 'lake' in the Republic of Serbian Krajina, which is linked to the Med through other lakes held by Croatia. Beach surveys take on a different meaning with armed, United Nations civilian policemen watching my every move—an Argentine would you believe! I had a very long pee off the beach into the lake and so managed a three page special report for DI4. Fascinating stuff!

To sum up, I am seeing things here I hope never to see again and meeting people I sincerely hope never to meet again but that is why we are here and, I believe, doing a most worthwhile job. But thank God for all my Royal Marines training and experience.

SITREP TO THE FCO

I thought it useful (although not required as I officially reported to the ECMM's HQ in Zagreb) to send a Situation Report of my first impressions to the FCO's Eastern Adriatic Unit (EAU) at King Charles Street. My letter of 4 February 1994 reads in part:

In common, probably with everyone else posted to former Yugoslavia, I was amazed at the length and breadth of the problem. In this current day and age, when most people are able to accept differences in order to live in peace, the hatred quite openly expressed and shown between the people of both sides (Croat and Serb) is horrifying.

It is always difficult for a newcomer to understand exactly what it is he is supposed to be achieving, and in the case of the Former Republic of Yugoslavia there are certainly a number of anomalies which do not help in this respect: the very quick turn round of monitors; the personal standard and commitment of some who are only here because they have been sent by their respective services to grow up is an example. My first team, from whom supposedly I was to learn the ropes, were very moderate indeed, with no active service experience, although the Frenchman always insisted he was trained to kill and not to monitor. Their only aims were to telephone their wives the moment we entered the Land Rover, distribute aid, then get home as quickly as possible.... Thank goodness for the FCO's vetting system and the fact that we (the UK monitors) are all volunteers, having retired following much foreign service and operational experience.

Some monitors, usually at the beginning of a presidency, are appointed with no experience at all into key positions. The case of the new HCC (Head of the Coordinating Centre) in Zadar (a Greek naval officer clearly with a very different and hidden brief) started with no understanding of the problems at all, and he was replacing an experienced British monitor.

Now for some constructive comments and observations: one thing that has become apparent to me in the RSK is that there are few if any people left with any understanding of international politics and relationships. On arrival in Split I found this to be just as relevant for Croatia.

Money = higher education = political awareness = an understanding of international affairs and interactions between neighbouring states. People with money on both sides have all left. Hence the dearth of sensible politicians able to know when to give a little. They do not have the diplomatic experience to know when to stop taking, to stop demanding...and to start listening.

On the coast a different style of monitoring is required from that in the RSK and I would sum up our work as follows:

Political monitoring with a view to helping international politicians and diplomats reach a negotiated settlement on the Krajina issue. This may expand if Dubrovnik comes under real threat again.

Economic monitoring in order to prepare the rebuilding of Croatia through the assistance of the European Union when the war comes to an end, and help the implementing of economic confidence building measures.

Humanitarian monitoring in order to orientate and coordinate and not to handle directly such aspects as the exchange of prisoners of war, the dead, and the reuniting of families.

While the present system of monitoring is well-established I believe that for some monitoring it is likely that we will achieve better results if we were not always dressed in white. I have noticed in intangible ways that when we walk into an office it is the uniform that often puts people on their guard. Because nobody on either side will ever believe that we are here for their own benefit I see this as a hindrance. People who are unwilling to talk to us in uniform are happy to dine with us in the hotel during which we can talk as equals with a consequent benefit to both sides, but this is an expensive, time-consuming, and sometimes invidious way of doing business.

This throws up two anomalies – probably more relevant on the coast... In Split I believe that it would make more sense for monitors to have a background in economics and politics – and perhaps even commerce. Not only would this ensure a higher standard of monitoring, but would provide a more professional image among those whom we monitor. The second, but allied, aspect is that monitors, particularly those away from the war, should spend as long as possible in their area. Political and economic monitoring only becomes useful after a lengthy study of an area's political and economic backing and filling.

However, as I am neither a politician nor an economist I have devised a style of monitoring on the coast that, I hope, hides these deficiencies in my background. I have developed a technique whereby I ask very few, if any, questions and treat the person to whom I am talking as a friend whom I wish to get to know better, and, through him, his country. An example was on the island of Brač, where I started by discussing whether or not I could get my yacht alongside the town quay. At the end of a fascinating morning I probably knew more about the island's problems than most of the islanders and was able to put them into a proper perspective.

One final thought. There has been a move by the Greeks to have the whole of the Dalmatian coastline under one Regional Centre. This is now the case as far as Ploče is concerned. However, for reasons to do with the war in Bosnia it has not been accepted by some that the Dubrovnik area should be monitored by those on the coast. This is not understood. Dubrovnik is the jewel in the

Dalmatian crown, and while it is accepted that, inter alia, aid moves inland from the area south of Ploče, where the Bosnian border reaches the sea (thus effectively cutting the coastline in half), the current monitors in that area do not, and I suggest cannot, cover the area of Dubrovnik at the same time. The monitors themselves admit that they are only interested in looking eastwards along the convoy routes. This cannot be in Dubrovnik's long-term interests. The whole of the coastline is linked, despite being cut in half, through common policies on tourism, fishing and canning, cement production, light industry, such as the plastic factories and the ladies underwear factories. Internal Croat trade takes place either by sea along the coast or, in penny packets, along the coast road. One inland Regional Centre can, if necessary, cover the humanitarian work in the port area, undisturbed by the monitoring team from another coastal regional centre covering economic and political aspects. My suggestion would be to downgrade the Regional Centre at Knin (but for local presentation purposes call it something important) turn Zadar into the coastal Regional Centre with (going south) a Coordinating Centre at Split with three teams covering the north as far Šibenik, the centre around Ploče and the south covering Dubrovnik. As I may have mentioned, there's been talk of Dubrovnik becoming an independent state with a status similar to, for instance, Monte Carlo.

On 9 February I received the following reply:

Thank you very much for your honest, and perceptive, letter of 4 February. Your comments, particularly those relating to the sense of hatred amongst the parties and the calibre of (some of) your colleagues chime loudly with my own impressions. Your letter indicating the sense of reward, often achieved at an unexpected moment as in your account on the island of Brač, is deeply satisfying.

Your comments about the isolation of RSK politicians are, sadly, very apposite. I hear similar sentiments about local politicians from other monitors working elsewhere in the Former Yugoslavia. Each monitor needs to find his depth and judge how best to swim the tide. I'm not surprised that your own particular technique has proved to be successful. One of the drawbacks of the professional technocrat – and I speak as a professional economist – is that they tend to go in with far too many direct questions at the outset. For the ECMM this has led to particular problems. As you will know from first-hand experience, attempts by ECMM to glean economic information have often been misinterpreted by the host as interference in internal affairs, or worse. The roundabout approach is often more effective.

I have much sympathy for your comments about the division of Regional Centre responsibilities along the Croat coast. A letter I have recently seen from the Mayor of Dubrovnik is clear that the community there is determined to pursue their immediate interest in an imaginative manner. But the issue is complicated by the schizophrenic attitude of the Croatians towards the ECMM. Croatia must accept that the ECMM's efforts to evaluate the economic situation and the potential of particular areas does require the country's cooperation.

With events beginning to alter swiftly, once I had moved from the RSK to Croatia's Dalmatian coast, I thought it high time that I updated the FCO's Eastern Adriatic Unit on the changing situation. On 10 March 1995, I wrote:

*As you know, I am now running Team Split, which seems to oscillate between two teams and one team with a movable number of monitors. The latest news is that we could now be divided up with one team based in Šibenik (*pace *the latest dictum), and the other team remaining here with responsibility for the area to the south-east. I am not sure that the ECMM quite realises the importance of the area for the future – but there we are.*

I met General Mike Rose yesterday who says he thinks he will be out of a job by August! My view that Croat troops can be released from Bosnia which will allow Croatia to reclaim, by force and damn the consequences, the Krajinas. Another possibility is that if peace can be brokered and the United Nations presence is no longer needed, they will be at liberty to get at each other's throats without interference. An extreme view, perhaps, but you will know better than I that nothing is ever stabilised here or, apparently, long-term.

There is more and more talk of Croatia being peace loving (compared to everyone else) but that the Krajinas are 'altogether something different'. This argument, they say, should have the backing of the world as it has recognised the legality of the Croat state as a sovereign nation inferring, naturally, that the RSK are terrorists for conducting an illegal 'occupation' of a properly constituted territory. (Nothing new here). I think that the war will be like nothing we have seen yet in my view. Fighting is inevitable and could start before the summer.[Again, I was early by almost exactly one year with my prediction.] *I notice almost every day an increasingly belligerent attitude towards the RSK and a rising anger at Europe's lack of support for its return to Croat rule. (Nothing new here either.)*

We have an identity problem on the coast which we have been working hard to reverse. Team Split is seen as a holiday camp and quite openly referred to as such among many and not helped by last summer's monitors being reported in the local press for spending too much of their time by the pool. This seems to manifest itself currently in a real lack of interest in the work we are trying to achieve. My staff paper (you were sent a copy) on the future of Team Split was an attempt to explain to the ECMM that the coast is central to any financial recovery and will be one of the most important places as far as regeneration is concerned, let alone any war. We find it difficult to get anyone to take the Split area seriously and I fear it is almost all due to the image it has held in the past. We have explained that we are serious monitors here to do a serious job in the second-largest Croat city that will be at the hub of economic growth. Their only answer is to reduce us by one monitor in advance of a natural reduction due to annual holidays leaving us with, on occasions, just one monitor.

The humanitarian problems are escalating with the lack of a dedicated humanitarian monitor in Split being badly felt. ECMM's policy towards, for example, the illegal occupation of private flats by the JNA oscillates considerably: the new HRC Knin, Jean-Pierre Thébault, has just reversed earlier appointments making steady monitoring a difficult task. This backing and filling, while accompanied by the quite unnecessary turn round of monitors, gives the Croat authorities here the impression of an unstable and unsteady organisation.

The SIS is well aware of my views on these matters, and while they might give the impression of constructive criticisms they are merely points that we are working on.

All 'sides' are subject to UN Arms Embargo 713 but some European nations, that should be jointly enforcing them, are themselves breaking them to support their various favourite or aligned, Balkan states. Very puzzling that the very embargoes we – a cross section of European monitors – are supposed to be monitoring are being broken by the countries we represent: except, as far as I can make out, the UK plus just one or two others. The main criminals in this respect seem to be the US, Italy, Germany, France and Greece plus of course some Middle East and North African countries such as Algeria and Iran – and Russia.

My contact in the FCO's East Adriatic Unit was kind enough to reply on 14 March:

Thank you very much for your letter of 10 March and the enclosed reports, which I read with interest. I have passed some onto the British Embassy in Zagreb.

I was interested in your comment about the belligerent attitudes of local Croats towards the RSK. As I understand it Split has long had a reputation for being a centre of hard-line Croat nationalism. Given that it is the area most directly threatened – both militarily and economically – an uncompromising stance is, perhaps, to be expected. Nonetheless, I wonder whether the fervour to reclaim the RSK by force is shared by the mainstream politicians in Zagreb. The indications are that moderates are in the ascendancy within the Zagreb government.

Your letter raises the question whether the RSK could be taken by force. When I was in Zagreb, the consensus was that the Croats could achieve only limited military objectives of a priority nature, like recapturing the Zagreb-Belgrade highway. Talk of resolving the RSK crisis militarily was brushed aside as unrealistic. The coastal region, of course, has a large number of displaced personnel who can only talk tough about regaining their birth right but I wonder whether such sentiments run so deep elsewhere in Croatia.

You are absolutely right about the Dalmatian coast's economic importance. I therefore understand your frustration at the lack of priority accorded to the area by the ECMM. You are clearly doing everything possible to redress the image problem. Jean-Pierre Thébault is not the easiest of men to work with but he has a reputation for defending his patch vigorously. I hope this will help your efforts to convince the ECMM headquarters that they should not neglect the Split area.

Sadly the EAU's assessments for any future conflict were not to be as the events of August 1995 were to demonstrate when, during Operation Storm, Croatia, supported, supplied and encouraged by the United States and Germany – among others – invaded the RSK and ethnically cleansed the whole Serb population from their 400-year-old homeland.

On 6 August, Jon Swain encapsulated the drama in a few simple headlines. In bold letters across the front page of *The Sunday Times*, he said:

BLITZGREIG IN THE FALKLANDS Tudjman's War. SERBS PANIC AS REARMED CROATS CAPTURE KNIN.

Finally, Jane's Information Group's Foreign Report, dated 21 September 1995, was headed:

CROATS TRY ETHNIC CLEANSING, before going on to say: *but their recent victories will cause nightmares for years to come.* The article then begins: *Once it was a defiant assertion of Serb power in Croatia: a large slab of controlled land protected – up to a point – by the United Nations. Now the Krajina is a wasteland. By one reckoning, man's inhumanity to man has left 95 per cent of the houses there in ruins, burnt and looted.*

Chapter 21

Captain Dragan of Serbia

Between 1993 and 1994 I was employed by the Foreign and Commonwealth Office as a European Monitor in the Former Republic of Yugoslavia, and to begin with, was posted to the Mission's regional headquarters based in Knin, the capital of the 'breakaway' state of the Republic of Serbian Krajina (RSK). Here I describe a meeting with Serbia's enigmatic Captain Dragan in his camp overlooking Croatian's Dalmatian coast:

> *Over the preceding days I had heard the name of a Serb army officer mentioned a number of times by other monitors, and whenever his name cropped up the interpretresses would, theatrically, pretend to swoon. However the answers to my questions had been vague. Nobody had ever actually met him, although some had occasionally pointed to a far hill overlooking the coastal plain while explaining that 'over there' is where he has his training camp. Training whom and for what? Nobody knew anything other than that Captain Dragan Vasiljković was a Serb idol, a war hero best left alone – supposedly a shady character who spoke with an Australian accent having served with the Australians in Vietnam.*

The French head of our Regional Centre was an urbane, diplomat named Paul Otolan, and one morning he must have done his homework, for as we drove away from Knin he turned and said in English: 'I hope this will please you. At last we are going to meet Captain Dragan'.

First we had to run the gauntlet of the local Canadian platoon commander. Lieutenant Kevin Brown was a prickly officer in whose United Nations' domain Captain Dragan lived, and my first impression of him was exactly as described. He did not like civilians in any form, nor of any nationality, and as I noted in my diary at the time, treated us all with disdain, if he bothered to take any notice of us at all. During our initial briefing it was clear that he was talking to us under sufferance, especially as a three-pronged attack was at that moment in progress from Croatia into the RSK, aimed at the Miranje crossing between the two belligerents. Indeed, from inside his briefing room we could hear an exchange of distant artillery fire. After his briefing, I felt it necessary to take Kevin aside and explain my military background, why I was there and why I was particularly keen to meet Captain Dragan. Quite suddenly, but as I hoped, we became confidantes. Shortly, he was to connive with me in fixing a second private, visit to 'the Captain', a visit that was to be known only by, and sanctioned only by himself and Paul.

Kevin drove Paul and me in his Mercedes jeep through the low mountain passes to Captain Dragan's camp at Golubič, accompanied by a well-armed Canadian escort, while Paul and I, in our ECMM white uniforms, were equipped only with my camera and a notebook. This was one of the rare occasions that I carried a camera, for if stopped by an RSK patrol they were in the habit of destroying them on the spot. As mine was my mother's 1934 Leica, I was not keen for this to happen. I also owned a modern Leica but it was rather less reliable.

The entrance to the camp was a surprise. Instantly it was obvious we were entering a well-disciplined military establishment unlike any I saw either in the RSK or later in Croatia. The front gate was robust, smart and well-guarded by uniformed, red-bereted, fit-looking soldiers, with clean, modern, Russian weapons. Standing just inside was the thin, almost gaunt, Captain Dragan, wearing 'patrol uniform' with a pistol and two grenades clipped to his belt. He shook our hands and greeted us enthusiastically. My immediate perception was that he spoke with a South African rather than an Australian accent, while my second impression was that he was too macho to be a good soldier, although I thought at the time, he might actually be a good leader. Later that evening I wrote:

> *There was something strangely suspicious about him that I cannot put my finger on as the result of this one visit.*
>
> *Dragan led us to his office where a westerly facing window looked out and down across Croatia's coastal plain towards the Adriatic. On the opposite side of the room the wall was largely covered by a huge map that depicted both sides of the Confrontation Line, while it was obvious, from the pile of them in a mug, that all the coloured pins had been removed for our visit.*
>
> *Over coffee Paul questioned him at length, in English (which they both spoke perfectly) about his political beliefs vis-á-vis the RSK and Croatia from which, in addition to other personal revelations, it was clear that he was*

*vehemently anti-German. I discovered later that he had a German wife or,
rather, had had a German wife whom he still saw in Belgrade. He believed,
passionately, that there should be a buffer zone along the Confrontation Line, a
form of 'green line' patrolled jointly by the UN and the RSK but not Croatia
(which might have been a flaw in his argument). He said that he would accept
the green line being almost anywhere providing that his camp was not re-aligned
into Croatia and that it stopped the killing.*

In the wider context, Dragan confirmed that all Serbs with money and intelligence
had quit the country, leaving a very low-grade population to run the army and
the government, which he said, was why his country was in such a poor state.
From all accounts, Croatia had the same problem, indeed this fact was one of the
more serious aspects hampering progress throughout the whole of the FRY. The
RSK, Dragan suggested, was not interested in the Dalmatian coast or its ports,
although I thought this was unlikely, as apart from Karen Plaza the country
had no outlet to the sea, for which all knew, it was desperate to possess. He
just wanted independence from Nazi-influenced Croatia and the end of all Nazi
symbols, signs and currency. [As I was to discover when later based in Croatia,
the swastika was prominent and even some soldiers wore it as an arm band.] If,
he explained, Croatia was to give up any pretence of returning to its Ustaše-style
outlook – in his view, the catalyst to everything that was happening – then the
RSK could accept being part of Croatia, but unless that happened independence
from Croatia was the only way ahead.

Dragan claimed to train the RSK's Special Forces and that he had, personally
and 'proudly' taken part in 140 missions into Croatia. He believed that Germany
would eventually take over the whole of Europe and that what was happening in
the FRY was an extension of the Second World. Former Nazis, with tacit German
support (although I suspected that the current German government would most
definitely not be approving the swastikas and other outward signs of quasi-Nazi
influence) were supporting Croatia in its bid to subjugate the Krajinas, as well
as joining the European Union. He believed, further, that if Croatia continued
to receive materiel support from Germany and the US, in contravention of UN
Arms Embargo 713 – at which point I listened even more intensely – it could
then crush the RSK through rigorous ethnic cleansing. It would be Greece's
turn next, followed by the rest of Europe, at which point I nodded politely but
thought he was becoming a touch carried away! Finally, he admitted that Greece
was continuing to help Serbia, a fact that was to come home to roost very firmly

with what were to become my far-from-delicate, seesawing relations with the new Greek monitor and my intermediate 'boss', Vassilis Dertilis.

After two most affable hours Kevin Brown returned us to our own transport and we set off for Knin in the Land Rover.

From my diary:

> *On the way back Paul asked for my initial comments but as soon as I began to state that Dragan spoke with a South African accent rather than an Australian one Paul immediately burst into Arabic (which luckily I understood) telling me not to say any more in front of the interpretress, who also spoke a modicum of French. He would discuss the matter in private on our return.*

In Paul's office I could offer no more information about Captain Dragan other than to confirm that he did indeed speak English with a South African accent: I never knew why this was important to Paul. My own interest, though, had taken a turn upwards and, privately, I was determined to find out more about this enigmatic man. That evening, I wrote to my SIS contact, a retired British army major and friend from the Falklands campaign, with whom, prior to this present posting, I had discussed various topics of interest to him. Now I suggested one of my own. Could he offer any information about Captain Vasiljković, if indeed he had ever heard of him? His reply was swift. He did know of him but 'as an Australian called Daniel Sneddon. Any more information would be invaluable'.

A day or so later and by some subterfuge I managed to get a message to Dragan via the civilian-despising Kevin Brown, asking for a private visit.

The remarkable outcome is that I have been asked, by Dragan Vasiljković, to call on him for a special one-to-one, private meeting tomorrow. I was instructed to wear civilian clothes.

Brown was now fully supportive and on this, my second visit, he treated me from the start as though I was still a serving Royal Marines lieutenant colonel, which I was not, and admitted that before our last visit he had mentioned my name to Dragan who seemed to 'know it from somewhere'.

On the morrow, and with Paul's enthusiastic agreement, I dressed in my white uniform, packed suitable civilian clothes for my visit to the Dragon's Lair, as I nicknamed it, and was driven in Team November Three's dodgy Land Rover to meet the now genial Kevin Brown. Jack and Jeff (the other two monitors in my team, respectively French and Belgium) were left with an ideal excuse to do nothing all morning. Having changed, Kevin drove me, just the two of us, in his own Mercedes 'jeep' through the shallow mountain passes. I was uncertain whether or not I was being set up for something altogether less than pleasant: unhelpfully, Kevin, who was at least armed, was of the same view. As this was a non-ECMM visit, and as far as I was concerned, I was off ECMM duty (if not SIS duty) and now in civilian clothes, I had considered asking to borrow a 9mm Browning pistol, or whatever the equivalent it was that Canadian forces carried, as a sidearm but, reluctantly, then decided against the idea.

Dragan was waiting for us at his main gate, still armed with pistols and grenades around his waist. Kevin dropped me with the promise that he would return in two hours – precisely! I was now alone and in the hands of one of the most unpredictable and – if rumours were correct – one of the most dangerous characters in Serbia.

To begin with, over coffee served in cups – with saucers, Dragan told me that because he knew of my Royal Marines' background, he was anxious to discuss our training methods. The quid pro quo was that in return he would be delighted to show me his camp, his training teams and the men under drill. He was also keen to discuss his operating procedures and current operations. Although he never said so, it was obvious that he wanted all of this to be reported back to the United Kingdom, by-passing the ECMM's convoluted and unreliable communications, of which he was suspiciously aware. I received the clear impression that he knew I was not only answering to the European Community Monitoring Mission but also direct to my own Foreign Office and SIS. I made no comment and let him talk on. That evening I recorded the following in my diary:

> *Absolutely fascinating – his camp can see the sea and thus all the Croat land in between. Dragan's men have so far (apparently) completed 116 missions into 'enemy' territory and have suffered no deaths or casualties due to enemy action. He is unpaid – I think – and runs this specialist camp with about 1,000 men under training although I have to say I think that this figure has to be a vast exaggeration. Every night patrols are sent from the camp to reconnoitre enemy artillery positions as we are, Dragan says, just outside 155mm artillery range of Croatia. This seems unlikely to me but I will check the ranges on the map now that I know where we are.*

By RSK standards, the men are drilled and trained very well and on passing the course as specialist infantrymen are awarded a red beret. He has difficulty with his own senior officers in Serbia, for they are suspicious of his overall motives but it does appear that he is slowly building up a cadre of junior officers who have reached a standard higher than any formal Serbian army training. He also runs the Dragan Foundation, for he claims, the wounded of all sides, and on today's showing I have no reason to doubt his sincerity in this. A glossy brochure is well supportive of this Foundation but does only show, as far as I can make out, those from Serbia being helped. If only half true, it does seem to be a noble gesture, and coupled with what I have heard elsewhere, explains why he is very much a hero in his own country, if not rather obviously, in Croatia.

Everything in his camp is done, built, acquired or made, through self-help. He is even given soldiers on punishment from the RSK to train them into better soldiers, but not, in their case, into red beret soldiers. They are here as a punishment and are employed only in the more menial tasks. Ten months ago the whole area was a burned-out clothes factory – funny how everywhere we find people living in old buildings that turn out to have been ex-clothes factories! It is a quite remarkable set up. All his red-beret men are trained as scouts – for which read reconnaissance troops. Helicopter drills are practiced I am told, but I never saw a helicopter, and as some of his descriptions of helicopter operations did not quite ring true to my understanding of such affairs, I doubt they existed.

The men are also trained in photography and I was shown some of their results, again assuming they are true. He uses GPS a great deal (which someone must have funded). He also has some Passive Night Vision Goggles, which will certainly need to be funded by someone. He also has (he claims) thermal imagers and laser target markers, although I was not shown these. It is though, the most spotless place I have seen since arriving out here, and that includes our own mission headquarters, and so full marks to Captain Dragan for his attitude to cleanliness. As he had explained during my first visit he has a great hatred of the Germans and an exceptional allegiance to our own Queen.

He claims that he himself has led a very large number of patrols into Croatia, although he insists that they were mainly to recce and destroy guns that were firing into the RSK. Interestingly, he can see the sea from his camp and must be within range of Croat artillery, despite his claims. The Croats must know where he is and yet he has never been targeted by Croat guns. Odd, as I don't give the Croats that much intelligence to be playing a game of double bluff, or that they have worked out that by not killing him it will do the Croat cause a greater deal of good. In the same way that Paisley has never been killed by the IRA.

Eventually, on the way back to the main gate and my lift home, I was shown a cadre of 'foreign' soldiers under training. They were, I was told with no hint of conspiracy, from the Italian Garibaldi Brigade, although I had already identified their nationality and unit from their uniforms. This mechanised infantry brigade had (and still has) at its core the 1st Bersaglieri Infantry Regiment, who formed (and still form) one of the elite infantry corps of the Italian army. This extraordinary sight, in the middle of Serbian-occupied Croatia, could not have been fabricated, and was a fact that I decided to keep from the ECMM but relay direct to my SIS contact. (Later *The Daily Telegraph* published a letter of mine detailing this 'discovery'.)

And what lay behind Dragan's desire to produce better-than-average Serbian soldiers? I asked the question, but his answer was perhaps understandably evasive. Possibly his real motive for excellent training lay beyond his own country and is best described in part of a letter of mine that was published in *The Daily Telegraph* on 20 November 2000:

Why, when as an FCO-employed European Community monitor in the Republic of Serbian Krajina, was I shown, in some secrecy by one Captain Dragan (whose name cropped up recently in Belgrade) in his mountain camp overlooking Croatia, a section of regular Italian soldiers being trained by him 'against the day Italy decides to take back that part of northern Dalmatia lost to the Germans at the end of the Second World War?' Dragan knew well that his revelations to me would reach the outside world but not via the European monitoring system.

One incident I did tackle Dragan on, in answer to his clearly stated view that the RSK was totally innocent of any war crimes, was the shelling of school children evacuated to an offshore island. I must have touched a nerve because he vehemently denied that he himself had committed any war crime, although he also admitted that he was accused of doing so. He made it plain to me that as he had no artillery, and certainly no weapons capable of reaching an offshore island, he could not be responsible for such an atrocity. It certainly seemed to go against all that he told me about his foundation and the desire to do, in Serbian eyes, good works.

Later I was to send a report on this visit to my SIS contact but it is necessary to paraphrase it here:

Dragan received me in a very friendly manner and provided me with a short introduction, followed by a thorough tour of the camp including parade grounds, operations rooms, briefing rooms, kitchens, the medical centre and even a prison. The camp was built by Captain Dragan's soldiers and is well organised, orderly and clean. The soldiers appeared well disciplined.

Dragan is an educated, English-speaking Serb who, he told me, had lived most of his life in Australia (although his accent is more South African). He has adopted many western military traditions as I believe that he served as a captain in the Australian army's Royal Victoria Regiment.

His motivation for serving in the RSK appears to be pride as a Serb and not for monetary reasons. He feels deeply that the world community has been treating the Serbs unfairly and that Croat propaganda (supported by Germany) has succeeded in creating a common opinion of the Serbs as bad people.

Dragan informed me that he joined the Serb army in 1991. In 1992 he established a foundation in Belgrade, which supports victims of the war and has thus gained great fame. In March 1993 he returned to Krajina in order to establish his special training camp to produce the 'red berets' of specially trained soldiers for he is convinced that Krajina needs a small army of disciplined soldiers with better basic skills.

Dragan appears to have a great influence, both in Krajina and in Serbia where he is, in his words, 'popular among the common people'. He is about 45-years-old, is very fit, articulate, logical – and convincing.

Training is at a basic level. A 14-day course (there is some confusion over the length of the various training courses) is conducted in specialist skills such as scouting (reconnaissance in depth) anti-tank, sniper and pioneer duties up to corporal level. This training includes practical exercises along the Confrontation Line. On completion of the training the Serbs are awarded the red beret which they wear with pride. Captain Dragan tries to raise the basic qualities of the soldiers and JNCOs to make the RSK's military more effective and efficient.

Captain Dragan believes that the RSK army should be cut to approximately 15,000 well-trained soldiers rather than 90,000 amateurs and, again in his words, who are little more than uniformed bandits.

A possible solution to the present stalemate, as (perhaps naively) offered by Dragan, is to establish a green line between Croatia and the Krajina occupied only by a strong United Nations force. This would permit both governments to stop the hostilities for the international community would not, then permit any armed hostilities from either side. Any violation of the green line would be met with immediate response from the strong international military force.

[Dragan was extradited from Australia in July 2015, then tried in Croatia for war crimes. He was sentenced to fifteen years in prison and released in March 2020.]

Chapter 22

Suicide (or Murder?) in Hotel Split

The following is an extract from *Paid to Predict* by the author.

Eventually I managed to get myself to the Dalmatian coast to be in due course, the head monitor of the European Community Monitoring Mission (ECMM) based in Split, which was precisely where the FCO and SIS wanted me. That side of my life was pretty straightforward, but the ECMM side of things rather less so.

My first evening in Hotel Split was thought-provoking. Via a circuitous route, I found my way to the upstairs ECMM dining room, a soulless, high-ceilinged space on the ground floor (the main dining room was one floor below, on the southern side, as the hotel is built on a steep slope) whose west-facing windows looked across a crumbling terrace of near-slum, two-storied dwellings. Along the windowless south wall was a lengthy, help-yourself table of cold meats and huge bowls of green and black olives, that I was to discover, would form the staple to my future diet. These delicacies surrounded three cauldrons that contained the 'dish of the day' but to my then untrained eye, looked more like thin soup in which floated small meaty croutons but whether they were fin, feather or fur would remain unsolved. This cafeteria arrangement was only for the use of the ECMM and was partitioned off from the remaining three-quarters of the large room that was never used by anyone. The room itself was at the end of a wide passageway that led from the lobby, along which, lines of refugees and displaced people queued for a form of gruel and bread. This 'pot mess' they took across the car park to their desperately overcrowded apartments.

The following is taken from my diary:

Dinner with Robert Lekeu (the other Split monitor and so utterly useless that he was to be sent back to Belgium) was difficult, as he has very strange ideas of what we are to do on the coast and they very definitely do not tie in with what Paul has told me to set up and then 'get underway'. The immediate future may be tricky, as Paul (my French head based in Knin in the RSK) has given me unofficial powers as it were, and yet I am again, number three in a team of three. Noble gesture though it might be, the distribution of teddy bears by Robert to displaced families is not what the ECMM is about.

On my way to bed via the staircase, raised voices were arguing vulgarly and vociferously by the Foyer Bar. I turned and watched two men dressed in Croat army combat clothes, screaming at each other across a table. From the expletives and accents I guessed they were drunk American mercenaries. My first reaction was to intervene, as I would have been obliged to do had I been the duty officer in a military establishment, but my diary explains otherwise:

Considered helping but decided that it was not the job of an ECMM monitor to get involved.

A single pistol shot had me turning my head again in time to watch one of the men fall to the ground. As he did so, a hand gun, probably a Croat army-issue HS95 9mm pistol, dropped to the carpet between the two. The women at the bar started screaming, while a number of similarly dressed soldiers fled towards the hotel's revolving front door. I was new to the Split scene and wisely continued to the staircase, guessing rightly as it turned out, that the hotel staff knew how to deal with what was probably a normal, if not an everyday, occurrence.

That is how I saw it, but the two protagonists were so close together, face to face, that it could well have been murder, although I was sure then, and am sure now, that it was suicide. The next morning, following the best sleep I had had since arriving in the Balkans, I walked across to the Foyer Bar on my way to breakfast, to stare at the bare floor where the bloodied carpet had been cut away. This exposed patch of stained cement served to highlight the incident rather than hide it. Noticing my interest, and my white uniform, a Croat policeman asked me if I had seen the game of Russian Roulette that had been played the evening before.

Heard that the drunk last night was apparently playing Russian Roulette, but as I pointed out to the Croat police, who were investigating the incident, you can only play Russian Roulette with a revolver, and not a 9mm Browning-type, automatic pistol. The police had no idea of the weapon used, and the surviving soldiers had long since fled the scene, as had the weapon. A piece of carpet where the victim fell and bled – dying – has been hacked out with a blunt knife, so now there is a large ragged-edged piece missing. The police took my point and my suggestion that they should look for an American mercenary, but they replied that there are simply too many of them. Nevertheless, I suggested that as they now knew the deceased's nationality it should be less difficult to chase his friends and colleagues. I left them to it.

Chapter 23

Šibenik Bridge Meeting

To continue my slide towards resignation, one of the most significant events of my employment by the European Community Monitor Mission (ECMM) now took place. On 12 March, I received an invitation – more like an order – to meet Vassilis Dertilis (the Greek naval captain and head of the Dalmatian coast monitoring teams) alone and in the middle of Šibenik bridge, which is a massive structure at 1,280 feet in length with a clearance above the Krka river of 131 feet. From my diary:

This is all rather melodramatic and 'cloak and daggerish' but both of us have no doubts that our various living quarters are bugged while equally certain that the middle of the bridge is not!

I had no idea in advance what Vassilis wanted to discuss, but it had to be important and sensitive. As this was to be the pivotal point in my employment by the ECMM, the moment I returned to Hotel Split's Room 519, I recorded the occasion in my diary, but I also wrote a narrative of the event in my Sinclair Cambridge Z88 laptop, before the facts became too hazy and even corrupted.

The following are excerpts of what I tapped into the word processor and wrote in my diary:

'Ewen' Turning his head, arms still resting on the concrete guardrail, Vassilis opened the impromptu meeting, 'Did you know that the Germans are importing Leopard tanks through the port of Pula in the north of Croatia?'

'Yes, Vassilis' I replied, 'I wrote it in yesterday's Daily Report that you will have received.'

I then added for emphasis, despite the unlikely chance that he had forgotten what else had been in my signal, 'along with the Americans sending fighter aircraft hidden in large shipping containers. I assume you, too, see the airfield monitors' reports from Pula?'

I then offered a form of report to Vassilis that went roughly like this:

What is going on in Pula is almost certainly going on in 'my own' port of Ploče, and the Pula team are anxious that I should be aware that these irregularities are taking place and that we should be forewarned. As it happens, Ploče has been on my list of places to visit since my arrival on the coast, but due to various internal shenanigans. I have done so only once, and that was really more of a reconnaissance for future visits. Now, of course, I have an imperative reason to institute a programme of in-depth monitoring of the port.

While the monitoring of Ploče was at the head of my unwritten agenda, there were one or two other factors that needed urgent discussion, far from prying or electronic ears, and where better than the middle of a bridge!

'Vassilis," I continued, "I have already begun to establish a monitoring program to include the port of Ploče. There seems to be an Irishman who I believe is responsible for port operations. The one time I have met him he was most friendly and keen to help. I'm damn certain that whether hidden in containers or not, little will escape his notice.'

'That is fine' Vassilis argued, 'but, as you know, Jean-Pierre (our new head, based in Knin – also French but of a very low calibre compared to his predecessor) has told us not to conduct such monitoring'. Vassilis was relaying nothing new, other that I was about to receive contradictory orders, from both this Greek naval officer and the French diplomat.

'Which is, of course, precisely why we are all out here in Croatia,' I interrupted. Vassilis knew this only too well.

'So that is why you must continue with your plans,' he said.

'Jean-Pierre has already told me not to continue with my plans!' I replied.

'I know, so I have a proposition to suggest', Vassilis responded.

'Which is?' I answered.

Knowing Vassilis, I was more than half prepared for his answer: 'You must continue to monitor any illegal imports through Ploče, but Jean-Pierre must not know that you have even visited the place, and he must certainly never know what you find there. So, I want you to continue monitoring as planned, but now you will need to falsify your Daily Reports by saying that you have been somewhere else. When you do go to Ploče, I want you to tell me, and me alone, what you have found.'

I needed no time to prepare an answer. 'Vassilis, you know my background well enough to know, that that is an impossible request for me to meet. Not only is it immoral but it goes against everything that the ECMM is supposed to represent.'

Vassilis remained silent, now staring down at the river, so I elaborated: 'There has to be a reason why the Frenchman does not want us to discover any embargo-breaking and there has to be a reason why only you, a Greek, need to know, and I don't like either of them.'

'I'll see if I can get Jean-Pierre to change his mind' was his unconvincing response. I know Vassilis will not try, and I also know that Jean-Pierre will not change his mind. There was a long silence and then Vassilis rather abruptly changed the subject.

'I am worried about my standing with your Foreign and Commonwealth Office in London and indeed with your head of department in Zagreb.'

I have no idea why my London office should be his concern but I have many ideas why my head of department in Zagreb should be.

'Oh really!' I feigned surprise, 'and what precisely do you want me to do about it, especially as you have just asked me to falsify my Daily Reports?'

Vassilis now presented a side of him that he had clearly been anxious to hide from me, ever since we had first met in Knin. I will not go so far as to say that I feel sorry for him, for much of his probably feigned unhappiness is entirely of his own making. Nevertheless, I do not, at the moment anyway, wish to make an enemy of him, as we have work to do over this illegal importing of tanks and aircraft.

'I'll square things away with my Head of the British Delegation, Vassilis, but in return you must abide by the original promises made to me by Jean-Pierre's predecessor, and just to remind you what those were, they include me staying at Split so that I can divide my current monitoring team into two, while also establishing a third monitoring mission in Dubrovnik.'

'I'll do what I can, and that is a promise,' he replied.'

I continued in my diary:

Vassilis also told me that the deputy Head of Mission (Operations) and the Chief of Logistics and Personnel have told Jean-Pierre that I was a 'known personality' and not a simple monitor (whatever that may mean), and that I was to stay in Split until the end of my mission. We'll see if that actually happens, but at least the ground rules are being laid down – or should I say that the status quo is being maintained, by HQ ECMM. Sadly though, I have my doubts that Jean-Pierre – a Frenchman – will take any notice of the Greeks in Zagreb. I sense trouble.

Ending this strange meeting, we walked back to our Land Rovers at each end of the bridge to drive off in opposite directions, leaving me, perhaps naïvely, with no clue that any promises would be kept and that I would still be required to falsify my Daily Reports. Then it was back to reality on my return to the hotel.

I knew then that one of the reasons why the Greeks and French, including Vassilis and now Jean-Pierre, wanted to clip my wings. Alone among all the monitors within the whole of the Knin's large Regional Monitoring Centre it must have looked odd, if not suspicious (for these things always got reported backwards, upwards, sideways, downwards and forwards within the ECMM) that I had the ear, not only of the British ambassador to Croatia, the British vice-consul in Zagreb, as well as the British and Italian consuls in Split, and now the British Secretary of State for Overseas Development. My friendship with the Commander-in-Chief Fleet and the Masters of RFAs *Resource* and *Sir Geraint* had not gone unnoticed either, and my private visit to Captain Dragan was becoming well known. As I have mentioned before, my room was certainly bugged, as was, without much doubt, the telephones not only in my room for local calls, but the one in Team Split's office which was connected to the international telephone network. It was not possible to keep anything secret – unless discussed in the very middle of Šibenik bridge. I resigned from the mission shortly afterwards.

Chapter 24

Reconnaissance of Brač Island's Secret Airfield, 1994

As part of my monitoring duties as I saw them, from both the European Community Monitoring Mission (ECMM) and the Secret Intelligence Service's (SIS) points of view, I was keen to investigate the rumoured presence of a 'secret' airfield on the island of Brač. Croatia had no airforce, nor the likelihood of procuring one for the foreseeable future. So, if true, why did it exist and who built it? The following is from *Paid to Predict* by the author:

The probability of a 'secret' airfield on Brač puzzled me more now and particularly, if it existed why did it exist. The SIS thought it lay 'possibly in a low lying plateau somewhere above Bol', which was a good enough excuse for me to go and have a look. The deputy mayor seemed to think it did not exist, or was he implying that it did not exist as far as civilian traffic was concerned? If this was the case, what was the military purpose for its existence? I had in mind the breaking of the UN arms embargo. Days earlier, when planning this 'patrol', I had mentioned the airfield to Sandra (the duty interpretress) as a monitoring project. Intriguingly she had stated that it was not a secret so much, it was just an unused military airfield, and as such, she advised against wasting our time, by which she meant wasting her time.

I disagreed and responded with the view that that was precisely a good reason to find out what it was, in truth, being used for, and what perhaps, it could be used for in the future. I had, too, reminded her, that the Croat Air Force had barely existed since 1991 when the Jugoslav National Army had left for Serbia – building a military airfield for an air force with no aircraft had to be questioned.

At 0900 the next day, 14 January, Willy (now my second useless, Belgium monitor) drove us via a rather peripatetic journey towards the airfield, retracing our track several times. There were good reasons for this. Neither Sandra or Willy knew where it was, although her assessment of the approximate position did, obviously unknown to her, coincide with that of the SIS. The airfield was not marked on any map despite construction having begun a few years earlier, and as we were eventually to discover, it was over one mile from the nearest marked track and over one-and-a-half miles from the nearest formal road.

Once we found what had to have been the route taken by the construction lorries, now very much overgrown, we actually covered a further two-and-a-half miles until, quite unexpectedly, the very rough path, for it was by now little more than stone-filled ruts, opened into a small, tarmacked car park below the control tower. Another reason why it had been difficult to find was that Willy, with his hangover, found driving confusing, nor was he helped by Sandra's map reading. I suspected that she did not want us to find the airfield, for she kept suggesting the least likely turning wherever there was a choice. In truth, she was so hung over that I do not think she cared whether we found the thing or not!

I was not surprised by the state of their health, for earlier that morning, at about 0300, they had created a considerable noise in the corridor outside my room which lay between theirs, arguing about whose bed they should share.

To reach the airfield we had driven along a switch-backed, boulder-strewn (on purpose?) track between wild olive groves, to find a modern but simple complex of aluminium-clad sheds, a baggage store and a rudimentary control tower perched on top of a wobbly-looking, large metal pole around which an equally unstable, metal, spiral ladder twisted upwards. There was not a soul around, and although it was clearly operational it was not actually in operation. I was though conscious that what I was about to do exceeded my ECMM mandate and could only be classified as intelligence-gathering. Nevertheless I was suspicious, and decided that the need to know why it existed outweighed the risk of being caught. Anxious to get a feel for the place, the length of the paved runway and its possible uses, it was a simple job to climb the perimeter fence and drop down the other side. Although glad that there was no one to prevent my snooping, I would have liked to have asked one or two, quite correct, monitor-style questions about the airfield's real purpose, for it had a very military feel to it. I was not to know, as I paced just over 4,700 feet of pristine runway, that it had been visited fourteen days earlier, as a subsequent article in the Croat weekly magazine, *Nacional*, described on 24 May 1994.

Considering that the US was more interested in the situation in Bosnia-Herzegovina than in Croatia, they asked Croatia to permit them to install a military base with unmanned aircraft. The basic condition was that this had to be the best kept secret, so that it would not appear that the US had taken sides in the war. The island of Brač was selected, as it could be well protected. There all the equipment and personnel led by the CIA experts, with the long-range unmanned aircraft which could cover the entire territory of Bosnia-Herzegovina to the Serbian corridor on the Sava River, were based. The entire Krajina region in Croatia was also in its range. At that time no one had any idea what was going on and what was being hidden on the island of Brač. Nor did the US's allies, the Germans, have any idea. They sent their Military Attaché there on 1 January 1994. He hired a car and drove the outer fence of the base and began taking pictures, thinking that the alertness of the base would have faltered on New Year's Day. However, he was quickly spotted and arrested. Only when he was brought in for questioning was it learned that he was the German Military Attaché in Zagreb, Hans Schwan.

I was obviously lucky, for unlike the hapless Hans Schwan, there was not a soul to apprehend me, although I could not help feeling that Sandra was longing for me to be caught and locked up! As the result of Schwan's arrest – and release – I was to learn much later that the airfield's security was then boosted in preparation for the arrival of the American Predator unmanned surveillance aircraft, prior to the invasion of the Republic of Serbian Krajina during Operation Storm in August 1995.

Chapter 25

The Merits of an Amphibious Capability

Written Evidence to the Parliamentary Defence Committee, 2017

In late 2017, I was invited to forward a paper to the Defence Committee on the merits of the United Kingdom having an amphibious capability. This is it:

Background

I am a retired Lieutenant Colonel who served in the Royal Marines between 1960 and 1992, commanding units within RM Commando Forces and RM detachments at sea. I also served, with the amphibious forces of the US, France, Norway, the Netherlands, Germany, Italy and Denmark. I commanded 3 Commando Brigade's 539 Assault Squadron from 1964-68, the 1st Assault Squadron in HMS *Anzio* in the Gulf 1963-64, and the 4th Assault Squadron in HMS *Fearless* 1971-74. I served as Officer Commanding Naval Party 8901, the Royal Marines garrison in the Falkland Islands, between 1978 and 1979. During the Falklands campaign in 1982, I was the navigational and amphibious adviser to Commander, 3 Commando Brigade, the Commodore Amphibious Warfare (COMAW), and was closely involved in the planning and execution of a number of amphibious operations including Operation Sutton, the initial landing at San Carlos. I later served on a four-year appointment as the first Royal Marines officer to the Director General Surface Ships (Amphibious Group). It was then that I wrote, on behalf of the Commandant General Royal Marines (CGRM), the Brigade Commander and COMAW, the Royal Marines' input into the Procurement Specifications for the current LPH (HMS *Ocean*), the two LPDs (HMSs *Albion* and *Bulwark*), the Mark 4 LCVP and the Mark 10 LCU. Following my retirement I served as editor of *Jane's Amphibious and Special Forces* from 1999 to 2015.

1. If I may, I will begin with a few basic statements that underline/underpin much of what I will say later.
    a) The expressions 'storming the beaches' and 'amphibious assault' worry me when uttered by (for instance) people such as Michael Fallon when

SoS for Def. If this is his perception of why the RMs exist, it is a dangerous and misguided, naïve even, misunderstanding. While the Royal Marines are the only force trained to conduct such operations, these would only be at the bottom of countless other options, depending on the threat or situation ashore. The storming of beaches and amphibious assault are expressions that smack of all-out war, whereas most future campaigns, and likely areas of disaster relief or emergency evacuation (what used to be known as 'military aid to the civil community) were surely covered by the then Secretary of State for Defence's statement that 'threats have intensified in other domains'. These other domains would suggest a lesser tempo yet one that could still require landing across beaches or through damaged ports.

b) While the current Royal Fleet Auxiliaries and other surface warships including HMSs *Queen Elizabeth* and *Prince of Wales* with their helicopters (that themselves are limited in their lift capability) can provide much invaluable help, none can lift ashore heavy equipment that might be needed such as lorries for the onward transport of aid, as well as plant equipment, tracked and wheeled, for the rebuilding of ports and the civilian infrastructure.

c) Only HMSs *Albion* and *Bulwark* with their shallow-draft landing craft and hovercraft (ideal for river work or in areas strewn with debris or whose underwater profile has been altered by earthquakes) can be of any practical and lasting value. Their Amphibious Beach Units are unique throughout the British armed forces, with their ability to build or rebuild beach landing sites or port facilities. The list goes on, for it is not just the ships that will be lost, but with them, the possibility of conducting any form of entry across hostile or damaged shores.

d) RFAs are civilian ships, and thus overt warfare may well affect their status, let alone the terms of service of their crews.

e) Amphibious warfare is at the scholarship level of all phases of war – bar none – for it takes place on the sea, beneath the sea, above the sea, in the air and in space and cyber space, with all enjoying at least one if not multiple interfaces with each other. At each of these interfaces, experts need to understand both sides of the various divides. Most significantly, its business is across the division between land and sea: a dangerous and complicated place in peacetime let alone in war. Weather and hydrography too, play vital roles not met in such intensity and importance as in other forms of warfare. Thus amphibious warfare, in its entirety, simply cannot be undertaken by the inexperienced, let alone by untrained amateurs.

2. It almost beggars belief that a maritime nation with world wide responsibilities is apparently considering reducing its amphibious capability. 'Vital' would not be too strong a word, for a lapsed amphibious capability cannot be conjured out of thin air when it is suddenly needed. Amphibious operations project power, support or relief, inland from sea river or lake, without the need for a port, airfield or over-flight rights. They can be militarily offensive or defensive. They are an effective method of deploying balanced forces to prevent a hostile landing, to remove an aggressive force or provide support to vulnerable neighbours. The very threat of an amphibious landing can be sufficient to deter hostile action, without the necessity of actually doing anything unless required or asked. An amphibious force can be deployed from its base to be in readiness elsewhere without commitment, it can land at a time of its choosing and retire without taking or losing ground. An amphibious response is a graduated response, and a response that can be delivered with complete surprise, at a location and with a combination of amphibious equipment of the force's choosing. Unlike other forms of warfare or disaster relief, amphibious operations can take place at large distances from the home base.

3. In optimal circumstances, amphibious operations require a mix of air-theatre entry and sea -theatre entry. Deletion of the ability to conduct sea-based theatre entry would have a devastating operational effect and would be impossible to achieve. If nothing else, amphibious operations are joint operations, the loss of any aspect of which, would spell disaster, and indeed make a successful amphibious operation impossible to achieve. Aims will not be achieved and men will die for no purpose. Think Gallipoli.

4. The placing of the two Albion-class landing platform dock ships into an alternating pattern of high-low readiness creates risk through the lack of continuity it would create, an inability to have one of the ships abroad at any one stage, training, showing the flag. This last item is often a much maligned attribute but in my view important. I have written elsewhere about the important role played by HMS *Fearless*, where, throughout her life, showing the flag was a necessary part of Britain's 'soft' but impressive foreign diplomacy. The same can be said for HMS *Intrepid* and indeed the

frigate and destroyer fleets which then operated worldwide. So often in the past, this soft approach has pre-empted trouble.

5. There is no substitute for purpose-built amphibious ships and there are no alternative platforms that exist for UK Armed Forces to replicate these capabilities. Amphibious warfare is at the scholarship level of defence. There is absolutely no substitute for the highly trained, well-exercised ships and men working as a cohesive team – from the Brigadier's and Commodore's staff downwards, to the very lowest levels. Some, in the Army, in the past have claimed that amphibious warfare exists only to keep the Royal Marines in business. That is of course rubbish, and has been proved to be rubbish time and time again. Look at 5 Brigade's appalling performance in 1982.

6. In terms of the comparison between the Albion-class LPDs and the Bay-class LSD(A)s, while the LSDs can carry more vehicles, they can only land them in very small penny packets at a time, whereas the LPD's can land a far larger, and importantly, balanced force in the first wave. The inability to do this latter would spell inevitable disaster. When I was helping write the Procurement Specification for the LPH and LPDs in 1988, we dealt mainly, in L and R over equivalents, but then had to offer to the shipbuilders, dozens of sample matrices of MBTs, 4-tonner lorries, amphibious beach unit vehicles, Viking over-snow vehicles (but they were a new concept), and rolls of Class 30 trackway. In summary, the LSDs are basic force multipliers and cannot offer a balanced first assault.

7. There is no comparison between the command, control and communications systems available on an Albion-class LPD to those on a Bay-class LSD. The LSD's communications systems are nowhere near enough for amphibious operations, covering as they do, surface, subsurface, air, ground and cyber space, let alone Special Forces and advance force operations, and the vast network of communications required for logistic resupply. All this is in addition to medical, diplomatic and political circuits (i.e. direct to COBRA), plus links to the command structure at for instance Northwood and the Ministry of Defence, as well as other single service headquarters. When being designed and built, the current LPD's comms fit was reduced by the Procurement Executive by about a third from that required by the military communicators for a standard amphibious operation. This reduction was due to costs – along with the hospital, the two Mexeflotes and the hangar. In short therefore, even the LPD does not have adequate communications for amphibious operations.

8. It is possible that the missing circuits and aerials have been retrofitted. Either way, the LSD is utterly unsuited to command and control this most complicated of all forms of warfare. When designing the Albion-class, as with all warships, they were built to accept considerable damage in order to still remain afloat and fighting. The same damage-control standards also apply, I believe, to the RFAs but these, inevitably, have large open spaces for stores and vehicles, which makes damage control more difficult. Admittedly, the LPD s also have large spaces for vehicles, but they are also designed to take on up to 3,000 tons of seawater when ballasting down, in order to flood the large dock, a dock probably four times the space of those in the LSDs.

9. There are many potential disadvantages to giving RFA ships tasks that are properly those of RN warships. Quite simply, LPDs are warships and manned and operated accordingly. They are designed to go in harm's way, whereas the RFA's are in effect, civilian ships and manned and operated accordingly. They are not designed to go in harm's way and are not usually armed, except lightly for specific tasks. The legal position of the RFA's crews would have to be very carefully investigated. If the argument that RFA vessels can stand in for warships is extended you might as well do away with the latter.

10. A single LPD and two Commandos (which is the current situation without any further reduction) does not constitute a sufficient force for training and exercising, to sustain amphibious capability at high readiness. I believe training has been curtailed to save money. It has always been accepted, that particularly training in the harsh Norwegian Arctic, bears fruit for operations throughout the rest of the world, like no other training area can. To lose this invaluable experience is verging on the criminal.

11. Although I am no longer serving in the Royal Marines, and the question on the effect on personnel that further reductions would have is best answered by those still serving, one can be fairly sure that these reductions would have a bad effect on morale and Service satisfaction. Cancellation of training programmes and uncertainty over future would take a toll on morale and I would have thought, effectiveness.

12. In terms of the effect of reductions on the communities where amphibious units and platforms are based, what is likely is a loss of local employment, a loss of social interaction and a loss of the civilian understanding of what the armed forces achieve. If the home of the Royal Marines is to be based

in a single area there will be social trouble. Why give up custom-built locations in order to cram everyone into one small space in South West Devon and South East Cornwall. This is a crazy concept that can only have been considered by blinkered politicians.

Lieutenant Colonel Ewen Southby-Tailyour, OBE, RM. 4 December 2017.

Chapter 26

Marine 'A'

On 15 September 2011, Sergeant Alexander Blackman of 42 Commando Royal Marines shot dead a dying Taliban terrorist in the Helmand province of Afghanistan. On 6 December 2013, Blackman (then known only as Marine 'A') was found guilty of murder by a court martial and sentenced to a minimum term of ten years. On 22 May 2014, the Courts Martial Appeal Court reduced his minimum term to eight years.

In March 2017, and following a vigorous campaign by many of us with battlefield experience, the conviction for murder was overturned and reduced to manslaughter. With time served taken into consideration he was released from prison on 28 April 2017. The following is just one of a number of essays and letters I wrote to the press as part of a larger campaign to have his sentence overturned.

SERGEANT ALEXANDER BLACKMAN, ROYAL MARINES
OPTIONS AND OBSERVATIONS
Putting aside for a moment, Sergeant Blackman's defence team failing to ask for the alternative charge of manslaughter to be brought, the rumour that members of the court-martial's panel were told to find him guilty, coupled to the alleged suppression of evidence for his defence, there is another factor in this unique and disturbing case. Quite simply, what else was Sergeant Blackman supposed to do with a mortally wounded terrorist?

Very few have condemned Sergeant Blackman while many thousands are actively supporting his bid for a review, yet no one (on either side) has been prepared to say what he should have done. A number have commented adversely on his actions, but unless they can answer this question, their statements are shallow to the point of being meaningless.

So, let me as, then, the second in command of 3 Company Desert Regiment, the Sultan of Muscat's Armed Forces (on loan from A Company, the Northern Frontier Regiment – which I was commanding) offer a few suggestions based on my own experience. On 11 January 1968 during the Dhofar War, and in the middle of a firefight (the first of three that day, of many days) I put to sleep my mortally wounded Arab (Muslim) sergeant major with an overdose of morphine. On reflection, I had roughly the same choices available to me in 1968, as I would suggest, Sergeant Blackman had on 15 December 2011 in Helmand.

His were these:

First, prevent the terrorist from dying through the application of first aid. The terrorist was dying if not already dead, so why prolong the inevitable at further risk to oneself. The patrol had nothing with which to do this, and the only morphine ampoules available were individual ones, strictly not to be used on anyone else. His back wound (courtesy of an Apache helicopter), was simply untreatable.

Secondly, call in a Chinook helicopter with an onboard Medical Emergency Response Team. By the time it would have arrived, the terrorist, if not dead already, would certainly have died. This would have been an unacceptable risk of an invaluable asset with no likelihood of a positive outcome. One of my nieces was a medic with a Medical Emergency Resuscitation Team (MERT), operating with Chinook helicopters in Helmand Province and would have been appalled had she been asked to fly into a killing zone to rescue a dead Taliban. I don't suppose the gallant RAF aircrew would have been too chuffed either.

Thirdly, drag him to safety. Safety from what? It might have been safe for the terrorist in his dying moments, while the team held his hand, but it would still keep Sergeant Blackman's patrol in the general killing zone, an area best left as soon as possible. If that means leaving a dying enemy behind, then so be it, as the safety of Blackman's men took priority. It was vital to get away from the area as soon as possible to regroup elsewhere, so that the enemy could then be engaged on Blackman's own terms.

Fourthly, put the dying terrorist out of his misery quickly, so that the patrol could leave the killing zone and continue with meeting the aim – a choice used down the centuries for friend and foe alike, with until now, little or no retribution. How?

Three more choices were available to Sergeant Blackman:

1. Crack on with the patrol and let the terrorist die in his own time – an inhumane act that would bring opprobrium.

2. Administer an overdose of non-existent morphine – peaceful but with the risk (these days) of a charge of murder.
3. Fire a single 9mm bullet direct to the heart – instant but with the risk (these days) of a charge of murder.

In other words, the choice was obvious and Blackman made the correct moral and military decision, if not, (as we are now obliged to accept) the correct legal one… or are there any others that I have failed to spot? Sadly though, it strikes me that Blackman was convicted largely on his own evidence, recorded on another marine's helmet cam, and yet I firmly believe that the 'patois' of an infantry battle, no matter how obtained, should never be produced as evidence in a trial.

Things are said before, during and after a firefight – for bravado, for effect, for release of tension through black humour, for encouragement – that should be inadmissible as evidence in the calm of a court, particularly so if that conversation can then be used for the very public damnation of the accused by the non-cognoscenti. An infantry battle's conversations might have seemed chilling to a judge advocate with no front line experience, but to those of us who do have such experience, they were perfectly normal, indeed, in most respects, rather mild.

Added to that, and against the view of the prosecuting QC at Blackman's court martial, the heat of battle, most emphatically, does not evaporate away the moment the last round has been fired, for it is then that the adrenaline, the fear and the nervousness often become far, far more intense – until the enemy is once more engaged, when one, again, becomes too occupied to be frightened.

There is perhaps a precedent for the exclusion of such evidence. In the case of Regina versus Litchfield for manslaughter, following the defendant's ship hitting rocks off the north coast of Cornwall on the 30 May 1995 with the loss of three lives, the High Court Judge, Mr Justice Butterfield, instructed the jury to disregard any decisions taken by Litchfield after his engines had failed, since these were decisions taken in extremis.

Another thought, relevant to the Blackman case, has to be at what stage, in legal terms, does a fatally wounded, possibly armed or booby-trapped terrorist, become a prisoner of war? The answer is 'never' if you are an Apache pilot or a sniper, but the niceties are not so clear if you are an infantryman on the ground, mopping up after an aerial rocket attack while constantly fearing deadly retaliation.

Finally, I do not accept that Sergeant Blackman's action put at risk other coalition personnel, as claimed at his court martial, by lowering himself to the level of the Taliban. He fired one shot. He did not torture, he did not maim, he did not disembowel, he did not behead, he did not dismember, and he did not put his handiwork on display. The Taliban's reaction would not have altered one jot as the result of Blackman's actions from that they were already exercising, and as we expected would happen to us in Dhofar in the 1960s – beheading and dismemberment. It could not have got any worse.

As a corollary, I will detail my own experience during the Dhofar War in 1968, which was not dissimilar, and yet is one that, I have no doubt, is also covered by the same legal definition as the actions taken by Alexander Blackman – and countless others before and since.

In 1968, across the Dhofar mountains, the Sultan of Oman's Armed Forces (SAF) were losing a desperate struggle against – courtesy of China and South Yemen – a determined, well-trained and well-armed insurgency, intent on controlling, eventually, the entrance to the Persian Gulf. I was with a Company of the Desert Regiment (on loan from the Northern Frontier Regiment where I was a company commander, seconded for two years from the Royal Marines) when on 11 January 1968, we were attacked by the enemy – the Adoo – in a strength and with a ferocity not previously experienced by the SAF.

I was driving a Land Rover with my Arab sergeant major in the passenger seat. Our job was to bring up the rear and collect those soldiers picketing the high ground either side as the company moved forwards in an 'advance to contact' formation.

Suddenly, our leading troops were engaged by machine gun and rifle fire. The sergeant major and I jumped out and raced to the crest of a ridge to assess the situation and offer what immediate mortar fire we could, while calling for air support. We too, then came under sustained and accurate fire from behind. The sergeant major, alongside me and perhaps ill-advisedly, wearing my Canadian army combat jacket, while I was dressed in similar clothes and headdress to our soldiers, was hit in the right side of his neck. He stumbled to the ground with blood spurting eighteen inches above his head. He might have been hit elsewhere but there was no time to check, nor was there time for lengthy thought. He was conscious and clearly in distress, but I had to weigh up the situation in purely military terms.

The legal niceties of the situation never entered my head and nor should they have done for the whole company was now under fire. The three rifle platoons, pinned down, needed directions, the mortars had yet to be given their fire orders – in Arabic, and I needed to call for vital air support if our 150 soldiers were to survive this wholly unexpected onslaught.

Yet I had a mortally injured man to consider, while there were others also across the battlefield, who although less seriously wounded, would die if not given first aid. The sergeant major was beyond help but his approach to inevitable death was slow, too slow. He needed pain killers and he needed gentleness. I injected my own phial of morphine into his right thigh, then with no thoughts of murder, manslaughter or mercy killing, called for more from the soldiers around me to hasten the process. Hard though it might sound, he needed removing from the equation, in our time and not in his time, in order that I could control my part of the battle and ensure that as many of my men as possible survived.

With the sergeant major's death I was able to meet up with the one other British officer and help the company win the day. In fact, the day was not yet won, for there were to be a further two infantry fire fights and more deaths on both sides, before the heavily blooded enemy called it a day at dusk and backed off, with their own dead and wounded, that in the end far outnumbered ours.

It was not until November 2013 and the verdict of Alexander Blackman's court martial that I revisited the events of 11 January 1968, when for the first time, I analysed my options. My conclusion was as clear now as it was then. My prime objective had been to fight and destroy the enemy with minimal cost to ourselves, my second aim during those few minutes, following the sergeant major being hit, was to make his passing as swift and painless as possible. Because of the pressing need – indeed my duty – to fight the battle, I should have left him alone, but that would have been inhumane. On the other hand I could not sit back and wait until he was dead. Speed was essential. Other, more crucial options were crying for attention.

I have no idea whether my action was murder, manslaughter or a mercy killing. All I knew then, and still firmly believe now, is that it was swift and peaceful, but above all and of the utmost importance, it was a combination of kindness and sheer common sense. Where is the criminality in that during a legal conflict that had been ordained, or as in Dhofar, had been supported by, the British government?

Chapter 27

Anton – A Royal Marines Dog

In 1944, my father, then Lieutenant Colonel Norman Tailyour, was commanding 27 Battalion, Royal Marines, as they fought eastwards through France and Germany.

At the time he owned a large French poodle called Anton. Very sadly, Anton was run over by an army lorry and killed. Such was his popularity as the Battalion's mascot, that he was buried among the other casualties of the time, and given his own headstone which simply read 'Anton' with beneath, the words, 'Royal Marines'.

Many years later, in the early 1970s, the Commonwealth War Graves Commission was reinterring a number of small graveyards into larger cemeteries, when they came across Anton's headstone. I was approached by the Commission who asked: 'If, by any chance, this was the grave of the officers' mess French cook?' They were surprised and not a little amused to know the truth. Sadly I have never discovered if Anton was also re interred along with his friends and admirers. I do hope so.

Selected Biography

Akehurst, John, *We Won a War: The Campaign in Oman*. Michael Russel, 1982

Alani, Mustafa, *Operation Vantage: British Military Intervention in Kuwait, 1961*. Surbiton, 1990

Alexander, Joseph, H., Sea *Soldiers in the Cold War: Amphibious Warfare 1945-1991*. Annapolis Naval Maritime Press, 1995

Amendolara, Dr Alejandro, *Inventiveness under Pressure: The Exocet Coastal Launcher in the Malvinas/Falklands War*. Acta International Commission of Military History, Bulgaria, 2012

Ashdown, Paddy, *A Brilliant Little Operation*. Aurum Press Ltd, 2012

Barker. A. J., *Suez: The Seven Day War*. Faber & Faber, 1964

Barker, Nick, *Beyond Endurance: An Epic of Whitehall and the South Atlantic Conflict*. Leo Cooper, 1997

Bartlett, A., *Amphibious Warfare*. United States Naval Institute, 1984

Bartlett, Merril, *Assault from the Sea: Essays on the History of Amphibious Warfare*. Annapolis Naval Maritime Press, 1983

Beaufre, Andre, *The Suez Expedition 1956*. Faber and Faber, 1969

Bicheno, Hugh, *Razor's Edge*. Weidenfeld and Nicolson, 2006

Blumberg, H. E., *Britain's Sea Soldiers*. Devonport, 1927

British Admiralty, *South America Pilot. Volume II. Sixteenth Edition*. Hydrographic Office, Taunton 1993

British Maritime Doctrine, Naval Staff Directorate, 1997

Brown, David, *The Royal Navy and the Falklands War*. Leo Cooper, 1987

Brown, Jeremy, *South American War*. Book Guild Publishing, 2013

Cable, James, *Gunboat Diplomacy 1919–1979: Political Application of Limited Naval Force*. Macmillan, 1981

Callwell, C. E., *Military Operations and Maritime Preponderance*. Blackwood, 1905

Clapp, Michael and Southby-Tailyour, Ewen, *Amphibious Assault Falklands*. Leo Cooper, 1996

Clifford, Kenneth, *Amphibious Warfare Development in Britain and America from 1920–1940*. Edgewood Inc, 1983

Connell, John, *The Most Important Country: The True Story of the Suez Crisis*. Cassell, 1957

Cordesman, Anthony and Wagner, Abraham, *The Lessons of Modern War: The Gulf War*. Westview Press, 1996

Darby, Philip, *British Defence Policy East of Suez 1947-1968*. Oxford University Press, 1973

Evans, Michael, *Amphibious Operations: The Projection of Sea Power Ashore*. Brasseys, 1990

Field, C., *Britain's Sea Soldiers Vols I and II*. Lyceum, 1924

Finlan, Alastair, *The Gulf War 1991*. Osprey, 2003

Foster, Simon, *Hit the Beach: The Drama of Amphibious Warfare*. Cassell, 1998

Fox, Robert, *Iraq Campaign 2003 – Royal Navy and Royal Marines*. Agenda, 2003

Fox, Robert, *Antarctica and the South Atlantic*. BBC, 1985

Freedman, Professor Sir Lawrence, *The Official History of the Falklands Campaign. Volume II: War and Diplomacy*. Routledge, 2005

Frost, John, *2 Para Falklands*. Buchan & Enright, 1983

Gates, David, *The Spanish Ulcer: A History of the Peninsular War*. Allen and Unwin, 1986

Gelder, George, *116 Infantry Brigade Royal Marines, North West Europe 1945*. Royal Marines Historical Society, 2020

Gelder, George, *Invasion: The Royal Marines and the Battle for Normandy 1944*. Royal Marines Historical Society, 2024

Grove, Eric, *Vanguard to Trident: British Naval Policy since World War II*. Bodley Head, 1987

Hastings, Max and Jenkins, Simon, *The Battle for the Falkland Islands*. Michael Joseph, 1983

Holmes, Richard, *Firing Line*. Jonathan Cape, 1985

Howes, Buster, *Operation Telic – 42 Commando Group in Iraq*. Association of Retired Naval Officers' Journal, 1994

Jane's Information Group, *Jane's Amphibious and Special Forces*. 1997-2014

Johnson-Allen, John, *They Couldn't Have Done it Without Us: The Merchant Navy in the Falklands War*. Seafarer Books, 2011

Ladd, James, *SBS the Invisible Raiders: The history of the Special Boat Squadron from World War Two to the Present*. Book Club Associates, 1983

Ladd, James, *The Royal Marines 1919-1980: An Authorised History*. Jane's, 1980

Lyman, Robert, *Operation Suicide: The Remarkable Story of the Cockleshell Raid*. Quercus, 2012

Longford, Elizabeth, *Wellington: Pillar of State*. Book Club Associates, 1972

Lovering, Tristan, *Amphibious Assault: Manoeuvre from the Sea*. Seafarer, 2005

McCart, Neil, *Canberra: The Great White Whale*. Patrick Stephens Ltd, 1983

MacIntire, John, *A Military Treatise on the Discipline of the Marine Forces when at Sea, Together with Short Instructions for Detachments Sent to Attack on Shore*. The Royal Marines Archives, 1763

Maisonneuve, Charles and Razoux, Pierre, *La Guerre des Malouines*. Éditions Larivière, 2002

Middlebrook, Martin, *Operation Corporate: The Story of the Falklands War*. Viking, 1985

Martini, Hector, Historia de la Aviación Naval Argentina: Conflicto Del Atlantico Sur. Departamento de Estudios Historicos ARA, 1992

Moulton, J. I., *Battle for Antwerp*. Ian Allen, 1978

Moulton. J. L., *Haste to the Battle: A Royal Marine Commando at War*. Cassell, 1963

Moulton, J. L., *The Norwegian Campaign of 1940*. Eyre & Spottiswoode, 1966

Muñoz, Jorge, *!Ataquen Río Grande! Operación Mikado*. Instituto de Publicaciones Navales, 2005

Neave-Hill, W., *British Support of the Amir of Kuwait, 1961*. Ministry of Defence Library, 1968

Neillands, Robin, *By Sea and Land: The Royal Marines Commandos: A History, 1942-1982*. Weidenfeld & Nicolson, 1987

Phillips, Lucas, *The Cockleshell Heroes*. Pan Books, 1957

Ramos, Javier E., *Isla Borbón: El Equipo de Combat Montalvo en Malvinas*. Ciudad Autónoma de Buenos Aires, 2013

Ratcliffe, Peter, *The Eye of the Storm*. Michael O'Mara Books, 2000

Reynolds, David, *Task Force: The Illustrated History of the Falklands War*. Sutton Publishing, 2002

Rivas, Santiago, *Wings of the Malvinas: The Argentine Air War over the Falklands*. Hikoki Publications (United Kingdom), 2012

Schenk, Peter, *Invasion of England, 1940*. Conway, 1990

Snelson, David, *Operation Telic: A Perspective from the UK Maritime Commander*. Association of Retired Naval Officers Journal, 2004

Speller, Ian, *The Role of Amphibious Warfare in British Defence Policy 1945-1956*. Palgrave, 2001

Southby-Tailyour, Ewen, *Blondie: The Life of Lieutenant-Colonel HG Hasler*. Leo Cooper, 1998

Southby-Tailyour, Ewen, *HMS Fearless: The Mighty Lion*. Pen & Sword, 2006

Southby-Tailyour, Ewen, *Reasons in Writing*. Leo Cooper, 1993

The Sunday Times Insight Team, *The Falklands War*. André Deutsch, 1982

Terry, Major Neri G. Jnr, USMC, *Selected Intelligence Issues from the Falkland Islands Conflict of 1982*. Faculty of the Defense Intelligence College, December 1989

Thomas, Peter, *41 Independent Commando, Royal Marines, Korea*. Royal Marines Historical Society, 1990

Thompson, Julian, *3 Commando Brigade in the Falklands: No Picnic*. Pen & Sword, 2007

Thompson, Julian, *The Royal Marines: From Sea Soldiers to a Special Force*. Sidgwick & Jackson, 2000

United States Marine Corps, *US Marines in the Persian Gulf, 1990-1999*. USMC History and Museum Division. 9 volumes from 1977-1997

Varble, Derek, *The Suez Crisis*. Osprey, 2003

Vaux, Nick, *March to the South Atlantic: 42 Commando, Royal Marines, in the Falklands War*. Buchan & Enright, 1986

Villar, Robert, *Merchant Ships at War: The Falklands Experience*. Conway Maritime, 1984

Warner, Philip, *With Wolfe to Quebec*. Phoebus, 1974

Woodward, John, *One Hundred Days*. HarperCollins, 1992

Young, David, *Four Five: The Story of 45 Commando, Royal Marines. 1943-1971*. Leo Cooper, 1972

Index

The front cover

What is the title of this book?

What do you think it wil
be about?

What can you see on the cover?

Why do you think there's a
candle in a cabbage?

What time of day is it? How do
you know?

The back cover

Let's read the blurb together.

What sort of things could
Owl organise for a quick
surprise birthday?

The title page

Look at the picture. What's
happened to the cabbage?
Who do you think might have
been eating it?

Let's read the title again.

What might happen at Rabbit's
surprise birthday?

LESSON 1

Read pages 2 to 5

READ

Purpose: To find out where Rabbit and Owl lived.

Pause at page 5

EXPLORE

Who is this story about? Where did they live? How did they share the tree?

What did they like to do all day? Find the sentence that tells you this. When did they meet and what did they do?

Which sentence tells you Owl and Rabbit had been friends for a long time? (*They had been very best friends for years.*)